OF HEAVEN AND EARTH

OF HEAVEN AND EARTH

RECONCILING SCIENTIFIC THOUGHT
WITH LDS THEOLOGY

Edited and compiled by
David L. Clark

DESERET BOOK COMPANY • SALT LAKE CITY, UTAH

Library of Congress Cataloging-in-Publication Data

Of heaven and earth : reconciling scientific thought with LDS theology
  / edited and compiled by David L. Clark.
        p.   cm.
    Includes bibliographical references and index.
    ISBN 1-57345-394-3 (hb)
    1. Religion and science. 2. Church of Jesus Christ of Latter-day
Saints—Doctrines. I. Clark, David Leigh, 1931–
BX8643.R39O35   1998
261.5'5'088283—dc21   98-30966
                                                                            CIP

Printed in the United States of America   72082-6379

10   9   8   7   6   5   4   3   2   1

CONTENTS

INTRODUCTION

───────────

S cientific questions interpreted to be in conflict with Latter-day Saint theology are centered on time and change. While there are many ramifications from these two themes that raise different but related questions, the age of the universe, our solar system, and Earth and the evolution of life on it are perhaps fundamental issues from which many, if not most, of the apparent and real controversies arise. It is not the purpose of this volume to redefine the details of all of the issues involved with time and change and the Church, for this has been done by many writers in a number of different ways.[1] Rather, this volume is intended to illustrate how members of The Church of Jesus Christ of Latter-day Saints who also have made significant contributions to their fields of scientific research reconciled challenging aspects of science and religion in their own lives.

There is a story concerning a man on the deck of the *Titanic* who watched as the few lifeboats quickly filled with frantic passengers. He proclaimed loudly that he was not the leaving the ship until someone explained to him exactly how the emergency had happened.

We all are probably sympathetic to this view because most of us feel the need to understand what is going on. If suitable explanations are not forthcoming, we may delay decisions because we look for explanations before we take serious action. The problem is that full explanations may come too late, and action may be needed before complete explanations are known.

Students of the physical and biological sciences who also are members of the Church often find themselves in an analogous circumstance to the man on the deck of the *Titanic*. Scriptural citations or even theological interpretations may appear to be in opposition to their scientific experiences. Full explanations for the apparent conflicts are not available or are unknown, and yet action in life is necessary before a complete understanding is attained. While looking for explanations should be encouraged, if we are really looking for excuses to justify weak faith, inactivity, bad actions, or just lousy attitudes, we need to alter our course. Probably it is a better idea to take positive actions on certain matters of life rather than wait for an explanation to save us.

It is said that going down with the ship is an accepted tradition for the ship's captain. For others on the deck, getting into the lifeboats before understanding everything may be the better idea.

It was late summer and I had just returned home from my lab where I had spent nine hours integrating newly generated $^{87}Sr/^{86}Sr$ isotope data with what little is known concerning the ventilation of the Arctic Ocean 65 million years ago. I had spent weeks trying to resolve a technical problem concerning the age of two Arctic Ocean samples that were critical for this research. One was either sixty-five or seventy million years old, and the other was either fifty or fifty-five million years old—certainly a minor point of interest for most folks, but of great significance for my interpretation of the history of the Arctic Ocean. In trying to resolve the question, I had used all of the tools of Earth science that were available to me, including stratigraphic position, age and correlation of fossils, geochemical dates with an error bar of five million years, and the comparison of these samples to similarly aged samples that had been collected from many parts of the world's oceans.

Many aspects of the questions were still on my mind when the phone rang and on the line was a committed member of the Madison Wisconsin Stake. After a brief chat, he asked for a short tutorial that addressed the age of Earth, the extent of Noah's flood, and the location of Kolob. After a few minutes of discussion, it was apparent that his real concern was the question of why science still appeared to be concerned with things that a number of prominent LDS writers claimed to be false. In response, I quickly drifted into an answer that had become routine during the past thirty-five years. I pointed him toward the writings of Elders James E. Talmage, John A.Widtsoe, and B. H. Roberts; quoted references to talks given by President David O. McKay and Elder Hugh B. Brown of the Quorum of the Twelve; told him to read a few essays of Henry Eyring and Lowell Bennion; and even reminded him of statements attributed to the Prophet Joseph Smith concerning the great age of Earth.

Although this seasoned response always provided me with a degree of instant gratification, it also created confusion in the mind of my caller, as was too often the case. He was still upset by the diversity of opinions, both past and present, concerning the age of Earth, life before Adam, and a variety of other things, and he was shaken to learn that faithful LDS scientists actually accept some of the most controversial aspects of what is considered to be the science/theology debate. Was it really possible that Earth was 4.5 billion years old, that Noah's flood did not explain all of geology, and that Abraham's discourse on Kolob was not necessarily the final answer for astrophysics? And if these things were true and believed by most twentieth-century LDS scientists (and at least some other faithful Latter-day Saints), why was this fact not more widely known? Why was there no recent statement referring to the Church's position on such things? Clearly confused by what he had anticipated would be a simple answer from his former bishop who was then a member of the stake presidency, the perplexed Church member promised to look up the references I had suggested and to get back to me with additional questions.

As the conversation ended, I thought about the number of times this kind of encounter probably was repeated daily throughout the Church. The long-awaited B. H. Roberts volume, *The Truth, the Way, the Life,* became available in 1994 (in two editions),[2] but Elder

Roberts was not a scientist, and much of his reconciliation of science and religion was based on nineteenth-century scientific thought. At the dawn of the twenty-first century, there are only a few compilations that address the apparent and real conflicts between LDS doctrine and current scientific thought, and it is evident that none of these texts is widely known or believed. How are many of the questions raised by modern science resolved by faithful LDS Church members who also are serious scientists?

There is a paradox in all of this, of course. Many LDS scientists spend their professional lives in research activity that is based on or assumes the validity of basic tenets that many Church members assume to be at best invalid and at worse a form of the doctrine of the anti-Christ. Yet these same scientists work side by side in a variety of Church callings with those who are suspicious of science and how it works. How does a paleontologist who devotes much of his life's energy and time studying the evolution of our planet's former inhabitants reconcile his research with the idea of special creation and no life before Adam? How does a geologist who works ten hours a day with the tools of science that indicate Earth is at least 4.5 billion years old confront the notion that Earth is young and that Noah's flood explains much of geology? Is it possible that astronomers who daily deal with light-years and the billions of years that this indicates, the Big Bang theory, and infinite space can even communicate with those who believe that Abraham's discourse on Kolob is about all that one needs to know about our galaxy? And what of other scientists whose research may not be directly involved with these traditional conflicts, at least on a daily basis, but who have needed to resolve some of these same problems for themselves and their students? What is their perspective on traditional and current science and theology problems?

What follows is a series of essays written by members of the Church who have specialized in Earth, Space, and a few related sciences and who have been concerned with the apparent and real conflicts of late-twentieth-century science and what has sometimes been assumed to be conventional LDS theology. These essays are written by internationally known scientists, a number of whom are members of the National Academy of Sciences, and all of whom have made significant contributions to their areas of research and yet are faithful Latter-day Saints. The contributors to this volume are researchers, professors, and university deans who also have served as bishops, stake presidents, Regional Representatives, and in a variety of other capacities. The writings presented herein are the personal resolutions of the century-old science and religion debate by some of the most outstanding scientists in the Church who also have served in the trenches of Church activity and have developed a strong testimony of the gospel. In none of the essays is there an attempt to define Church policy or a formal position on perceived theological problems. The essays are a personal account of how devoted LDS Church members interpret modern science and use it in their professional lives. This volume claims only one thing: that resolution of modern scientific thought with LDS theology is possible. These essays describe how a few believing scientists have accomplished this.

David L. Clark
Madison, Wisconsin
September 1997

NOTE

1. See, for example, James L. Farmer, ed., "Science and Religion," *Dialogue* 8, no. 3 and 4 (1973): 21–143; Wilford M. Hess, Raymond T. Matheny, and Donlu D. Thayer, eds., *Science and Religion: Toward a More Useful Dialogue*, 2 vols. (Geneva, Ill.: Paladin Press, 1979); Erich R. Paul, *Science, Religion, and Mormon Cosmology* (Urbana: University of Illinois Press, 1992); Gene A. Sessions and Craig J. Oberg, eds., *The Search for Harmony: Essays on Science and Mormonism* (Salt Lake City: Signature Books, 1993).

2. See B. H. Roberts, *The Truth, the Way, the Life: An Elementary Treatise on Theology*, ed. John W. Welch (Provo: BYU Studies, 1994).

PHILIP F. LOW studied at Brigham Young University, the California Institute of Technology, and Iowa State University. Although most of his professional life was spent at Purdue University, where he taught soil chemistry, he also served as guest professor at the University of California, Berkeley; North Carolina State University; the University of Florida; and at universities in Argentina, Jerusalem, India, China, and Australia. He made significant contributions to his field through his more than one hundred published papers on different aspects of soil chemistry and clay mineralogy.

In 1992 he was elected to the National Academy of Sciences. In addition, Dr. Low served as president of the Soil Sciences Society and received the Distinguished Service Award from BYU, the Herbert Newby McCoy Award of Purdue University, the Bouyoucos Distinguished Soil Science Career Award, and the Distinguished Service Award of the Soil Science Society of America.

Dr. Low's family includes his wife, Mayda Stewart, six children, twenty-five grandchildren, and six great-grandchildren. He served as counselor in several Indiana district presidencies, as the first stake president of the Indianapolis Indiana Stake, and, from 1976 to 1983, as a regional representative of the Church. More recently he served as a stake missionary, high priests group instructor, and Gospel Doctrine instructor. Dr. Low passed away in 1997 while this volume was being prepared.

CHAPTER 1

PERSPECTIVES ON SCIENCE AND RELIGION

PHILIP F. LOW

For the forty-five years I was on the faculty at Purdue University, I taught classes on the physical chemistry of soils and conducted research on that subject. Throughout my life I have been an active member of The Church of Jesus Christ of Latter-day Saints and have served in several of its administrative offices, including district president, stake president, and regional representative. Being deeply involved in both science and religion for so long, I have often observed how they seem to reinforce and contradict each other. For peace of mind, I have been obliged to develop a philosophy in which science and religion can be integrated in a rational way. My purpose in writing the present article is to share this philosophy in the hope that it might be helpful to someone else. Naturally, the religious aspects of the philosophy are based on the tenets of The Church of Jesus Christ of Latter-day Saints.

UNCERTAINTY IN SCIENCE AND RELIGION

So much has been said about the conflict between science and religion that it is almost axiomatic that such a conflict actually exists. However, truth cannot be in conflict with itself. It follows that whenever a claim is made that science and religion conflict with each other, the claim—if it is a valid one—must be based on some kind of misunderstanding in science or religion or both. In this context, conflicts can exist only between

1. False religion and true science.
2. False science and true religion.
3. False religion and false science.

Since truth and error can be intermixed in any scientific or religious philosophy, the challenge is to determine which aspects are true and which are false. This seldom can be done with certainty.

Many people have the impression that scientific findings are indisputable because they can be repeated again and again and are obtained with the five senses or with instruments that extend those senses. But this impression is contrary to fact. Some degree of uncertainty always exists about the reliability of experimental results. This uncertainty may arise because the method of measurement disturbs the system being measured. For example, the arrangement of particles in the soil can be studied by obtaining a soil sample, but the act of removing the soil from the ground may disturb the delicate arrangement. Uncertainty also may arise because the measuring device used in an experiment may not be sufficiently sensitive. Although an analytical balance is not sensitive enough to detect the loss of mass in a chemical reaction, a loss of mass does in fact occur.

In addition, regardless of how many experiments support a given concept, there is always the possibility that the next experiment will disprove it or require that it be modified. Even Newton's laws had to be modified with the advent of the theory of relativity. Thus a scientist must be content with gathering evidence in favor of an idea. As evidence accumulates, the idea may achieve the status of a theory and, eventually, of a law. Even so, the idea can never be proved unequivocally.

In addition to any uncertainty about the reliability of experimental results, there is uncertainty about their interpretation. Experimental results are seldom so definitive that only one interpretation is possible. Depending on their previous experience and prejudices, different scientists will have different interpretations. Thus, opposing schools of thought develop, and reconciliation of these schools of thought occurs very slowly. I am inclined to agree with the famous German physicist Max Planck, who said, "A new scientific truth does not triumph by convincing its opponents and making them see the light, but rather because its opponents eventually die, and a new generation grows up that is familiar with it."[1]

Members of the LDS Church are often unwilling to recognize any uncertainty in their religious beliefs. But uncertainty does exist. In Church history we see that beliefs once regarded as certainties had to be forsaken or substantially modified. In this regard, it is noteworthy that the return of the Saints to Jackson County, Missouri, was postponed, the United Order no longer exists, polygamy as an earthly practice was abandoned, and worthy males of all races may receive the priesthood. But why should we expect it to be otherwise? Conditions change, new problems requiring new solutions arise, and God reveals to his prophets what should be done. Only the most fundamental principles remain constant.

A factor that complicates the separation of truth from error and promotes uncertainty is the spread of information throughout the Church by word of mouth. In this process historical facts can become exaggerated or garbled, private scriptural interpretations may be accepted as doctrine, misinterpretations of the spoken or printed word may become widespread, and so on. Members of the Church constitute a close-knit group in which all kinds of information, true and false, are readily transmitted. Consequently, we often "know" something that isn't true and can be troubled by assumed conflicts that do not exist. To paraphrase a statement of Will Rogers: It isn't what you don't know that will hurt you—it's what you know that isn't so.

Although we would be well advised to heed the words of the prophets, uncertainty is not always eliminated when they speak. President J. Reuben Clark, former counselor in the First Presidency of the LDS Church, observed that there is only one way we can be certain that Church leaders are speaking the mind and will of the Lord: "I have given some thought to this question, and the answer thereto so far as I can determine, is: We can tell when the speakers are 'moved upon by the Holy Ghost' only when we, ourselves, are 'moved upon by the Holy Ghost.' In a way, this completely shifts the responsibility from them to us to determine when they so speak."[2]

In the same address President Clark cited the following quotation from Brigham Young: "I am more afraid that this people have so much confidence in their leaders that they will not inquire for themselves of God whether they are led by Him. I am fearful that they settle down in a state of blind self security, trusting their eternal destiny in the hands of their leaders with a reckless confidence that in itself would thwart the purposes of God in their salvation, and weaken that influence they could give to their leaders, did they know for themselves, by the revelation of Jesus, that they are led in the right way. Let every man and woman know, by the whisperings of the Spirit of God to themselves, whether their leaders are walking in the path the Lord dictates, or not."[3]

In addition to potential uncertainty about the spoken word, there can also be uncertainty about the written word as found in the scriptures. On one occasion the Prophet Joseph Smith said: "I believe the Bible as it read when it came from the pen of the original writers. Ignorant translators, careless transcribers, or designing and corrupt priests have committed many errors."[4] Furthermore, the title page of the Book of Mormon includes this statement: "And now, if there are faults they are the mistakes of men." This is tacit admission that the Book of Mormon may not be entirely faultless. However, I hasten to add that it would be presumptuous as well as fruitless for any uninspired person to try to identify any faults in it.

In calling attention to the uncertainty that exists in both science and religion, it was not my intention to disparage either one. Quite the contrary, I have the utmost respect for both. My only purpose was to provide a basis for the assertion that dogmatism is unwarranted in both areas. Whenever a conflict seemingly exists between science and religion, the wise course is for one to remain open-minded and to reserve judgment until more information becomes available. Dogmatism can only serve as an impediment to true understanding. Like the apostle Paul, we should recognize that "now we see through a glass, darkly; but then face to face: now I know in part;

but then shall I know even as also I am known" (1 Corinthians 13:12).

The element of uncertainty in religion posed a problem for me when I was younger. To be scrupulously honest, I avoided using the phrase "I know the gospel is true" when I bore my testimony. Instead, I would use words to express my sincere belief or great confidence in the truthfulness of the gospel. My faith was strong, but it fell short of a perfect knowledge. As time passed, I realized that I knew the principles of the gospel to be true as much as I knew any set of principles to be true, including those espoused by science. Therefore, if the word *know* was to have any place in my vocabulary, I reasoned, I could legitimately and appropriately use it in bearing my testimony. Since then I have had no qualms when I have said, "I know the gospel is true." The foregoing experience illustrates the fact that, since absolute knowledge is seldom attainable in mortality, people may have different degrees of certainty when they say they know something.

METHODS OF SCIENCE AND RELIGION

The methods of science and religion are similar in two important ways. Both require faith and experimentation. The necessity of faith is well recognized in religion but not in science, whereas the necessity of experimentation is well recognized in science but not in religion. Regarding faith in science, consider the following statement by Vannevar Bush, retiring president of the Carnegie Institute of Washington, in his final report to the board:

> For the scientist lives by faith quite as much as the man of deep religious convictions. He operates on faith because he can operate in no other way. His dependence on the principle of causality is an act of faith in a principle unproved and unprovable. Yet he builds on it all his reasoning in regard to nature. . . .
>
> So, back of all other motivations, there is a deeper one, vague in outline, seldom expressed, often denied, yet powerful in its influence. Its ultimate expression is beyond our ability. For the present it can be expressed in the faith that man can learn to

know and to understand and that it is good to exercise that power and to strive for the extension of our wisdom.[5]

Concerning experimentation in religion, the Book of Mormon prophet Alma had this to say:

Now, as I said concerning faith—that it was not a perfect knowledge—even so it is with my words. Ye cannot know of their surety at first, unto perfection, any more than faith is a perfect knowledge.

But behold, if ye will awake and arouse your faculties, even to an experiment upon my words, and exercise a particle of faith, yea, even if ye can no more than desire to believe, let this desire work in you, even until ye believe in a manner that ye can give place for a portion of my words.

Now, we will compare the word unto a seed. Now, if ye give place, that a seed may be planted in your heart, behold, if it be a true seed, or a good seed, if ye do not cast it out by your unbelief, that ye will resist the Spirit of the Lord, behold, it will begin to swell within your breasts; and when you feel these swelling motions, ye will begin to say within yourselves—It must needs be that this is a good seed, or that the word is good, for it beginneth to enlarge my soul; yea, it beginneth to enlighten my understanding, yea, it beginneth to be delicious to me.

Now behold, would not this increase your faith? I say unto you, Yea; nevertheless it hath not grown up to a perfect knowledge. . . .

And now, behold, because ye have tried the experiment, and planted the seed, and it swelleth and sprouteth, and beginneth to grow, ye must needs know that the seed is good.

And now, behold, is your knowledge perfect? Yea, your knowledge is perfect in that thing, and your faith is dormant; and this because you know, for ye know that the word hath swelled your souls, and ye also know that it hath sprouted up, that your understanding doth begin to be enlightened, and your mind doth begin to expand.

O then, is not this real? I say unto you, Yea, because it is light; and whatsoever is light, is good, because it is discernible, therefore ye must know that it is good; and now behold, after ye have tasted this light is your knowledge perfect?

Behold I say unto you, Nay; neither must ye lay aside your faith, for ye have only exercised your faith to plant the seed that ye might try the experiment to know if the seed was good. . . .

And because of your diligence and your faith and your patience with the word in nourishing it, that it may take root in you, behold, by and by ye shall pluck the fruit thereof, which is most precious, which is sweet above all that is sweet, and which is white above all that is white, yea, and pure above all that is pure; and ye shall feast upon this fruit even until ye are filled, that ye hunger not, neither shall ye thirst." (Alma 32:26–29, 33–36, 42)

Note from this scripture that faith, with its inherent uncertainty, must precede the attainment of perfect knowledge and that perfect knowledge is attained by performing the necessary experiments. In other words, we must experiment with the words of God if we are to know of their surety. For example, by putting the principles such as love, service, forgiveness, and repentance into practice, we become aware that these principles are valid. But it is self evident that in our individual lifetimes we cannot perform all of the experiments required to substantiate for ourselves every principle of either science or religion. We must rely on the experience of others. In science we rely on the experience of people like Pasteur, Newton, Darwin, and Einstein. In religion we rely on the experience of people like Moses, Isaiah, Paul, and Joseph Smith. To advance our knowledge of the truth in either field, it is vital that we read the pertinent literature.

Science has revealed many physical laws that express the order found in the universe. Some scientific laws bear the names of the great scientists who discovered them—the laws of Mendel, Maxwell, Newton, van't Hoff, and Einstein, to name a few. There are also laws that express the order found in the universe of the spirit. These laws were revealed by God. Among them are the Ten Commandments and the laws that require us to love our neighbor, forgive one another, repent of our transgressions, and so on. Both kinds of laws have stood the test of time. It is generally recognized that physical laws are inviolate. However, it is not always recognized that spiritual laws, although not inviolate, cannot be violated with impunity. The ultimate penalty is always unhappiness.

Scientific truth is discovered by means of the five physical senses or by the use of instruments that extend these senses. However, man is more than a body of flesh and bones with physical senses. A divine spirit resides within him, and this spirit is sensitive to communications from the Holy Ghost. Thus it may be said that man has a sixth, or spiritual, sense. This sense can be the means by which he discovers religious truth. The scientific and religious methods of discovering truth are not mutually exclusive. However, the physical senses alone are not sufficient to discover religious truth, and the spiritual senses alone are not sufficient to discover scientific truth. For example, one can neither prove nor disprove the existence of God entirely by his physical senses. Nor can one determine the mechanism of a chemical reaction entirely by his spiritual senses. Religion and science are two complementary and equally important ways of finding the truth, and wisdom dictates that in order to fully understand ourselves and the universe about us we should use all of our senses. One who is willing to do this can be a scientist and yet be religious at the same time.

THE AGE OF EARTH
AND THE CREATION OF MAN

Conflicts between science and religion seem to arise mostly in regard to the age of Earth[6] and biological evolution. I cannot speak authoritatively on how these conflicts can be resolved because I am not a geologist, nor a biologist, nor an official apologist for the LDS Church. Further, it is unlikely that sufficient information currently exists to allow any permanent resolution to be reached. If the scriptures could be entirely reconciled with the scientific theories of today, they could not be entirely reconciled with the scientific theories of tomorrow, because these theories are constantly changing. Nevertheless, I will offer a few tentative ideas about the creation of Earth and the creation of man.

Although the scriptures tell us that Earth was created (organized) as a habitat for God's children, they were not intended to be text-books of geology, and so they do not tell us how our planet was created. The details of creation were left for us to seek as we search for truth. As some of these details have come into focus, they sometimes appear to contradict the scriptures. In particular, the scriptures seem to support the concept that Earth was created in a period of six days, but scientific findings support the concept that it took millions of years for Earth to reach its present state. The evidence for the latter concept is overwhelming, and I subscribe to it. Therefore, I am of the opinion that the scriptures in question have suffered from errors in writing, translation, or interpretation.

Regarding the scriptural account of Earth's creation, I would like to make two observations. Both are based mostly on the Pearl of Great Price because its account of the creation is more informative and likely more accurate than that given in the Bible. An excerpt from the creation account in Abraham 4:1–8 follows:

> And then the Lord said: Let us go down. And they went down at the beginning, and they, that is the Gods, organized and formed the heavens and the earth.

> And the earth, after it was formed, was empty and desolate, because they had not formed anything but the earth; and darkness reigned upon the face of the deep, and the Spirit of the Gods was brooding upon the face of the waters.

> And they (the Gods) said: Let there be light; and there was light.

> And they (the Gods) comprehended the light, for it was bright; and they divided the light, or caused it to be divided, from the darkness.

> And the Gods called the light Day, and the darkness they called Night. And it came to pass that from the evening until morning they called night; and from the morning until the evening they called day; and this was the first, or the beginning, of that which they called day and night.

> And the Gods also said: Let there be an expanse in the midst of the waters, and it shall divide the waters from the waters.

And the Gods ordered the expanse, so that it divided the waters which were under the expanse from the waters which were above the expanse; and it was so, even as they ordered.

And the Gods called the expanse, Heaven. And it came to pass that it was from evening until morning that they called night; and it came to pass that it was from morning until evening that they called day; and this was the second time that they called night and day.

One possibility is that after Earth was organized and formed, it may have remained in an empty and desolate condition before the accounting of time began. Hence, it could have aged in this condition for unmeasured eons. Now consider the creative periods that followed. In verses subsequent to those cited, the Gods continued to redefine night and day after each creative period, and they continued to equate the number of creative periods with the number of times they had defined night and day. What significance can be attached to this unusual procedure? Did the definition prescribe the units of time that should be used in measuring the duration of the creative period? Also, how long was the duration of each creative period in conventional units? The answers to these questions would certainly be helpful in resolving arguments about the age of Earth.

Now let's consider the creation of man in light of the following scriptures:

So God created man in his own image, in the image of God created he him; male and female created he them. (Genesis 1:27)

And the Lord God formed man of the dust of the ground, and breathed into his nostrils the breath of life; and man became a living soul. (Genesis 2:7)

And God saw these souls that they were good, and he stood in the midst of them, and he said: These I will make my rulers; for he stood among those that were spirits, and he saw that they were good; and he said unto me: Abraham, thou art one of them; thou wast chosen before thou wast born.

And there stood one among them that was like unto God, and he said unto those who were with him: We will go down, for there is space there, and we will take of these materials, and we will make an earth whereon these may dwell;

And we will prove them herewith, to see if they will do all things whatsoever the Lord their God shall command them. (Abraham 3:23–25)

So the Gods went down to organize man in their own image, in the image of the Gods to form they him, male and female to form they them. (Abraham 4:27)

And the Gods formed man from the dust of the ground, and took his spirit (that is, the man's spirit), and put it into him; and breathed into his nostrils the breath of life, and man became a living soul. (Abraham 5:7)

From these quotations we learn that spirits existed in the presence of God before Earth was organized, that man (and woman also) was formed in the image of God, that he was formed from the dust of the earth, that his spirit was put into his body, and that he became a living soul when the breath of life was breathed into his nostrils. But we do not learn the process by which the body of man was formed. I suggest that this process could have involved some aspects of evolution as described by modern science and that it could have continued until the body was "in the image of God," at which point it was a fit abode for a divine, preexistent spirit. Then the spirit of Adam, our common progenitor, was put into his body, and he became a living soul. By reason of his divine spirit, Adam was distinguished from all forms of life that preceded him. This spirit endowed him (and his progeny) with special attributes, particularly the ability to reason. As a result, he could "subdue" the earth and "have dominion . . . over every living thing that moveth upon the earth" (Genesis 1:28).

Regardless of the means by which Earth and man came into being, I believe that God was in charge. This belief stems from my religious philosophy, but there also is scientific support for it. In science there is a quantity called the entropy. This quantity is a measure of the degree of disorder, randomness, or disorganization of the matter in any system (region in space). The higher the entropy, the greater the degree of disorder. Thermodynamic theory dictates that the entropy of a closed system (a system with boundaries that are impermeable to matter) increases as the system proceeds *spontaneously* toward equilibrium and that the entropy is at maximum at equilibrium. If Earth was a closed system, the original Earth should have become progressively more disordered with the passage of time. But the opposite is true. Earth now exhibits order and beauty, whereas it was once chaotic according to science and "without form, and void" and "empty and desolate" according to religion (Genesis 1:2; Abraham 4:2). It is reasonable to conclude, then, that Earth's development from a chaotic condition to an orderly condition did not proceed spontaneously. Because of energy from the Sun, Earth is not a closed system. In my opinion that additional force or influence emanated from God.

MODERN SCRIPTURES AND SCIENTIFIC PRINCIPLES

Science was in its infancy during the lifetime of the Prophet Joseph Smith. For example, little was known about atomic theory, the conservation of matter and energy, and the nature of light. Moreover, what was known to science was probably unknown to Joseph Smith, because his formal education did not extend beyond the third grade. Yet modern scriptures that have come forth through his instrumentality are remarkably consistent with scientific principles. This fact is illustrated by the following examples.

The Eternal Nature of Matter

"We will go down, for there is space there, and we will take of these materials, and we will make an earth whereon these may dwell" (Abraham 3:24). In refuting the idea that Earth was created out of nothing, this scripture is consistent with the scientific principle of the conservation of matter, which, simply stated, is that matter cannot be created or destroyed.

"For man is spirit. The elements are eternal, and spirit and element, inseparably connected, receive a fulness of joy" (Doctrine and Covenants 93:33). With only slight modification, this scripture, like the preceding one, is in harmony with the scientific principle of the conservation of matter.

The Extent of God's Creations

"And worlds without number have I created; and I also created them for mine own purpose; and by the Son I created them, which is mine Only Begotten" (Moses 1:33). The galaxy as viewed with modern telescopes testifies to the scientific truthfulness of this scripture. If God's purpose for creating other worlds was the same as that for creating this world, we may also assume that at least some of the other worlds are inhabited, i.e., that there is life on other planets. The question of life on other planets is one that is currently commanding scientific interest.

The Glory of God

"The glory of God is intelligence, or, in other words, light and truth" (Doctrine and Covenants 93:36). This statement implies that God's glory was derived from his infinite knowledge of the truth. Contributing to this knowledge are all the spiritual laws, social laws, and physical laws presently known and yet to be discovered. This omniscience enabled him to be the creator of all things.

Light and the Spirit of Christ

He that ascended up on high, as also he descended below all things, in that he comprehended all things, that he might be in all and through all things, the light of truth;

Which truth shineth. This is the light of Christ. As also he is in the sun, and the light of the sun, and the power thereof by which it was made.

As also he is in the moon, and is the light of the moon, and the power thereof by which it was made;

As also the light of the stars, and the power thereof by which they were made;

And the earth also, and the power thereof, even the earth upon which you stand.

And the light which shineth, which giveth you light, is through him who enlighteneth your eyes, which is the same light that quickeneth your understandings;

Which light proceedeth forth from the presence of God to fill the immensity of space—

The light which is in all things, which giveth life to all things, which is the law by which all things are governed, even the power of God who sitteth upon his throne, who is in the bosom of eternity, who is in the midst of all things. (Doctrine and Covenants 88:6–13)

In his book *Joseph Smith as Scientist*, Dr. John A. Widtsoe relied on the foregoing scripture when he compared the Spirit of Christ with the ether—a hypothetical medium through which light was supposed to be transmitted. Then, to reinforce the idea involved in this comparison, he quoted LDS Church apostle Parley P. Pratt:

As the mind passes the boundaries of the visible world, and enters upon the confines of the more refined and subtle elements, it finds itself associated with certain substances in themselves invisible to our gross organs, but clearly manifested to our intellect by their tangible operations and effects. . . . The purest, most refined and subtle of all these substances . . . is that substance called the holy spirit. . . . It is omnipresent. . . . It is in its less refined particles, the physical light which reflects from the sun, moon, and stars, and other substances; and by reflection on the eye makes visible the truths of the outward world.[7]

Dr. Widtsoe also quoted President Charles W. Penrose, an accepted writer on Church doctrine: "It is by his holy spirit, which permeates all things, and is the life and light of all things, that Deity is everywhere present. . . . By that agency God sees and knows and governs all things."[8]

Since Dr. Widtsoe wrote his insightful book, our knowledge about light has expanded, and it is now known that the ether does not exist. Nevertheless, some comparison of light with the Spirit of Christ may still be warranted. In the following paragraphs I have tried to bring this comparison up to date by using modern concepts of light.

The word *light* is commonly applied to electromagnetic radiation in the ultraviolet, visible, and infrared portions of the electromagnetic spectrum, but I will apply it to the entire electromagnetic spectrum from gamma rays to radio waves. The energy of the light is proportional to its frequency. Light of various frequencies, visible and invisible, comes from the sun, moon, and stars and travels through the immensity of space before it reaches Earth. When it strikes matter, the light is either reflected, absorbed, or transmitted, depending on the composition of the matter and the frequency of the light. So it may be said that the unreflected light either remains within or passes through the matter. In some cases the absorbed light is changed and induces photochemical reactions, such as photosynthesis, that are essential to life. Therefore, if we identify the Light of Christ with physical light, we see that the Light of Christ is in the sun, moon, and stars; that it fills the immensity of space; that it is in all things and through all things; and that it gives life to all things. Further, we can catch glimpses of how the energy in the Light of Christ might be used to govern all things.

In keeping with what has been said, I would like to hypothesize that light radiates from all three members of the Godhead, namely, God the Eternal Father, Jesus Christ, and the Holy Ghost. Although each of them is an individual being and can be in only one place at a time, the light radiating from them may be the common means by which they each may communicate with man and extend their influence throughout the universe. In this view it is easier to understand why the members of the Godhead are described as being surrounded by intense light and why such terms as the *Spirit of God*, the *Spirit of Christ*, and the *Holy Spirit* are often used interchangeably.

In regard to communication between members of the Godhead and man, the following scriptures are pertinent:

> There is no such thing as immaterial matter. All spirit is matter, but it is more fine or pure, and can only be discerned by purer eyes. (Doctrine and Covenants 131:7)

> . . . that which is spiritual being in the likeness of that which is temporal; . . . the spirit of man in the likeness of his person. (Doctrine and Covenants 77:2)

From these scriptures we see that the spirit of man is composed of matter that is finer and purer than the gross matter composing his body. It is possible, therefore, that the light that quickens a person's understanding has a frequency that his spirit is sensitive to, while his physical senses remain insensitive to it. Just as visible light in one part of the spectrum communicates information to the eye, nonvisible light in another part of the spectrum may communicate information to the spirit.

BIOCHEMISTRY AFFIRMS GOD'S CREATIVE ROLE

My son Philip S. Low holds the rank of Distinguished Professor of Chemistry at Purdue University, where he teaches and conducts research in biochemistry. He is an active, orthodox member of the LDS Church, and we often discuss the issues of science and religion. I would like to present a few of the ideas that he has shared with me.

The concept that life evolved from a single living cell may seem to simplify the theory of evolution, but it does not answer the fundamental question of how the living cell originated. The probability is infinitesimally small that (1) elements like carbon, hydrogen, oxygen, and nitrogen came together accidentally in the right proportions, arrangements, and energies to form simple molecules like amino acids; (2) that such simple molecules came together accidentally in the right proportions, arrangements, and energies to form complex molecules like proteins; (3) or that such complex molecules came together accidentally in the right proportions, arrangements, and energies to form extended, organized structures like the nucleus or mitochondrion.

And since the probability of a succession of events is the product of the probabilities of the separate events, the probability that the components of the living cell were formed accidentally is virtually zero. But even if this probability had a finite value, an intriguing question would still remain: what causes these components to perform the vital functions of the cell in a cooperative and harmonious way? In other words, what endows the cell with life? The above questions are more easily understood if we recognize the influence of an omnipotent, omniscient creator.

The concept that the spirit of man gives life to what would otherwise be an inanimate body is consistent with what is known about the chemistry of life's processes. Biochemists endeavor to understand and describe the molecular processes that collectively constitute a living organism. They have found that, with proper precautions, the organelles, cells, enzymes, and substrates within a tissue can be maintained in good functioning condition for hours, if not days, after their isolation from the tissue. This finding demonstrates the durability of the chemical structures and reactions that contribute physically to life. Virtually all biochemists will agree that the biochemical systems in the body lose their functionality slowly and that the biochemistry of the body remains unchanged from one second before death to one second after death. However, death is always an event that occurs in a moment, regardless of whether it is caused by heart failure or a severe blow to the head. Consequently, the most plausible explanation for the suddenness of death is the separation of the body from the spirit that gives it life.

Another religious concept that seems to defy scientific logic but that is actually consistent with scientific observations is the concept that our bodies will be immortalized following this earthly existence. Biological immortality has been a well-established fact for a long time. For example, many years ago a woman named Henrietta Lacks died of cervical cancer. So that the cause of her cancer could be studied, the malignant tissue was removed and cells derived therefrom were proliferated in a nutrient-rich growth medium. Since the cells multiplied rapidly, they were frequently separated into batches, transferred to fresh media, and shared with other interested scientists.

Now, decades later, these so-called HeLa cells are maintained in culture in numerous research laboratories around the world for use in the study of cancer. Simply stated, HeLa cells from the cancer of Henrietta Lacks are immortal and will live and grow for as long as they are nourished. Further, there are many other cell lines that have arisen from other patients' cancers that are equally immortal. It is important to note that this kind of immortality is not characteristic of normal, nonmalignant cells. Normal, nonmalignant cells express genes that ensure cell death at the end of a definite life span. To be specific, genes encoded in the DNA of normal cells ensure that the cells can divide fewer than one hundred times before they must die. In other words, they confer mortality on the cells. Cellular immortality arises when one or more of these genes mutates to a dysfunctional state, thereby allowing the cell to live indefinitely. Thus death is clearly a predetermined process prescribed by specific genes in all living organisms, and it is destined to occur unless these genes are changed or removed. Consequently, it is tempting to speculate that immortality can be imparted to man by the simple deletion of a select few mortality genes. It is also interesting to consider that the gradual shortening of the life span of man documented in the Old Testament could have arisen as mortality genes were gradually induced and expressed themselves.

THE SOIL AFFIRMS GOD'S CREATIVE ROLE

Most living things depend directly or indirectly on the soil for their sustenance. This makes soil a very important part of nature, one that should manifest the handiwork of God if, indeed, he was the Creator. Let's consider how the soil lends support to the concept of a divine creation.

Clay particles in the soil are so small that the combined area of their surfaces can reach eight hundred square meters per gram. Many of these particles are composed of very thin crystalline layers that are stacked one above the other like the leaves in a book. When such particles are placed in contact with water, the water penetrates between their superimposed layers and forces them apart. As a result the clay swells. In a fully swollen clay, the interlayer of water can be forty times thicker than the layers themselves, and the weight of the water can be more than fifteen times that of the clay. Thus clay is able to hold enormous amounts of water. Moreover, the process of soil formation tends to concentrate the clay in a region just below the soil surface. The overall result is that rainwater is retained in the root zone of plants and thus is more available to them.

Clay particles carry a net negative charge of high density due to ionic substitutions within their crystalline layers. Consequently, cations (positively charged atoms) are strongly attracted to them.

This attraction keeps the cations from moving away from the layers. Since many of the major and minor plant nutrients are cations, they tend to remain where the clay is concentrated, in the root zone of plants. In this manner plant nutrition is facilitated.

The source of many plant nutrients is the rocks from which the soil is formed. For these nutrients to become available to plants, the mineral constituents of the rocks have to dissolve in the soil solution. Water is the ideal solvent for this purpose. No other solvent known to man would be as effective. Furthermore, water is ubiquitous. Without its solvent action in the soils of Earth, the processes that sustain life would stop.

The amount of heat required to raise the temperature of a substance by one degree is called the specific heat capacity. Water has a high specific heat capacity, and this characteristic allows it to serve a useful purpose. The presence of water in the soil prevents sudden or extreme changes in soil temperature because more heat has to be absorbed or released to effect a given change in temperature. Therefore, water helps to ameliorate the climate of the soil.

The strong interaction between clay surfaces and the adjacent water depresses the freezing point of the water. As a result, water next to the clay surfaces remains unfrozen at sub-zero temperatures even though the water farther removed from these surfaces freezes. Thus, a film of unfrozen or liquid water is interposed between clay surfaces and ice in a frozen soil. The thickness of this film depends on the temperature. It becomes thicker as the temperature rises. Minerals can still dissolve in this water, ions can still diffuse through it, and it can still flow along a pressure gradient. This means that during the winter, plant nutrients can be replenished and active plant roots can be supplied with nutrients and water, albeit at a slow rate.

Microorganisms in the soil decompose organic matter incorporated therein. In the process of decomposition, plant nutrients are released from the organic matter. Also, organic acids are produced, and they promote the release of plant nutrients from soil minerals. But the decomposition does not go to completion. A residue of partially decomposed organic matter, called humus, resists further decomposition. Humus gives the soil its black color, which is conducive to the absorption of radiant energy. It also stabilizes soil aggregates and thereby improves the tilth and permeability of the soil.

Another important function of soil microorganisms is to decompose the vegetative litter that would otherwise accumulate and eventually kill the plants that produce it. Accumulated vegetative litter would prevent sunlight from reaching the plants and reduce their supply of oxygen.

From what has been said, soil is obviously much more than what appears to the naked eye. Its properties, and the reactions and processes that occur within it, make it an ideal medium for plant growth. Without it, life as we know it could not exist. In this regard it is important to note that although plants and animals may have adapted to the soil, the soil did not adapt to plants and animals. Consequently, the soil could not have evolved like life is supposed to have evolved, for example, by natural selection. Under any given conditions, the characteristics of soil millennia ago must have been the same as they are today. When Earth was formed, these characteristics came into being either by design or accident. In view of this, I believe they came into being by the grand design of God.

A SCIENTIST'S TESTIMONY

The ideas presented in this article are arguable, and they may not be sufficiently convincing to change the beliefs of anyone who is predisposed to challenge them. It is my hope, however, that they will help persuade people with scientific convictions to be more tolerant of religion, and people with religious convictions to be more tolerant of science. It is also my hope that the material I have presented will help modify the impression that science and religion are inherently incompatible and help relieve the concerns of those who are troubled by presumed conflicts between science and religion. As one who is well acquainted with both science and religion, I have found them to be quite compatible. Indeed, they complement each other in my philosophy of life. I recognize both as being integral parts of the entire body of truth known and used by an omniscient God. Because my religious beliefs are more important than science to my eternal happiness, I would like to testify of their truthfulness.

In the many years I have lived, my experience with the principles of the gospel of Jesus Christ has convinced me that they are valid. My knowledge of them is not perfect. I still have to exercise faith. But my knowledge is sufficient to justify the assertion, without any qualms of conscience, that I know the gospel is true. Its truthfulness has also been confirmed by the Holy Ghost. Therefore, I believe that there is a God in heaven who hears and answers my prayers. I believe that Jesus Christ is his divine Son, whose atonement made it possible for me to be forgiven of my sins. I believe that both God and Jesus Christ appeared to Joseph Smith in the Sacred Grove, revealed their true identities to him, and informed him that he would be the instrument by which the pristine truths of the gospel would be restored. I believe that Joseph Smith was this instrument and that he translated the Book of Mormon under divine direction. And I believe that, like Joseph Smith, his successors in the presidency of the Church have also been prophets. These beliefs are precious to me, and I recommend them to anyone who is seriously seeking truth.

NOTES

1. Max Planck, *Scientific Autobiography and Other Papers,* trans. Frank Gaynor (New York: Philosophical Library, 1949), pp. 33–34.

2. J. Reuben Clark, "When Are Church Leaders' Words Entitled to Claim of Scripture?" *Church News,* 31 July 1954.

3. Ibid.; also in Brigham Young, *Journal of Discourses,* 26 vols. (London: Latter-day Saints' Book Depot, 1860), 9:150.

4. Joseph Smith, *History of The Church of Jesus Christ of Latter-day Saints,* ed. B. H. Roberts, 7 vols. (Salt Lake City: Deseret Press, 1964), 6:57.

5. "Report of the President of the Carnegie Institute of Washington," in Carnegie Institute of Washington, *Year Book No. 54, July 1, 1954–June 30, 1955* (Baltimore: The Lord Baltimore Press, 1955), pp. 6–7, 9.

6. Editor's note: In many of the chapters of this book, the word *Earth* will be capitalized as the proper name of our planet. We capitalize names of the planets Venus, Mars, and so forth; and many scientists feel strongly about capitalizing Earth as well.

7. Quoted in John A. Widtsoe, *Joseph as Scientist* (Salt Lake City: YMMIA, 1908), p. 26.

8. Ibid.

B A R T   J.   K O W A L L I S received degrees from Brigham Young University and the University of Wisconsin and has taught geology at BYU since completing his doctoral work in 1981. In 1996 he was named chairman of the Department of Geology at BYU. He has done field work in Africa, Spitsbergen, Mexico, and western North America and has specialized in studies of rock microstructure and fission-track dating of rocks from different parts of the world. He has lectured in the United States, Australia, Japan, and France and has published extensively on his research interests.

He served as a missionary in Canada, counselor in a branch presidency at the Missionary Training Center, stake high councilor, elders quorum president, and in many positions in the Church's auxiliary programs. Currently he is a counselor in a Provo, Utah, bishopric. He has been active in youth activities, Scouting, and Utah politics. He married Julee Clark and is the father of four children.

CHAPTER 2

THINGS OF THE EARTH

BART J. KOWALLIS

Yea, verily I say unto you, in that day when
the Lord shall come, he shall reveal all things—

Things which have passed, and hidden things
which no man knew, things of the earth, by which
it was made, and the purpose and the end thereof—

Things most precious, things that are above,
and things that are beneath, things that are in the earth,
and upon the earth, and in heaven.[1]

I wait anxiously for the day when these "things of the earth" will be revealed. But in the meantime, how can I, as a scientist, continue to practice and believe in my religion? Are science and religion "incompatible and mutually exclusive," as biologist Edward O. Wilson proposes?[2] Or can they "live harmoniously together in the human soul," as suggested by author and eminent physicist Freeman Dyson?[3]

I certainly cannot do much toward helping resolve the debate on the compatibility of science and religion. However, my intent here is to provide some justification for why I continue to believe in God, in the Book of Mormon, in Joseph Smith, and in the modern hierarchy of the LDS Church when I have been trained in the fundamental tenets of science and accept them as being true. In my profession I teach and study geology. I have specialized in the study of Earth's architecture (structural geology) and in understanding the ages of rocks and minerals (geochronology). Much of what I have learned from my studies and believe to be true is seemingly incompatible with the scriptures. I say "seemingly" because I believe that all apparent contradictions between religion and science will disappear as our understanding approaches God's understanding.[4]

In particular I will focus on the concepts and challenges of determining the age of things, and I will discuss some religious implications of the enormous span of geologic time. During the past few years, my research has focused on determining the age of rocks and minerals. In 1983 I established a laboratory at Brigham Young University dedicated to geochronology, and during the past decade I have used isotopic dating techniques numerous times, such as to obtain more precise ages for the dinosaur bones found in Utah and Colorado,[5] to determine the rate of movement along the Wasatch Fault zone,[6] to help calibrate the geologic time scale.[7] In all of my studies I have found no reason to doubt the reliability of the methods used. I believe that the ages obtained by these methods—often registering in millions or hundreds of millions of years—are reflecting events that happened on this world since its creation. The principles that govern isotopic decay and the use of this decay for determining ages are as well established, accepted, and understood as are the laws of motion and the law of gravity. These ideas cannot be dismissed as mere scientific nonsense, unless we are willing to throw out the whole of science itself.

My laboratory at BYU specializes in a type of isotopic dating called fission-track dating. Like all isotopic dating methods, fission-track dating relies on the decay of radioactive isotopes.[8] In this kind of dating, the isotope of interest is uranium-238. When certain minerals (e.g. zircon and apatite) crystallize from liquid magma, they contain trace amounts of uranium-238. With the passage of time, the uranium-238 (called by scientists the parent material) decays to produce a new isotope (called the daughter material), usually by emitting an alpha-particle but occasionally by spontaneous fission. The rates (half-lives) of alpha decay and of spontaneous fission for uranium-238 have been measured independently in many laboratories around the world and are well known. When a uranium-238 atom decays by spontaneous fission, the atom breaks into two positively charged, highly energetic fragments. These fragments crash through the crystal that contained the uranium-238 atom and leave an ionization trail (called a fission track) behind. It is these tracks that are used in fission-track dating.

So how do we date a rock or mineral using fission tracks? And what does the age mean when we have obtained it? Let me use, as an example, granite from the Little Cottonwood stock located in the Wasatch Mountains east of Salt Lake City. This granite was quarried by the first settlers of Salt Lake City and used in building the Salt Lake Temple. The granite is mostly made of quartz, feldspar, and biotite, but it also includes small amounts of zircon, sphene, and apatite, minerals that contain enough uranium-238 to be useful in isotopic age determinations. A sample of granite is crushed and processed through a series of mineral separation techniques to obtain a concentrate of the uranium-bearing minerals. The minerals are then mounted in epoxy and carefully polished; the fission tracks are revealed by etching the mineral with acids or bases. The tracks found in a mineral grain are counted, and this number is used, along with data on the amount of uranium-238 in the grain and the isotopic decay rate, to calculate an age. The fission tracks tell us how much daughter product was created by the decay process, the amount of uranium-238 represents the amount of parent isotope remaining, and the decay rate (or half-life) allows us to link these two pieces of information into an age.

The fission-track ages we obtained from apatite grains in the Little Cottonwood granite ranged from about 6.5 million years to about 11 million years.[9] This range in age for the granite is substantial and may appear as a failure of isotopic dating systems. Indeed, these differences in age obtained on the same rock body have been used by some to attempt to discredit geologic time and the science behind it. Why do we obtain different ages on the same rock body? Which age is right?

Actually, all the ages are correct. Each age is simply telling us something about the cooling history of the granite. The apatite fission-track ages on the temple granite change systematically from 6.5 million years near the base of the Wasatch Mountains at about 5,000 feet elevation, to 8 million years at about 7,000 feet elevation, to 11 million years at 11,000 feet elevation. This change in age with elevation reflects the fact that the Wasatch Mountains have been uplifted along the Wasatch Fault for millions of years. As the mountains were uplifted, the underlying granite was brought to the surface of Earth. Temperatures inside Earth are warmer, and so as the granite was uplifted it cooled. When the apatite grains in the granite cooled below about 100° C, they began to preserve fission tracks. This temperature is called the "closure temperature," and it is different for each mineral and each type of isotopic decay. Before the apatites cooled below 100° C, uranium atoms were still decaying and producing tracks, but the tracks were not stable because the temperature was too high. Only when the mineral cooled below 100° C did tracks begin to accumulate in the apatite grains. The reason the apatite fission-track ages are older at the top of the mountain than they are at the bottom is because the mountaintop came up to the surface of Earth first. The rock at the top cooled below 100° C about 11 million years ago, while the rocks at the bottom cooled below that temperature only 6.5 million years ago.

All isotopic dating systems are sensitive to temperature—some to fairly low temperatures like the apatites in my example above, and others only to much higher temperatures. It is important to remember, however, that the ages obtained are not the ages of the elements themselves, nor necessarily of the time the rock first formed. The ages obtained by using these isotopic clocks are ages of thermal events, ages for the last time the rock or mineral was heated above and then cooled below its closure temperature. Every isotopic dating system has its limitations, but once we understand them they can provide a wealth of information about the history of Earth.

Before I continue to discuss the concepts of geologic time, I would like to share with you a small part of my personal history.

FIRST ENCOUNTERS

My purpose in writing here is to strengthen the faith of my students, to understand more completely my own faith, and to build the faith of any others who may chance to read these pages. I write from the standpoint of a scientist who believes deeply in the truths and theories of science and yet sees no serious conflicts between science and religion. Others may have written as adversaries of some scientific ideas and theories. Nonetheless, we all agree that when the truth is known, all conflicts between science and religion, be they apparent or real, will disappear.

The variety of views on science and religion was a significant influence on my own early perceptions of science and scientists. However, in order to explain the influence of different views of science and religion in my life, I need to travel back for a few moments to my youth—to the time of my introduction to life, science, and religion in the small Mormon town of Pleasant View.

Pleasant View, Utah, spreads out like a warm and careworn patchwork quilt along the foothills at the base of a mountain called Ben Lomond. From almost anywhere in town you can see far out over the valley until the view disappears into the waters of the Great Salt Lake. It is indeed a "Pleasant View." The residents of nearby Plain City and Far West always claimed that the view was pleasant because we saw them when we gazed out from up on the hills. To me, however, the best view was not out over the valley, but straight up 900 West Street, past my home, and up into the towering Wasatch Mountains. Ben Lomond was almost like Pleasant View's own mountain; it defined the town and set us apart from all the other communities stretching out along the Wasatch Mountains. As a youth I did not know why Ben Lomond was different from the rest of the nearby mountains. I did not know that it marked the end of one segment of the Wasatch Fault and the beginning of another because it protruded prominently out to the west of the main trend of mountains marching on southward. I only knew that it was a beautiful mountain and that we were its guardians.

In the hills above Pleasant View, and in the narrow canyons cut back into Ben Lomond above these hills, I discovered something magnificent. I discovered rocks. I brought them home with me. They were my greatest treasures. Some, I was certain, were extremely valuable. Each one I collected had its own special personality and character. I still have many of those rocks on my shelves today. In fact, on a recent visit my father said he had discovered yet another box of rocks in a corner of the basement and suggested that I was now old enough to store them at my own home. Opening that box with two of my own children was like an early Christmas present. We talked and sorted and touched each rock while I told them what they were and where they came from.

My mother and father encouraged my interest in rocks while I was still very young. They let me bring rocks into the house and keep them in my room! Mother would often examine them with me and try to help me identify them. They bought me books and kits on mineral and rock identification; they took me to rock shops and to gem and mineral shows; they made stops of geologic interest a regular part of our family vacations; and, although I never realized it at the time, they enjoyed rock collecting as much as I did.

At fourteen, when I went to receive my patriarchal blessing, the stake patriarch asked me a number of questions before giving the blessing. The only question I still remember was "What do you want to be when you grow up?" My answer was sure and unequivocal: "I am going to be a geologist." My faith in patriarchal blessings increased substantially that day, for when he gave the blessing he told me that I would indeed be a geologist.

At the time of the blessing, I don't suppose I really knew what geologists did or what they believed. Had I known that, I might have chosen a different career. All I really had in mind as a young boy was that geologists got to collect rocks for a living, and I couldn't think of anything more wonderful than that. I knew nothing about controversies surrounding the age of Earth or evolution, concepts that are central to the science of geology. In fact, what little

I did know of these topics came from my mother. I was taught that evolution was really "evil-ution"—a doctrine of the devil used to mislead us and destroy our belief in God. I was also taught that the scriptures were plain in describing the age of Earth; it was, at most, a few thousand years old. I firmly believed that these were fundamental teachings of the Church. As I grew up, I heard them repeated in Sunday School classes, in sacrament meeting talks, and during seminary. Warnings were given about the things we would be taught at school, but it was really not a problem. I don't remember these topics even coming up at school. Perhaps it was because the science teachers I had at school were Latter-day Saints and they steered away from evolution and other controversial topics. I had no idea that any alternative points of view existed in the Church or had been presented by other General Authorities. In my home these were questions that had already been answered.

The first time I was confronted by someone with a different perspective was during my mission to Quebec. The Quebec Mission was formed by splitting the Ontario-Quebec Mission about six months after I arrived in Montreal. Because the mission was new, we had a small group of only about fifty missionaries. I knew the names of all the missionaries and was well acquainted with most of them. One missionary, Elder Clayton, was exceptional in his work ethic. He was known mission-wide because he and his companions always worked more hours and wasted less time than anyone else. He would prepare enough food for the week (usually a big batch of franks and beans) on preparation day and store it in the refrigerator. He had no apparent fear of people and would stop and talk to anyone at anytime even in the most uncomfortable and unlikely settings. He always greeted every missionary with a warm handshake and the words "I love you, Elder." I always felt a little uncomfortable around Elder Clayton, as did many other missionaries. We referred to him as "Enoch"; we were certain he already had his application in for translation.

One day while I was working with Elder Clayton on an exchange, we tracted out some potential investigators in an apartment building. They invited us in, and we began to have a lively discussion. At one point in our conversation, one of them asked us what our church taught about evolution. I responded that we believed it to be a false theory and that as a church we could not accept it. Elder Clayton, in his calm and pleasant manner, interjected that he believed I was wrong. His understanding was that the LDS Church took no official stand on evolution. I was completely astounded and distraught, and I felt the blood rushing to my head as I checked my anger, for this was heresy to me. We left, and on the way back to our apartment I let him know that the Church could not tolerate such doctrine. I pointed out the obvious implications that evolution had for fundamental tenets of the gospel like the Fall and Atonement, the creation story, and our relationship to God. He said he understood what I was saying, but he stuck by his belief that the Church had not taken an official position. Although I felt vindicated that day, his comments had a profound effect on me: they opened a crack in my mind with thoughts that had not been there before; they helped me to be more open and willing to listen the next time a similar discussion occurred. I am indebted to him for the day we shared together.

The next encounter I had with these theories of Earth was on my return to BYU in the winter of 1974. I enrolled in a historical geology class taught by Dr. Lehi F. Hintze and was cruising along in the course, doing quite well, feeling only occasionally uncomfortable about the vast ages that were proposed for the periods of geologic time, when Dr. Hintze decided it was time to talk more pointedly about evolution and the age of Earth and to give us his view of the LDS Church's position. It was a difficult and challenging week for me. During our discussions, I again felt flushed and uncomfortable, but I couldn't simply ignore what Dr. Hintze was saying, for he had built a firm foundation of geologic facts and evidences during the earlier part of the course, and now he backed up his LDS views with quotes from apostles and other General Authorities. Elder James E. Talmage, he pointed out, had written and talked about the creatures that "lived and died, age after age, while the earth was yet unfit for human habitation."[10] Elder John A. Widtsoe had written about the "vast periods of time" required for each class of animals to arise, dominate Earth, and then become extinct, and he felt that millions of years were needed to accomplish the task.[11] Many other quotes and articles were presented, but perhaps the most significant for me was the copy of a letter sent by President David O. McKay to Professor William Lee Stokes, an LDS geology professor at the University of Utah. The letter, dated 15 February 1957, stated that "on the subject of organic evolution the Church has officially taken no position."[12] Elder Clayton, my one-day mission companion, had been correct! I felt embarrassed by what I had said to him, and yet I began to feel a great sense of relief to know that I could continue to study geology and to learn and believe its fundamental theories without throwing out my religion in the process.

And so I became a geologist, as my patriarchal blessing said I would. I have never regretted the decision. As I have continued to learn, grow, and study in the two decades that have followed that historical geology class, I have found that my study of science has sometimes forced me to rethink other beliefs and to challenge other long-held tenets of my faith. But I believe the outcome of this process has always been to eventually strengthen my testimony of the gospel, to make me a better person and a more understanding teacher, and to bring me a bit closer to the truth.

WORLDS AND TIME WITHOUT END

Geologists today believe that Earth is about 4.5 to 4.6 billion years old.[13] For most of us, including the scientists who determined these ages, this vast expanse of time is totally incomprehensible. What is a billion? How big of a number is it? Suppose that you could view the history of Earth in its entirety with only one change from the original version: each year of Earth's history would be viewed in just one second. How long would it take to see all 4.6 billion years? Well, if you didn't stop for eating, sleeping, or anything else, but just watched twenty-four hours a day, you could view just over 31.5 million years of Earth history each year. To see all 4.6 billion years at this one-year-a-second pace would take you almost 150 years!

Even big numbers like a billion don't seem so big when we begin to contemplate the numbers of stars, planets, and galaxies in the known universe. There are perhaps 400 billion stars in just our own Milky Way Galaxy, with an estimated 300 billion planets that could support some type of life.[14] The number of total galaxies is not known but has been estimated to be at least 100 billion, and in each galaxy, on average, there are 100 billion stars. This gives us a rough estimate of 10 billion trillion stars—or 10,000,000,000,000,000,000,000 stars![15] Can the mind of man comprehend such numbers? It is certainly beyond my capabilities. But in attempting to understand these numbers, I think I begin to understand something about God. I begin to understand what he means when he says that his works are "innumerable . . . unto man"[16] and that his name is "Endless," for he is "without beginning of days or end of years; and is not this endless?"[17]

In general I am a firm believer in the idea propounded by Galileo, and reiterated more recently by Elder James E. Talmage, that the holy scriptures are not textbooks of science, nor were they ever intended to teach scientific principles. Galileo, in his letter to Castelli on 13 December 1613, stated that "scripture deals with natural matters in such a cursory and allusive way that it looks as though it wanted to remind us that its business is about the soul and that, as concerns Nature, it is willing to adjust its language to the simple minds of the people."[18] Elder Talmage said: "Let us not try to wrest the scriptures in an attempt to explain away what we cannot explain. The opening chapters of Genesis, and scriptures related thereto, were never intended as a text-book of geology, archaeology, Earth-science or man-science. . . . We do not show reverence for the scriptures when we misapply them through faulty interpretation."[19]

Most misconceptions that arise between science and religion could be avoided if we kept these ideas in mind. Sometimes, however, I believe we can gain useful and interesting insights by combining science and the scriptures. This is apparent in trying to understand how our belief in God is compatible with the vast stretches of geologic time, the huge numbers of stars and galaxies now known to exist, and the enormous reaches of space. The Book of Moses in the Pearl of Great Price describes one of the most glorious experiences that a mortal man could possibly have and gives some pertinent insights into these ideas of time, space, and very large numbers.

Moses was "caught up into an exceedingly high mountain."[20] (There could have been no better place to have the type of vision Moses was about to have than up among the rocks—rocks that had probably been around during much of the history that Moses was about to witness.) And Moses "saw God face to face, and he talked with him."[21] What he then saw was the world in intricate detail, from the beginning to the end. For God said to Moses:

"I will show thee the workmanship of mine hands; but not all, for my works are without end. . . .

" . . . [But] this one thing I show unto thee, Moses, my son, for thou art in the world, and now I show it unto thee.

"And it came to pass that Moses looked, and beheld the world upon which he was created; and Moses beheld the world and the ends thereof, and all the children of men which are, and which were created; of the same he greatly marveled and wondered."[22]

When the vision ended, Moses was drained and did not recover his strength for several hours. In contemplating this experience later, he stated, "Now, for this cause I know that man is nothing, which thing I never had supposed."[23]

Man was nothing! This was the Moses who gathered up a huge group of disorganized, uncooperative, and often belligerent people; led them out safely from the clutches of the Egyptians; and helped preserve them in the desert. This was the Moses who with God's help brought down devastating plagues on Egypt. This was the Moses who heard the voice of the Lord speak out of the burning bush and received instructions from him on many other occasions. This was the Moses, a former prince in Pharaoh's court, who may justifiably have thought that he was something, that he was somebody, that he had accomplished quite a bit in his life. What a shock this vision must have been! For now Moses realized man was nothing, something he had never supposed. I believe he was beginning to see the immensity of God's creation, and it brought home to

Moses the same feeling I get when I stand outside on a clear night and contemplate the stars, or when I hike up into the mountains and look at rocks that were first formed billions of years ago.

Later in the Book of Moses, after Moses had been visited and tempted by Satan, his vision of God and the world reopened and God showed him the "earth, yea, even all of it; and there was not a particle of it which he did not behold, discerning it by the spirit of God."[24] At this point Moses was bold enough to ask God a question. He asked him why he had made all these worlds and planets and people and how they were made. It appears that God was not going to give Moses a complete response. I often take this approach with my children when they ask me a question that will take too long to explain. God said, and I paraphrase, that he did it "just because." Yes, he had his reasons, but they were for his "own purpose" and according to the wisdom that "remaineth in [him]."[25] However, God did explain, among other things, that the creative work had been accomplished by the "word of my power, . . . which is mine Only Begotten Son."[26] Moses, like my children, wanted to learn more: "Tell me concerning this earth, and the inhabitants thereof, and also the heavens, and then thy servant will be content."[27] At this point God revealed to Moses the great plan, the reason behind all of creation:

"And the Lord God spake unto Moses, saying: The heavens, they are many, and they cannot be numbered unto man; but they are numbered unto me, for they are mine.

"And as one earth shall pass away, and the heavens thereof even so shall another come; and there is no end to my works, neither to my words.

"For behold, this is my work and my glory—to bring to pass the immortality and eternal life of man."[28]

This vision of Moses is simply packed with ideas that were unknown or only in their infant stages in the scientific community at the time of Joseph Smith. For example, what did God mean by "the heavens, they are many"? The wording of this passage makes me believe that God was not just referring to the stars we see in our own heavens at night, but to some other heavens as well. I can see other possibilities. First, the heavens spoken of here may represent galaxies, and we certainly know today that "they are many." However, it was not until the early part of the twentieth century that scientists were even certain that other galaxies existed.[29] Will these galaxies "pass away"? Before the development of modern theories of cosmology, it was believed that the heavens were static and immutable. Today it is believed that galaxies have a finite lifetime— they are born, they live for several billion years, and then they will die in either a general collapse of our universe or in a slow burnout as the universe continues to expand.[30]

An alternative hypothesis is that the heavens spoken of in this passage of scripture represent different universes of which ours is only one of many, and that each of these universes has a finite lifetime. As strange as this idea may sound, it is today one of the prominent scientific theories for the origin and demise of the universe. Physicist Andrei Linde, one of the proponents of this theory, wrote: "Just a few years ago there was no doubt that the universe was born in a single Big Bang singularity. . . . Now it seems more likely that the universe is an eternally existing, self-producing entity, that is divided into many mini-universes much larger than our observable portion."[31] Each of these mini-universes has a finite existence in space and time, appearing and disappearing over billions of years.

Moses also learned in his vision that there are worlds without number that come and go on the eternal stage, and he learned that the inhabitants of Earth are "numberless as the sand upon the sea shore."[32] These were certainly not well-known facts in Moses' time, nor even in Joseph Smith's time, but they are beginning to be established today. These interesting concepts would make good items for further discussion, but I want to come back to the most important idea that Moses was taught during his vision—the purpose for all of creation, which was "the immortality and eternal life of man." I believe that in his vision Moses glimpsed what eternity was like, and this glimpse was one of the main reasons he was left to exclaim that "man is nothing." Eternity is a concept that is frequently talked about but seldom, if ever, comprehended. But what better way could God have found to impress upon Moses the idea of eternity and immortality than by showing him a small part of creation. Compared to eternity, a few billion years of Earth history are nothing—a mere drop in a huge bucket. Compared to infinity, what are a few billion trillion stars and planets? They do not even scratch the surface of the totality of creation.

So do we as members of The Church of Jesus Christ of Latter-day Saints have a problem with an Earth that is 4.6 billion years old? Unequivocally no! How can we be concerned with a mere 4.6 billion years when we believe in an eternal God, when we believe in the immortality and eternal life of man?[33] Elder Bruce R. McConkie, in a general conference address in 1982, suggested that the six days of creation were more properly thought of as periods of time. He said: "What is a day? It is a specified time period; it is an age, an eon, a division of eternity; it is the time between two identifiable events. And each day, of whatever length, has the duration needed for its purposes. . . . It seems clear that the 'six days' are one continuing period and that there is no one place where the dividing lines between the successive events must of necessity be placed."[34]

We should not, therefore, worry about accepting these concepts of science, concepts that deal with vast ages and very large numbers, for they help us to gain a small but important insight into one of the main characteristics of God and godhood: the concept of eternity. To me these wonderful discoveries of science add to the greatness of God, lift and inspire me, and help me to see that I am indeed nothing compared to God and his creations. Carl Sagan, the late eminent astronomer and unbeliever, had some interesting words of advice for those of us who are believers. He said:

> How is it that hardly any major religion has looked at science and concluded, "This is better than we thought! The Universe is much bigger than our prophets said, grander, more subtle, more elegant. God must be even greater than we dreamed"? Instead they say, "No, no, no! My god is a little god, and I want him to stay that way." A religion, old or new, that stressed the magnificence of the Universe as revealed by modern science might be able to draw forth reserves of reverence and awe hardly tapped by the conventional faiths. Sooner or later, such a religion will emerge.[35]

I don't think we need to wait for that religion to emerge; it is here already. Dr. Sagan had obviously not read the Book of Moses, nor was he acquainted with the teachings of the modern prophets. We do not believe in a "little god," and our prophets have always emphasized the greatness and beauty of the universe God has created. For us, each new discovery of science should be as a new revelation; each discovery gives us a new and more complete understanding of how God works and teaches us his ways. Our God is not a God only of the supernatural, miraculous, or mysterious. He is a God of truth and knowledge; he encourages us and desires for us to learn and gain knowledge. Mormonism "embraces every true science and all true philosophy. . . . True science, true art, and true knowledge comprehend all that are in heaven or in Earth, or in all the eternities. . . . All truth is ours."[36] "We are open for the reception of all truth, of whatever nature it may be, and are desirous to obtain and possess it, to search after it as we would for hidden treasures."[37]

We believe that "it is impossible for a man to be saved in ignorance,"[38] that "whatever principle of intelligence we attain unto in this life, it will rise with us in the resurrection," and that "if a person gains more knowledge and intelligence in this life through his diligence and obedience than another, he will have so much the advantage in the world to come."[39] We have been taught to "study and learn, and become acquainted with all good books,"[40] to "seek not for riches but for wisdom,"[41] and to ponder and study things out in our own minds before we ask God.[42] After all, God has challenged us to become like him—to become gods,[43] to gain his glory—and his glory is intelligence.[44]

As science demonstrates the order and law of the universe, we should not feel threatened but should gain through these natural descriptions a greater reverence and awe for the marvelous work of the Creator,[45] for "he comprehendeth all things, and all things are before him, and all things are round about him; and he is above all things, and in all things, and is through all things, and is round about all things; and all things are by him, and of him, even God, forever and ever."[46]

NOTES

1. Doctrine and Covenants 101:32–34.

2. Edward O. Wilson, "Evolutionary Biology and Religion," lecture given at Catholic bishops' meeting, 1987. See David M. Byers, ed., *Religion, Science and the Search for Wisdom* (Washington, D.C.: United States Catholic Conference, 1987), pp. 47–62.

3. Freeman Dyson, *Infinite in All Directions* (New York: Harper & Row, 1989), p. 11.

4. This statement is paraphrased from Henry Eyring, *The Faith of a Scientist* (Salt Lake City: Bookcraft, 1967), p. 99.

5. See Bart J. Kowallis and Julia S. Heaton, "Fission-Track Dating of Bentonites and Bentonitic Mudstones from the Morrison Formation in Central Utah," *Geology* 15 (1987): 1138–42. See also Bart J. Kowallis, Eric H. Christiansen, and Alan L Deino, "Age of the Brushy Basin Member of the Morrison Formation, Colorado Plateau, Western USA," *Cretaceous Research* 12 (1991): 483–93.

6. See Bart J. Kowallis, Jeffrey Ferguson, and Gregory J. Jorgensen, "Uplift along the Salt Lake Segment of the Wasatch Fault from Apatite and Zircon Fission Track Dating in the Little Cottonwood Stock," *Nuclear Tracks and Radiation Measurements* 17 (1990): 325–29.

7. See Bart J. Kowallis et al., "Age of the Cenomanian-Turonian Boundary in the Western Interior of the United States," *Cretaceous Research* 16 (1995): 109–29.

8. See G. Wagner and P. Van den Haute, *Fission-Track Dating* (Dordrecht, The Netherlands: Kluwer Academic Publishers, 1992), p. 285.

9. See Kowallis, Ferguson, and Jorgensen, "Uplift along the Salt Lake Segment," p. 327.

10. See James E. Talmage, "The Earth and Man." Address delivered in the Salt Lake Tabernacle on Sunday, August 9, 1931, and later printed in the *Deseret News*, 21 November 1931. Reprinted for the BYU Geology Department in 1976 by BYU Printing Service.

11. John A. Widtsoe, *Joseph Smith as Scientist*, manual distributed by General Board of the YMMIA (Salt Lake City: The Church of Jesus Christ of Latter-day Saints, 1908), p. 52.

12. This letter to Professor Stokes and others like it have been widely distributed, but they have also been criticized as not being official Church documents. These letters are private correspondences signed only by President McKay, not by the entire First Presidency. For me, however, at the time I first read one of these letters, it carried a great deal of weight, because it came from the prophet and president of the Church. I still find them to be useful and important documents today.

13. See G. Brent Dalrymple, *The Age of the Earth* (Stanford, Calif.: Stanford University Press, 1991), p. 474. This is one of the most recent of several books dealing with the age of Earth. Some new data have appeared since the publication of the book, but the general conclusions have not changed.

14. See Carl Sagan, *Cosmos* (New York: Random House, 1980), pp. 298–301.

15. See ibid. pp. 5–7.

16. Moses 1:35.

17. Moses 1:3.

18. Quoted in Giorgio de Santillana, *The Crime of Galileo* (Alexandria, Va.: Time-Life Books, 1955), p. 39.

19. Talmage, "The Earth and Man," 3.

20. Moses 1:1.

21. Moses 1:2.

22. Moses 1:4, 7–8.

23. Moses 1:10.

24. Moses 1:27.

25. Moses 1:31.

26. Moses 1:32.

27. Moses 1:36.

28. Moses 1:37–39.

29. See George Abell, *Exploration of the Universe,* 2nd ed. (New York: Holt, Rinehart, and Winston, 1969), p. 608.

30. See Tony Rothman, "This Is the Way the World Ends," *Discover,* July 1987, pp. 82–93.

31. Andrei Linde, "Particle Physics and Inflationary Cosmology," *Physics Today,* September 1987, p. 68.

32. Moses 1:28.

33. Brigham Young said: "I am not astonished that infidelity prevails to a great extent among the inhabitants of the earth, for the religious teachers of the people advance many ideas and notions for truth which are in opposition to and contradict facts demonstrated by science, and which are generally understood.

"You take, for instance, our geologists, and they tell us that this earth has been in existence for thousands and millions of years. They think, and they have good reason for their faith, that their researches and investigations enable them to demonstrate that this earth has been in existence as long as they assert it has; and they say, 'If the Lord, as religionists declare, made the earth out of nothing in six days, six thousand years ago, our studies are all in vain; but by what we can learn from nature and the immutable laws of the Creator as revealed therein, we know that your theories are incorrect and consequently we must reject your religions as false and vain. . . . '

"In these respects we differ from the Christian world, for our religion will not clash with or contradict the facts of science in any particular. You may take geology, for instance, and it is a true science; not that I would say for a moment that all the conclusions and deductions of its professors are true, but its leading principles are; they are facts — they are eternal; and to assert that the Lord made this earth out of nothing is preposterous and impossible. God never made something out of nothing. . . .

"If we understood the process of creation there would be no mystery about it, it would be all reasonable and plain, for there is no mystery except to the ignorant . . . How long it [Earth] had been organized is not for me to say, and I do not care anything about it. As for the Bible account of the creation we may say that the Lord gave it to Moses, or rather Moses obtained the history and traditions of the fathers, and from them picked out what he considered necessary, and that account has been handed down from age to age, and we have got it, no matter whether it is correct or not, and whether the Lord found the earth empty or void, whether he made it out of nothing or out of the rude elements; or whether he made it in six days or in as many millions of years, is and will remain a matter of speculation in the minds of men unless he gives revelation on the subject" (in *Journal of Discourses,* 26 vols. [London: Latter-day Saints' Book Depot, 1860], 14:115–17).

34. Bruce R. McConkie, *Ensign,* June 1982, p. 11.

35. Carl Sagan, *Pale Blue Dot: A Vision of the Human Future in Space* (New York: Random House, 1994), p. 52.

36. Brigham Young, in *Journal of Discourses,* 14:280–81.

37. John Taylor, in *Journal of Discourses,* 14:337.

38. Doctrine and Covenants 131:6.

39. Doctrine and Covenants 130:18–19.

40. Doctrine and Covenants 90:15.

41. Doctrine and Covenants 6:7.

42. See Doctrine and Covenants 9:8.

43. See Doctrine and Covenants 132:20.

44. See Doctrine and Covenants 93:36.

45. See Richard H Bube, *Putting It All Together: Seven Patterns for Relating Science and the Christian Faith* (Lanham, Md.: University Press of America, 1995), p. 66.

46. Doctrine and Covenants 88:41.

H E N R Y   E Y R I N G   received degrees from the University of Arizona and the University of California at Berkeley. Following a brief period at the University of Wisconsin, he taught at Princeton until 1946, when he became dean of the graduate school and professor of chemistry at the University of Utah. His publications number more than six hundred. He was awarded fifteen U.S. and international honorary degrees, and he received eighteen prizes that include the National Medal of Science, the Priestly Medal, the Berzelium Medal of the Swedish Academy, and the Israel Wolf Prize. He was a member of the National Academy of Sciences and served as president of the American Chemical Society and the American Association for the Advancement of Science.

Dr. Eyring married Mildred Bennion and raised three sons. Following the death of Mildred, he married Winifred Brennan. His Church work included service as a branch president, district president, and member of the General Board of the Sunday School of the Church.

Dr. Eyring, who passed away in 1981, wrote two books that record his views concerning the integration of twentieth-century science with LDS theology. The following two essays, "The Physical and Spiritual Worlds" and "Faith and God," are adapted from those books, Reflections of a Scientist *and* The Faith of a Scientist, *respectively.*[1]

CHAPTER 3

WORLD OF EVIDENCE,
WORLD OF FAITH

HENRY EYRING

ESSAY 1: THE PHYSICAL AND SPIRITUAL WORLDS

My wife and I have a lot that is sixty feet across the front, one hundred feet deep, and extends straight up to the limits of space, so far as I know. Clearly, this qualifies me to speak on the broader aspects of the universe.

We live in a series of six worlds, from the infinitesimally small to the infinitely big. They can be represented by a point surrounded by five circles. This essay deals with the five physical worlds of the nucleus, the atom, the living cell, everyday experience, and the stars, as well as the sixth, or spiritual, world.

The Nucleus

The first, or central, world is the world of the atomic nucleus. The nucleus is where most of the weight of the atom is situated. One hundred thousand atomic nuclei touching each other in a line extend only across one atom, and it takes one hundred million atoms to make one inch! Vibrations inside the nuclei of atoms are about a million times more frequent than the vibrations between atoms.

It is natural to wonder how anything as small as the nucleus can have structure, and even if it does, how we can find out about it. The procedure for finding out is to shoot electrically charged atoms or electrons at nuclei and see how they bounce. This tells us a great deal about the kinds of forces that are acting between the colliding particles.

When a particularly violent collision results in penetration into the nucleus and causes it to fragment, we can watch the tracks left by the fragments in a cloud chamber. In this way we find out that the nucleus is made up of positively charged protons and uncharged neutrons of virtually the same weight.

For twenty-five years, scientists accepted *parity,* the principle that an atom does not know which end is up and has the same properties in all directions. However, an experiment suggested by Yang and Lee, for which they were given the Nobel Prize, showed otherwise. If we put radioactive cobalt sixty in a magnetic field, its nuclei line up with their south poles pointing toward the north pole of the earth. Every once in a while, one of the cobalt nuclei shoots out an electron. If the nuclei were indeed symmetrical, they would be equally likely to eject the electron through the north pole as through the south pole. However, a Geiger counter similar to the kind used to prospect for uranium reveals that the electrons are shot out preferentially through the nuclear south pole. Thus, the principle of parity must be given up.

Now the scientists have introduced *quarks,* fractional particles having a charge of one-third. When quarks were proposed in the early 1970s, they were conceived of as being undivided particles, although their charge was fractional. More recent observations have indicated the existence of one-dimensional conductors called *solitons,* which have fractional charge and a fractional electron number.

By such experiments we come to understand something of the complexity and intricacy of this almost unimaginably tiny world of the nucleus. One hesitates to speculate whether we have even yet found the indivisible building blocks of the physical world.

The Atom

The second world is the world of chemistry, made up of atoms and molecules. This, too, is a tiny world. I noted earlier that it would take one hundred million atoms placed side by side to make an inch. A molecule finishes one of its vibrations in about a ten million millionth of a second. We call this length of time a *jiffy* for lack of a better name. The quartz-crystal watch you wear on your wrist derives its great accuracy from such rapid vibrations.

An example of the exactness with which the universe works is found in the ammonia molecule. Ammonia consists of a nitrogen atom sitting on three hydrogen atoms. The startling fact is that this umbrella-like molecule turns wrong side out almost twenty-four thousand million times a second. If you beam radar through a tube containing ammonia, the signal fades just when the radar frequency equals the inversion frequency of the molecules. In this way the ammonia molecules can be used as a clock to break time up into twenty-four thousand millionths of a second with unprecedented accuracy. It is interesting that this ammonia molecule turns wrong side out just as often whether it is at room temperature or at the lowest temperature obtainable in the laboratory, whether in Soviet Russia or the United States, and whether this country is Democratic or Republican. Many things we think are important don't seem to affect the ammonia molecule much. The accuracy and order of the universe continue without regard to fashions in hairstyles, clothes, politics, science, or religion. What's true is true. What works, works.

When I went to Berkeley in 1925 to pursue my Ph.D., no one could explain more than a tenth of the attraction of two hydrogen atoms for each other. We knew that each hydrogen atom was uncharged, being made up of a positive nucleus whose charge was just neutralized by the charge on a negative electron. True, the atoms could distort each other and give about one-tenth of the observed binding energy, but the remaining part of the bond was a mystery.

The complete answer supplied by quantum mechanics was that the electron pair, by keeping out of the way of each other as they circulated around the two nuclei, could spend enough time between the two positive nuclei to glue them together to just the observed amount.

In order for the pair of bonded atoms to exchange partners with a similar pair, thus making a new compound, the pairs must approach each other closely. Accordingly, as two pairs of bonded atoms bump into each other, they can only approach and change partners if one or the other pair of electrons is pushed out of the way into an upper state. This collisional work that has to be done so a chemical reaction can take place is called the *energy of activation.*

Using this picture of the energy of activation accompanying a chemical reaction and building on the labors of my many able predecessors, it was possible for me, in 1935, to write down the general equation for the rate of all chemical reactions. This equation has become an integral part of chemistry, used universally.

The excitement of standing, in imagination, at a pass between two energy valleys representing the initial and final states in a chemical reaction and counting the activated complexes as they make their way over the pass in shattering collisions in which atoms are exchanged between the two colliding molecules is the thrill of a lifetime.

Further, to find that wave mechanics and thermodynamics, which have had so many other triumphs, are the same tools that enable us to quantitatively explain this all-pervading aspect of the material world in which we live brings a feeling of awe at the order and exactness of the universe that is never forgotten.

The Living Cell

The third world in which we live is the world of the living cell, the world of biology. Cells vary in size, but typically they are about a micron across, that is, about one ten-thousandth of a centimeter. An active cell divides into two cells about every twenty minutes.

The word *life* itself conjures up animation, movement, excitement, and perhaps a little mystery. Discussions of the origin of life disturb some people. Some are particularly disturbed by scientists who "tamper with creation" and actually try to start life in a laboratory. It would disturb me more to find that life *couldn't* be started in a laboratory. If life can't be started somehow in this physical world, then how did I get here? You see, I *think* I'm alive, although some of you might observe me dozing at my desk and wonder.

The human cell has near its center a nucleus containing forty-six chromosomes. Twenty-three of these come from the father and twenty-three from the mother. The chromosomes are made up of about a million genes that constitute our inheritance. A gene controls the synthesis of essential molecules, such as enzymes, that build and regulate our unbelievably complicated bodies.

A colleague, Frank Johnson, and I once wrote a paper of evolution and rate theory, "The Critical Complex Theory of Biogenesis." This paper outlines a theory of prebiological evolution. One of the principal questions addressed is why living things are optically active.

The body is made up of many types of molecules, just as a large building may be made up of many types of brick. Many of these molecules are asymmetrical, and frequently one optical isomer is found to occur in living things to the virtual exclusion to its mirror image. We can understand this selective choice of building blocks if we recognize that the body is built up by molecules that are incorporated into the body from the food we eat. This section is made by a process of fitting the molecules to the enzyme much as a left hand selects a left-hand glove and rejects a right-hand glove.

Muscles and enzymes are made by joining amino acids together into long chains called proteins. There are twenty different amino acids that are joined together in different proportions to form the links in the various types of protein chains. Of these twenty amino acids used by the body, all but one are asymmetric. Further, all the nineteen asymmetric amino acids used are like the left-hand glove and are called l-amino acids. In every living thing, the opposite optical isomers, which are called the d-amino acids, if present in the food, are rejected by the enzymes that build proteins, and are eliminated from the body. We therefore call this world we live in an l-amino acid world. The l comes from *laevo,* the Latin word for left; and d stands for *dextro,* or right.

Using absolute rate theory, Johnson and I arrived at a reasonable rate of appearance of these optically active templates, given assumed concentrations of certain chemicals in the primordial "soup."

The interesting thing is that from any given pot of "soup" it is as likely that a d- as an l-type world will start up. We can readily imagine a d-amino acid world. In fact, if we look into a large mirror, the world we see is a d-amino acid world, since every object, including the molecules, is the mirror image of those in the real world. Obviously, everything in the d-amino acid world would work exactly as well as everything in our real world, and it is a matter of no obvious consequence which world we happen to have. If there are other worlds that support life, there is no reason for supposing that they may not be d-amino acid worlds. If so, such worlds would be completely inhospitable to us, since we could not digest their foods, and marriages between people coming from d and l worlds would necessarily be sterile. On the other hand, there is, of course, no reason why people from two such worlds might not converse with each other with complete understanding, and one could not tell the two types of people apart by their appearance.

The fact that in our world every living thing, from the tiniest living cell to man, uses only the l-amino acids along with the d-sugars highlights the unity running through the living world. Everything that grows collects those particular optical isomers needed for food and rejects the opposite isomers. Here again, we catch a glimpse of the unity that everywhere characterizes the cosmic design.

Everyday Experience

The fourth world is the world of everyday experience. Here, we measure time in seconds or minutes, and distances in feet or miles. This is the world we know most about.

Since Sir Isaac Newton discovered the universal law of gravitation and developed the laws of mechanics, his successors have been able to calculate the motion of the planets in their orbits to any desired degree of accuracy. Astronomers predict exactly when an eclipse will occur. Using this knowledge, men make great preparations, assemble expensive scientific equipment, and move to the ends of the earth when told that an eclipse is imminent. They get their cameras ready to take pictures and open the shutters at the right moment, and the eclipse begins at the predicted instant. If the eclipse were ever so little off schedule, it would make headline news around the world.

These same laws that enable astronomers to compute eclipses tell precisely, of course, how a satellite goes around in its orbit. A man who makes a good running broad jump only misses becoming an earth satellite by not running fast enough. Thus, if instead of running twenty miles and hour he ran twenty thousand miles an hour, he would find that as he jumped, the earth would curve away beneath him faster than he could fall toward it. Our jumper would settle into an elliptical orbit extending around the earth, except for one thing—the air resistance would slow his speed and set him on fire. To avoid air resistance, the satellite is shot above the atmosphere. This is the only reason for sending it up six hundred miles.

Satellites like *Sputnik* and the moon have a terrifically frustrating job. The moon has been falling toward the earth and overshooting the mark for billions of years and still has no prospect for a successful hit. Man has not succeeded in sending satellites up to such complete frustration yet. The reason is simple. Even at altitudes of six hundred or a thousand miles there is still a trace of hydrogen left. As the satellite circles the earth, it bumps into gas. When it has bumped into a weight of gas equal to its mass, its momentum is cut in half, except that by falling closer to the earth it picks up additional speed. Still, it is a remarkable human achievement to launch a satellite and in a small degree become a partner in creation.

All such achievements rely on the fundamental belief that the everyday world is exactly predictable. We may not yet know or completely understand the rules of when earthquakes occur, or what causes surprises for the weatherman, but we are sure that such events are not really capricious. The more we learn, the better we understand and the closer are our predictions.

The Stars

If we look at the stars, we see the fifth world. Men have probably always looked up and wondered: How far away are the stars? What makes them shine? How long have they been there? Will they exist forever? Some have believed that the stars were gods who controlled their destiny. Others noticed the regularity in the grouping of stars and used their knowledge of stellar movement to help mark the passage of the seasons and fix the times of planting and harvesting. The early Greeks believed the stars were fixed like nails to the vault of the heavens. Aristotle maintained that celestial objects were permanent, immutable, and perfect. He so convinced the Greeks of this that when a new star appeared in 134 B.C., it was attributed by its discoverer to an omission by his predecessors.

In the Middle Ages, Copernicus showed that the earth was not the center of the solar system. But Aristotle's thinking continued to dominate astronomy until the 1500s when new stars were discovered, and then in the seventeenth century when Galileo used his telescope to discover spots on the sun—demonstrating that the solar complexion was somewhat less than perfect—and to prove that the sky was filled with stars that could not be seen with the naked eye.

Just so you know how old I am, I can remember when astronomers, using ever-larger telescopes, discovered that some of the "stars" thought to be part of the Milky Way were actually other galaxies—each containing billions of stars and lying far beyond the Milky Way's outermost limits.

Even so today, as we look out at the universe, the first impression is one of stupendous size. By using such instruments as the huge two-hundred-inch optical telescope on Mount Palomar and new radio, X-ray, and gamma-ray telescopes, modern-day stargazers have pushed the frontiers of understanding ever closer to the edges of the universe and into the very cores of stars. We can see out so far that the light reaching our eyes started on its journey toward us almost twelve billion years ago. You remember how fast light travels: 186,000 miles a second; it goes around the earth, a distance of twenty-four thousand miles, seven and one-half times in a second. A light-year is the distance that light travels in a year—about six trillion miles. If you multiply twelve billion years by six trillion miles, you get a seven followed by twenty-two zeros for the number of miles you can see in any direction you care to look. The known radius of the universe in miles is even bigger than the national debt. It is a very long distance indeed.

When you walk outside on a clear moonless night, all the celestial objects you can see with the naked eye are either planets or stars, or, if you have superman vision, you might be able to see the

Andromeda galaxy that looks like a fuzzy star. All the stars you see are part of our own Milky Way galaxy. The closest star, other than our own sun, is Proxima Centauri, four light-years away. At our present rates of space travel, this journey would require one hundred twenty thousand years. Consequently, we seem to be marooned in our solar system, at least for the time being. Present missile travel, which proceeds at a speed about a thousand times as fast as man can run, will need to be speeded up by another factor of a thousand before we can undertake trips beyond our solar system.

Some scientists believe that the universe is the expanding remnant of a huge fireball created 20 billion years ago by a giant explosion. The stars and planets are the products of that cataclysmic blast and its aftereffects. In 1929 astronomer Edwin Hubble used shifts in the spectral lines of light coming from distant galaxies to calculate that these islands of stars are moving at tremendous speeds away from the earth—and from each other—like dots painted on the surface of an expanding balloon. Scientists at Bell Laboratories have even listened with their sensitive radio antenna to radiation interference, which amounts to the hissing echoes of creation: "In the beginning God created the heaven and the earth. And the earth was without form, and void; and darkness was upon the face of the deep. And the Spirit of God moved upon the face of the waters. And God said, Let there be light: and there was light" (Genesis 1:1–3).

Most cosmologists—scientists who study the structure and evolution of the universe—agree that the biblical account of creation, in imagining an initial void, is uncannily close to the truth. I might add, it is as if the one who wrote those words was there, or at least had talked to Someone who was.

Are we the only worshippers in this great cathedral called the universe? Professor Harlow Shapley, emeritus professor of astronomy at Harvard University, has written an interesting book, *Of Stars and Men* (New York: Washington Square Press, 1960), in which he estimates that there are one hundred million, million, million, million suns in space. Shapely has very conservatively estimated that at least one sun in a thousand should have acquired planets. Most of these satellites are at such distances from their suns that they are either too hot or too cold to support life as we know it. Still others lack life-giving water, while others lack the necessary oxygen. However, Shapley has estimated that of those suns with planets at least one in a thousand has a planet at the right distance for life.

Of those having a planet at the right distance, at least one in a thousand should have a planet large enough to hold an atmosphere; and, finally, one in a thousand of those having a large enough planet at the right distance should have an atmosphere of the right composition to support life. Thus, he concludes that there should be at the very minimum one hundred million planets that could support life, and the number is probably many times more. From the scientific point of view, it is hard to doubt that myriads of worlds are suitable for human habitation.

It is accordingly natural to conclude that the universe is filled with intelligent beings and, presumably, always has been. Any unfolding of intelligences on this earth only repeats what has happened previously elsewhere. Even if we believe beings on distant planets have progressed far beyond us, still the barrier to travel posed by interstellar distances seems quite sufficient to explain why mortal space travelers have not visited us.

So we envision a still-expanding universe that began almost twenty billion years ago, extends for twelve billion light-years, and contains ten billion galaxies—each one an island of hundreds of billions of stars. Actually, we also need to add the dimension of time. We see our nearby sun as it looked a little more than eight minutes ago. We see Proxima Centauri as it was about four years ago, and some of the farther galaxies as they looked billions of years ago. The farther out we look, the further we are looking back in time. Some objects we see may no longer exist.

With all that we do know, it is obvious to the serious student that there is a great deal more that we don't know. To the ultimate question—what existed before the big bang—most of modern science is mute. It's as if it were against the rules to ask questions when there isn't any scientific way to approach the answers. It's still a nice question though, isn't it?

From nucleus to galaxies, the universe is complex, orderly, consistent, and very, very interesting. It is also full of energy and motion. There is something peculiar about that.

If you picked up a watch far from human habitation and found it running, you would ask not only "Who made this watch?" but "Who wound it up?" So it is with the universe. The universe is running down. It is a universe of change. People are born and pass from the earth, and stars, too, come into existence and pass away.

The sun is about half hydrogen; the rest of it is composed of other materials. The hydrogen bomb shows us what happens to hydrogen down in the center of the sun where the pressures and temperatures are enormous. Four hydrogen atoms come together to make helium, and in the process a little of their weight is changed into energy. This energy falls on the earth as sunlight and makes the plants grow.

Thus, the sun is a giant furnace with a supply of hydrogen for fuel—quite a good supply. But if the sun ever burns out, it is going to be very cold in Salt Lake City. You might like an estimate of the fuel supply on hand. I would say the supply should last at least five billion years, so we don't need to worry about it right away.

This picture of the sun as a furnace with a limited amount of fuel poses interesting problems. The second law of thermodynamics is a formal statement of the familiar fact that if energy is being obtained continuously from some source, then the supply of energy must run out sometime unless it is replenished from an outside source. As with any woodpile, if you keep burning up the hydrogen on the sun, it must ultimately be used up unless it is replenished. There is evidence that in the last billion years the sun's temperature has never varied by the small amount that would make the earth unfit for habitation.

It is a well-known fact of experience that if we set a pot of boiling water on a table in a cool room, the pot cools, and when once cooled it never returns to the boiling point without being reheated. In just the same way, the sun is giving off its heat and very gradually growing colder. When the sun ceases to shine, all living things will die; all changes will cease, and the world will reach a deadly, monotonous uniformity. This state is called the *heat death* and is a consequence of nature always moving toward more probable states and never in the reverse direction toward less probable states.

An interesting calculation illustrates the complete improbability of a hot sun arising by change. We suppose that in order to become hot again, the sun must accumulate an amount of heat equal to that which it gives off during its lifetime. This must be accumulated from its surroundings, which we shall assume in the heat death drops to a temperature of seven hundred degrees centigrade. Then, using the straightforward theory of chemical reactions, we find that a length of time in years equal to at least one with a hundred thousand billion, billion, billion, billion, billion zeros must elapse before a hot sun has a 50 percent probability of occurring again by chance. This is almost no chance at all! A universe *filled* with hot suns is no more likely. It is evident that our hot sun, or this universe, did not arise by such a chance fluctuation.

In a very real sense, then, the universe is like a clock that has been wound up. If it is self-winding, it is unique in scientific experience. In a talk before the National Academy of Sciences, I raised the obvious question, "How did the universe get wound up?" No one chose to answer. After the talk, I repeated my question privately to three scientists. President Millikan of the California Institute of Technology said, "I, like you, am a religious man." Professor Van Vleck of the Harvard physics department said, "Of course, one doesn't know." The third man said, "Don't you believe in your religion?" I answered, "Yes, but I wondered about yours."

The Sixth, or Spiritual, World

The five physical worlds display order and complexity. The second law of thermodynamics tells us that, even if we can explain this complexity, we have a problem of how it all got started within the working of the natural laws as we understand them. This leaves scientists no better off than anyone else. We *all* have to rely on a very small measure of information and a very large measure of faith.

This brings us, then, to the sixth world, which includes and surrounds all the others. This is the world that existed before the "big bang." It is the world of the Creator, who provided the energy to wind up the watch and the knowledge and power to establish the complex order we have come to understand in the five physical worlds. As far as we know, this sixth world is without beginning and end of space and of time. Presiding over all is the Creator, whom we worship. Holding everything together are the eternal laws, which will require an eternity for us to master.

One of the first Soviet cosmonauts who circled the earth in space boasted on his return that he hadn't seen anything of God on his journey. This raises the interesting question of where the sixth world and its inhabitants are. Is heaven part of the physical universe as we know it, or is it in some other time and space—in another dimension?

Let's consider the notion of postulates. Postulates are those fundamental propositions that are assumed without proof, generally because there is no way to prove them other than to see if the theories built on them predict events that are then verified by experiments. For example, we all learned as part of our high school geometry class the postulate that parallel lines never meet. This is a postulate of euclidean geometry. However, if you're willing to walk far enough, I can show you a problem. If you and a friend both start out at the equator and walk due north, you are walking parallel paths. You both start out a right angles to the equator. But, you will meet at the North Pole! (You can check this out by looking at two different degrees of longitude on a globe. Each intersects the equator at a 90-degree angle, but they meet at the poles.) The problem is that plane geometry works only on a plane—a flat, two-dimensional world. It doesn't work when the plane curves into a third dimension.

This points up the importance of examining our postulate, our assumptions. Whether or not a particular theory actually predicts reality is more a function of the underlying assumptions than of the elegance of the proof itself. Thus, euclidean geometry is perfect for the flat world for which it was designed, but it results in poor predictions in a three-dimensional world.

The avenue to religious faith lies in the examination of evidence. The Lord himself outlined the procedure when He said, "If any man will do his will, he shall know of the doctrine, whether it be of God, or whether I speak of myself" (John 7:17).

The existence of the sixth world is necessary to an understanding of the other five. Put another way, the existence of the five worlds can be adequately explained only if we assume the existence of the sixth world. Of course, we can also look for evidence of the sixth world in history, and we can look for the evidence directly, by exercising that part of us that shares that other, spiritual dimension.

I worship the wisest being in the universe. I know there is a wisest being in the universe because you can take the wisest person in a room and say, "This is the smartest man in the room—and his wife is smarter." And then you can find the smartest person in the city, then state, then country, then world, then universe. I worship the wisest being in the universe. I know there is such a being. How could there not be? People are different in understanding, and there are lots of them. There must be one who is the smartest.

So I know there is a God. You say, "That still isn't religion." I say, "It is to me, because I can't believe that this wisest being in the universe wants anything except justice." You see, I know some things about Him. If you went out in your car tonight and were hit by a drunk driver and killed, there are others who would say, "Isn't it a tragedy that he couldn't live out his life, that he was cut off?" And do you know what they would do if they could? They'd give you another chance.

The wisest being in the universe is surely as compassionate as these good neighbors that we have. He must like justice and not injustice. So I know there is a God. Because otherwise the world would be unjust. This idea takes us a long way toward understanding God. He exists. He is compassionate. He loves justice and relates to us. We are His children. Isn't that a comforting thought? I'm sure of it, but you don't want to believe anything I say unless it's true.

I can say that I am certain that God is just as real as anybody I know, and that He likes me. And that He likes you too. Those are my postulates for the sixth, spiritual world. They perform exactly the same function in helping me understand the sixth world as the postulates of science do in helping me understand the other five.

ESSAY 2: FAITH AND GOD

The more I try to unravel the mysteries of the world in which we live, the more I come to the conception of a single overruling power—God. One can come to this point of view by prayer and the testimony of the Holy Ghost, or because there seems to be no other explanation of the unity and wonder of the universe, or by the pragmatic method of science that the Savior suggested long ago—try it and you will know.

I have often met this question: "Dr. Eyring, as a scientist, how can you accept revealed religion?" The answer is simple. The gospel commits us only to the truth. The same pragmatic tests that apply in science apply to religion. Try it. Does it work? The conception of a God ruling the universe and concerned with how it works is impossible for me without the corollary that He should be interested in man, the most remarkable phenomenon in the world. Being interested in man, God naturally provided a plan for man's development and welfare. This plan is the gospel of Jesus Christ.

This immediately raises many questions. At best, men are faltering and imperfect. The Savior stands alone as the perfect example. The gospel is indeed the plan which the Creator of the universe has devised to guide His children and bring them back to Him. Through the ages, He has chosen from among His worthy sons prophets to act as guides to his children. Today, The Church of Jesus Christ of Latter-day Saints is presided over by good and wise men who instruct and counsel those who have the wisdom to listen.

In the great council of the premortal life, a tremendous decision was made that man was to have his free agency. This brings with it many interesting problems with tragic results. War and catastrophe are taken by some people to be evidence against the existence of God, or at least His unconcern for the evils that overtake man. I think this should be thought of in a completely different light.

Lucifer promised to bring salvation to every soul, whether the person to be saved desired it or not. Dictators have been operating in the same way from time immemorial. Never has there been a more concerted effort to take away free agency than in the modern communistic world where about 1 percent of the population rules through force and terror. God's non-intervention in human affairs is not a sign of His absence or His disinterest. Rather, it exemplifies one of His greatest gifts—free agency, which enables us to work out our individual salvation. If Lucifer were ruling the world, no one could doubt his presence.

There is a related argument that interests me. One sees good people cut off by death in their prime. This seems to me to be evidence for a life after death. It is impossible to reconcile such incompleteness with any other idea than that we will live again and that what we have lost through no fault of our own will be made up to us in full by a just God.

The wonderful gospel plan as advocated by the Savior in the premortal life, known by His prophets down through the ages and announced by him personally during his earthly ministry, has again been restored by the Prophet Joseph Smith, working as an instrument of the Father. With it we have a rational understanding of life. Eternal progression as a result of wise choices through the use of free agency gives the complete and satisfying explanation of the world in which we live and the struggles we are called upon to make. The success of man in sending satellites into space is arresting evidence of the great capabilities of and the destiny of man, the spirit child of God.

I, as mere man, instruct others. I am dedicated as a scientist, and the significant thing about a scientist is this: he simply expects the truth to prevail because it is the truth. He doesn't work very much on the reactions of the heart. In science, the thing is, and its being so is something one cannot resent. If a thing is wrong, nothing can save it, and if it is right, it cannot help succeeding.

So it is with the gospel. I had the privilege of serving with four other Church members in a conference in which, as a group, we undertook to answer the questions the assembled young folk might ask us.

One of the questions was addressed directly to me. A young man said: "In high school we are taught such things as pre-Adamic men, that kind of thing, but we hear another thing in church. What should I do about it?"

I think I gave the right answer. I said, "In this church, you only have to believe the truth. Find out what the truth is!"

If there is anyone else who is trying to teach anything else with authority, this church is not the least worried about that question or any other kind of question, because the Church is committed only to the truth. I do not mean to say that as individuals in the Church each one always knows the actual truth, but we have the humility sometimes to say we do not know the answers to these things. No Latter-day Saint needs to worry about any question of that kind, because the Church is committed to the truth.

Some have asked me: "Is there any conflict between science and religion?" There is not conflict in the mind of God, but often there is conflict in the minds of men. Through the eternities, we are going to get closer and closer to understanding the mind of God; then the conflicts will disappear.

In the great council in heaven, already referred to, two plans were offered—one whereby the minds of men would be compelled to accept the truth. There would be no choice. Man would make no error. The other plan was set forth by God. In His plan, man would have his free agency. He could decide between the Church of God and all other ways of operating in the world.

God rules from heaven. He does it with such silken threads that some think He has lost the reins. Some people do not even know that He exists. Others wonder whether He exists. I have often thought that a condition like this could never have come about if a dictator such as Hitler or Stalin were ruling.

God is so gentle, so dedicated to the principle that men should be taught correct principles and then govern themselves and take responsibility for their own mistakes, that His children can actually question whether He exists. I cannot think of anything that more wonderfully typifies His mercy, His kindness, His consideration for us, His concern for us, than that He does it all with bonds that are like the strongest steel but are so gentle that you cannot see them.

I do know that He exists. It *is* true, as great mean have known throughout the ages, that this great world we live in is governed by powers more powerful than those of the world. I ask you to look at the wisest man you know and ask yourself whether you believe he is the greatest intellect in the universe. Do you think the tremendous order and wonderful things that have come into the world were created by something with no more understanding than this wise man you know? Of course you do not. It is unthinkable.

I worship the Supreme Intelligence of the universe, and I am convinced that, wise as men are and in spite of the wonderful things they have done, the Creator of this universe goes so far beyond anything that men understand that it is ridiculous to talk of the two in the same terms. So far as I have been able to observe, those who study deeply into scientific matters are often of that persuasion.

The Prophet Joseph Smith was indeed the inspired instrument in restoring the gospel of the Savior, as is shown by the way it works in the lives of men. Since all truth has a single source, the apparent conflicts that often trouble us reflect only our incomplete understanding and must eventually be happily resolved. Eternal progress is man's destiny.

NOTE

1. *Reflections of a Scientist* (Salt Lake City: Deseret Book Co., 1969), pp. 63–80; *The Faith of a Scientist* (Salt Lake City: Bookcraft, 1969), pp. 41–45.

WILFORD R. GARDNER *studied at Utah State University and Iowa State University and received degrees in physics, mathematics, and soil physics. He worked as a physicist for the U.S. Department of Agriculture in Riverside, California, following graduate school and then served as professor of soil physics at the University of Wisconsin, as head of the Department of Soil and Water Science at the University of Arizona, and as dean of the College of Natural Resources and director of the agriculture and natural resources programs at the University of California, Berkeley. He retired in 1994.*

Dr. Gardner was elected to the National Academy of Sciences in 1983. He published more than 150 papers on different areas of soil physics and served as president of the Soil Science Society of America in 1990. He was a Senior Fulbright Fellow in Belgium, and in 1972 he was awarded the Medal of Honor by the University of Ghent. He continues to work with a number of international committees concerned with water resources and soil physics in western Europe, Russia, Australia, and Asia.

Dr. Gardner married Marjorie Cole and has three children. He has served as Sunday School president in six different wards, served on three stake high councils, served as bishop of a California ward, and taught a number of classes.

CHAPTER 4

SCIENCE AS A WAY TO GOD

WILFORD R. GARDNER

To conclude, therefore, let no man out of a weak conceit of sobriety,
or an ill-applied moderation, think or maintain, that a man can
search too far or be too well studied in the book of God's word,
or in the book of God's works; divinity or philosophy, but rather
let men endeavor an endless progress or proficience in both.
—FRANCIS BACON, *Advancement in Learning*

And when ye shall receive these things, I would exhort you
that ye would ask God, the Eternal Father, in the name of Christ,
if these things are not true; and if ye shall ask with a sincere heart,
with real intent, having faith in Christ, he will manifest
the truth of it unto you, by the power of the Holy Ghost.
—MORONI 10:4

INTRODUCTION

The first quotation above is from my father's copy of the sixth
edition of Charles Darwin's *The Origin of the Species*. The second will be recognized by most readers as a verse from the
Book of Mormon. Together they define the themes I wish to address.
Also on my bookshelf is a collection of essays by Henry Eyring, Carl

J. Christensen, Harvey Fletcher, Joseph F. Merrill, Frederick J. Pack, John A. Widtsoe, and Franklin S. Harris. [1] These men were among the most distinguished LDS scientists and educators of their generation, and they were also leaders among the members of The Church of Jesus Christ of Latter-day Saints. After one reads these thoughtful and eloquent discourses on the putative conflict between science and religion, one might well suppose that no more need be said on the matter. Science and LDS religious doctrine both seek and promulgate truth; and truth, by its very nature, cannot be in conflict with itself.

However, as an educator I am well aware that each generation must seek and learn truth for itself. Borrowed truth such as the truth we learn from our parents can carry us only so far through life. At some point we must find and live by our own truths. I will not try to defend science, although I would submit that it is useful and desirable to raise the scientific literacy of all members of society. Those who would defend their scientific or religious truths often do their cause a disservice with bad arguments, buttressed by bad science, bad religion, or both. This I will attempt to avoid, knowing that any scientific arguments I make at this time will sound sadly outdated in a very few years. I will not try to achieve what Eyring and his fellow authors accomplished, which is to demonstrate that science and the religious doctrines of the Church of Jesus Christ are not in conflict with the scientists' own personal philosophies. Rather I would like to discuss the process by which I came to similar conclusions.

For some scientists, there never has been a conflict in their minds. But seemingly very wise people on all sides of the issues have asserted that there is or has been a conflict. I have always desired such resolution of the issues as I could obtain. Everyone who seriously seeks this goal will have to do it his or her own way. Perhaps a brief account of my own efforts will encourage others to believe that the struggle is worth the effort.

The philosopher Søren Kierkegaard observed that "life can only be understood backward, but it has to be lived forward." [2] In my own search for truth, whether sacred or scientific, I too have had to live forward, not knowing what was yet to come, nor why. Only after reflection, analysis, and much thought have I eventually understood some of the lessons to which I have been exposed. At each stage in my life I have looked back at my past thinking and have found errors, truths, partial truths, and errors mistakenly thought to be truths. There were frequent periods of doubt interspersed with times when I was blessed with insight and understanding.

In order to give the reader a sense of my personal approach to the search and integration of religious and scientific truths, I must resort to a series of flashbacks. It is not so important that I recall exactly what happened and how. What is important is what effect my thoughts and reactions to events had upon my philosophy of life, and upon the actions resulting from that ever-evolving philosophy. My scientific and religious education have usually worked together, mostly in harmony, to bring me to a modest understanding of this universe and its inhabitants.

It is essential to differentiate between the approach to the search for truth in religion and the search for truth in science by distinguishing between the nature of scientific truths and the nature of religious truths. Each sphere of truth has its own validity, its own goals and objectives, and its own means or methods of searching for truth. Although we as Latter-day Saints are taught to accept all truth, in an important sense the two spheres of truth meet only in the human soul. Failure of mankind to understand this dichotomy has been the cause of much unnecessary contention and disputation.

In science we repeat an experiment under controlled conditions until we get what we consider reproducible results, albeit the results may be negative. In life we get results without the opportunity to control the conditions and often without the opportunity to repeat or control the experiment. It is true that there is a lot of repetition in life. As one of my friends often observed, "If you keep doing what you have always done, you will keep getting what you have always gotten." Like all good aphorisms, there is a kernel of truth encapsulated within that husk of simplism.

However, cumulative effects of repetitive behavior sometimes lead to totally unanticipated results. We learn religious truths from both repetitive and unique experiences. From each of life's events it is for us to do the sifting and winnowing to separate the wheat from the chaff and find those precious kernels of truth bound up inextricably with each experience. If we are wise, we will also learn from the experiences of others and avoid undesirable consequences or achieve desirable outcomes.

At various stages in my life I have looked back and realized how naive were my earlier opinions and ideas. I have come to realize that even in my more mature years I am still far from where I need and want to be in my understanding of truth. This essay is an attempt to recount the more significant parts of that backward look, insofar as it relates to the intersection of science and religion.

I would like first to place my own "pilgrim's progress" in the historical context in which it was lived. In 1633 Galileo was placed under house arrest for advancing the Copernican view that the earth revolved around the sun and was not the center of the universe. The events of Galileo's life illustrate the vital point that the most serious clashes between religion and science occur when one appears to threaten the very essence and being of the other.

Charles Darwin's *Origin of the Species*, published in 1859, seemingly eliminated the need for a Creator in order to explain the existence of life on this planet. The book provided the basis for perceived threats to the doctrines of Christian churches. Many philosophers and scientists, particularly biologists, took up the debate, and their legacy is still our intellectual misfortune.

At about the same time, the concept of "Higher Criticism" of the Bible was spreading throughout northern Europe, further threatening Christian beliefs. The rationalism of this movement led the historian Will Durant to comment, "The result of two centuries of discussion seemed to be the annihilation of Christ."[3] Durant dismissed this extreme view with his own conclusion: "That a few simple men should in one generation have invented so powerful and appealing a personality, so lofty an ethic . . . would be a miracle far more incredible than any recorded in the Gospels. After two centuries of Higher Criticism the outlines of the life, character, and teachings of Christ remain reasonably clear, and constitute the most fascinating feature in the history of Western man."

Defenders of the Christian faith have resorted to various tactics. In 1925 John T. Scopes was tried and convicted in Dayton, Tennessee, for violating a state statute forbidding the teaching of evolution in the schools of the state. The verdict was reversed on an appeal, but the statute stayed on the books until 1967.

Since the discovery of the double helical structure of DNA, the building blocks of the genetic code, our understanding of evolutionary biology has been revolutionized. There is no longer a "missing link" between man and the apes; through comparing DNA base pairs, biologists can calculate the relationship between any two species of organisms. The availability of more powerful telescopes has allowed astronomers to see further into the past and describe the evolution of the universe from the first few seconds of its existence. Many churches now openly embrace such scientific concepts as evolution.

On the other side, many scientists of our day are more conscious of the limitations of science than were scientists of the past, and many scientific establishments go out of their way to avoid denigrating religion.[4] In the United States the battle between science and religion continues to be carried into the courts over the question of what can be taught in public schools without violating the Constitutional prohibition of favoring one religion over another. Having failed to achieve the right to give equal time to the biblical account of the Creation, some Christian churches have invented a concept they call Creation science, for which they demand equal school time. The Supreme Court has determined that this concept does not qualify as science, even when it is modified to admit a limited evolution. Thus in the forty years since publication of the book *Science and Your Faith in God,* the context and the debate have changed significantly. The rule of law has placed the debate in its proper venue. Individual believers on all sides must make their cases by force of reason, logic, and faith. It is the realm of faith which I first seek to address.

MY PERSONAL VOYAGE

The first significant religious experience which I can recall is my baptism into The Church of Jesus Christ of Latter-day Saints. It took place in an irrigation reservoir on the outskirts of Fort Collins,

Colorado, in June of 1934, four months prior to my ninth birthday. It was the first and only baptism performed by either of two elders serving in a relatively hostile mission. Thus it is understandable that their instructions to me were a bit sketchy. They assumed I was more informed as to what was going to happen than was the case. I had seen pictures of Christ and John the Baptist in the River Jordan, with John's arm raised to the square as he prepared to baptize Christ. Waist deep in the water, their upper bodies appeared dry. Remembered pictures of Jesus after his baptism, showing the Holy Ghost descending in the form of a dove, did not depict the Lord dripping wet. I innocently assumed that as soon as Elder Rose had recited the appropriate incantation, I would have faithfully and fully fulfilled my part of the ordinance.

Suddenly, and entirely without warning, Elder Rose thrust me under water and attempted to drown me. At least that's the way I interpreted it. The fact that he failed to ensure that either of my hands was restrained made my struggle for survival all the more vigorous. This only caused him to redouble his efforts to hold me firmly on the bottom of the lake. At long last, he seemed to have a change of heart and pulled me upright and led me sputtering and bewildered out of the water. He and his companion exhibited a sense of satisfaction which I did not share. My emotions were a combination of surprise and relief. The fact that my mother seemed to sanction the entire process fixed in my mind a less-than-theologically-accurate connection between misbehavior, atonement, and baptism.

We had hardly started for home when the elders' ancient vehicle ran out of gas. After a short deliberation the junior companion agreed he would walk the two miles (and back) to the nearest gas station. Upon his return he confessed that he had brought only enough gas to get back to the station. Lacking funds, he had had to leave his watch with the owner as security. My mother set that matter right, and we proceeded homeward with everyone else appearing rather self-satisfied if not downright joyful, while I tried to make sense out of the afternoon. I must have been confirmed sometime afterwards, but that part of the ordinance has been lost from my memory.

This inauspicious beginning proved to be characteristic of many of my religious experiences. I have learned since that it is not unique to encounter a significant religious experience ill prepared for what is to come. A sense of bewilderment and bemusement is often my initial reaction. I have frequently found myself, as a result of compliant and complacent willingness to go along with the wishes of family, friends, and associates, suddenly thrust into situations where my very future was cast into uncertainty and doubt; and on these occasions I have wondered about the meaning of it all. My immediate concern was more often with how to get out of or survive the situation than how or why I got into it in the first place. However, this mode of encounter has served to fix such events firmly in my memory.

Our family was one of the first LDS families to settle permanently in Ft. Collins, and my religious training in our exceedingly small branch was acquired haphazardly and over strong objections and resistance on my part. I never had LDS classmates in school near my age with whom I could associate. There was no Primary, no Young Men nor Young Women programs, no seminary classes, no Scouting. With great perseverance, my mother managed to get me, my sister, and my brother to what passed for church services—a combination of Sunday School and sacrament meeting held in the leftover Saturday night smoke of the Odd Fellows Hall.[5] We seemed never to pursue any other course of study than Church history. We undoubtedly had a Book of Mormon in the house, though I don't recall where it was kept.

Whatever our religious training may have lacked, our moral training was another matter. No children ever had two parents with more unflinching senses of integrity and honesty. It was clear from my earliest years that in our family there were certain things (a large number, in fact) we simply didn't do, whatever the standards of the rest of the world. My mother's technique with me, which was incredibly effective, was to explain in a greatly sorrowful tone of voice how mortified she had been by my behavior (behavior deserving of this response was often exhibited during church). I did not know for a long time what *mortification* meant, but to my young mind it sounded as though mortifying one's own mother was just about the worst thing a child could do. As a parent, I have not changed my feelings on that subject.

After high school I entered engineering training at Stanford University on a "full scholarship," courtesy of the U.S. Army. Prior to my departure from home, the branch president thought it might be a good idea if I were ordained a priest. This was done, and thus it was that as an eighteen-year-old freshman at Stanford, I blessed the sacrament for the first time. At the time I was a temporary member of the Palo Alto Ward.

The four-year college education promised by the army was replaced after a single semester by an assignment to an infantry regiment and later a combat engineer battalion. After being exposed to the subject of physics at the college level, I knew I wanted to be a physicist, whatever it might take to achieve that goal. Only later did I learn that many of my relatives had already entered that field of science.

At the end of hostilities in Europe, my battalion left Germany and embarked from Marseilles, France, for the Philippine Islands, from which we were to participate in the invasion of Japan. War is a sobering and unforgettable experience. It leaves impressions that do not dim with age and which become an integral part of one's own being. Seeing the death and destruction in Germany prepared me, I believe, for my next and my most significant religious experience. My personal copy of the Book of Mormon was still rarely opened, with large parts unread. However, I could never again read scriptural accounts of ancient battles dispassionately. Never again could I take life for granted nor leave its meaning unquestioned.

During the next two months, the only shipboard activity of any interest, other than eating, reading, and watching the flying fish, was the glee club directed by the chaplain's assistant (another shipboard activity, dice games played with large amounts of real money, both amazed and frightened me). The price for participation in the glee club was attendance and performance at the interdenominational Sunday services. During services one Sunday[6] I idly contemplated the fact that I was really an imposter. Everyone else who belonged to the singing group was a Jew, a Catholic, or a Protestant. My dog tag declared me to be a Protestant, but my religious training had drummed into my head that we Mormons were *not* Protestants but that we were somehow related to the Jews.

While I mused on such thoughts, a very foreign idea entered my mind. For the first time in my life, the thought occurred to me that I didn't have to be a Mormon, or a Christian, or anything else. I could go home and inform my family that I was no longer a Mormon. It was a liberating thought which opened up endless vistas and opportunities. I knew I wouldn't need to drink alcoholic beverages; most of my friends of other Christian denominations in Ft. Collins didn't. Nor would I need to smoke. While I didn't really care for coffee and beer, I thought I could learn to fake that part of the non-Mormon lifestyle.[7] As for girls, they were still largely merely a part of my fantasy life, but a whole new dimension of fantasies had been opened up. I cannot explain the sense of freedom I felt at that moment.

As the chaplain's sermon came to a close and we prepared to sing the closing anthem, my joys were dashed as quickly as they had arisen. I thought that my parents would accept my decision, though there was still the possibility that my mother might feel mortified. More important was the overwhelming realization that both the Lord and I *knew* that I was forever and unquestionably a Mormon. Reason and desire were irrelevant. Some heretofore-unappreciated agent for transmitting knowledge and truth from the Lord had acted upon me. I still didn't know what kind of a physicist or what kind of a Mormon I was destined to be, but my future course seemed foreordained, however mixed my feelings.

MY EDUCATION BEGINS

Had I been in doubt about my future vocation, both religious and secular, upon discharge from the army, I would have stayed in Colorado. There a college scholarship was available, and I could have lived at home, enjoying my mother's cooking. Instead, I entered Utah State University, where I could acquire a degree in physics (something which Colorado State did not offer, whereas at Utah State my Uncle Willard Gardner was chair of the Physics Department) and a Mormon wife (which Ft. Collins also did not appear to offer).

Once enrolled at Utah State, I did not take religious classes at first; I had calculated that by taking the maximum number of *real* courses I could finish my degree in three years. During my senior year, however, I decided to audit (unofficially, since I was already over the course limit) an LDS Institute course in the Old Testament from Heber C. Snell. The main motive was not so much to learn anything about religion but to be able to share a course with Marjorie Cole, a freshman whom I had identified as my future spouse. Snell was, arguably, the best Biblical scholar in the Church at the time. He had been among those promising scholars encouraged by the Church to go east a generation earlier for advanced training at Chicago and other top centers of learning. With his dry wit and gentle manner, Snell opened my eyes to the world of religious scholarship. He dealt honestly with the seeming inconsistencies in the scriptures and helped us to separate the important concepts from troublesome interpretations. He led us to an appreciation of the historical, religious, and philosophical truths of the Old Testament. We learned to appreciate its beauty and poetry as well. I am forever indebted to Professor Snell for ignoring the letter of the university's law and obeying the spirit by allowing my participation in his class. From him I learned the critical difference between reading and studying the scriptures.

Dr. Snell's course helped me to realize that one source of my occasional uneasiness with the knowledge that I was a Mormon was an uncomfortable feeling that there were truths known to the philosophers and the prophets that were missing from my own simplistic and very limited knowledge of Mormon doctrine. It was to be some years before I really managed to redress this situation to any significant extent.

Meanwhile, I entered Iowa State University for graduate work in physics and mathematics. My father, a very wise man (and a soil chemist) had suggested that I could probably make a fair-to-middling physicist. On the other hand, were I to take a degree in physics and enter the field of soil physics, of which his older brother Willard had been a pioneer, I might make a very good future for myself. At that time few soil physicists had more than a year of college physics. At Iowa State the physicist Don Kirkham, son of the distinguished

Mormon educator Francis Kirkham and nephew of Oscar Kirkham, a General Authority, held a joint appointment in both the agronomy and the physics departments. Kirkham had become interested in soil physics through a brief association with Willard Gardner while Kirkham was teaching physics at Utah State. Kirkham was an important reason for my choosing Iowa State, and a very sound reason he proved to be. By happy coincidence, Marjorie later was to become Don Kirkham's secretary, an added bonus. One of Don's daughters later became one of my students.

I discovered at Ames that Mormon scientists were represented in most of the agricultural sciences far beyond the proportion of Mormons to the general population of the country. These men were moving into positions of international prominence.[8] With some exceptions, most were still strongly identified with the religion of their birth. Kirkham was already acknowledged to be the top mathematician among the soil physicists and was eventually to train more soil physicists than any other single individual. Thus, my newfound Mormon friends were largely a subset of my scientific colleagues, and they created a very congenial and tolerant intellectual atmosphere.

Equally tolerant was the science faculty. I recall one lecture on quantum mechanics given by J. F. Carlson (of whom we were all much in awe, inasmuch as he had been a student of Robert Oppenheimer). After Professor Carlson had presented the surprising results of an interesting calculation, one of the students burst out spontaneously, "Why is that?" Carlson replied in a matter-of-fact tone, "I can teach you how it is. Only God can tell you why it is." It was said in such a manner that it left open the possibility that, to Carlson's way of thinking, God did indeed exist and did bear responsibility for why things are as they are.

At about that time I read a comment attributed to the distinguished Princeton physicist John Wheeler.[9] Wheeler suggested that the size of the universe was dictated by the requirements for the existence of mankind. Very large and complex molecules are required for the existence of life on earth. Very large molecules require a very long time to evolve and to be organized into life forms. Long times, in an ever expanding universe, require very large distances. In a very real physical sense, therefore, the existence of mankind requires a universe billions of years old and of immense size. In the words of the physicist Freeman Dyson, "The universe knew we were coming."[10] I found very intriguing the theological implications of this concept.

I initially eschewed attendance at priesthood meetings in the Ames Branch. My excuse was that the course of study was Church history and that the class was taking longer to get across the plains than the 1847 journey. I was taught an important lesson in the ways of the Church when I responded to the question "What would you rather study?" My mistake (at least I thought so at the time) was to suggest that I would rather study something much different, such as the priesthood and Church government. Two weeks later I was the teacher of such a class. The experience forced me to begin the process of filling the gaping voids in my religious background.

Upon graduation I received several job offers in my primary field of training, solid state physics. However, I elected to take a position in soil physics that would allow me to work for a year (which ended up to be thirteen years) under the tutelage of L. A. Richards with the USDA in Riverside, California. Richards was a direct descendent of Willard Richards, who was a cousin of Brigham Young and was also President Young's personal physician, and who is perhaps best remembered for having been one of the four men incarcerated in the Carthage Jail at the time of the martyrdom of the Prophet Joseph Smith. L. A. Richards was recognized as the foremost experimental soil physicist in the world. He had taken his M.S. with my Uncle Willard at Logan and his Ph.D. in physics from Cornell University and had preceded Dr. Kirkham at Ames in the same faculty position. Once again, my scientific and my religious worlds were intimately interwoven. Kirkham represented the best in theory and Richards the best in experiment, and both possessed, one might say, distinguished Mormon pedigrees. My daunting scientific challenge was to find a niche somewhere in between the two men.

With so many relatives and friends sharing both my scientific and religious heritage, I also faced the challenge of determining where I fit into the ecclesiastical spectrum of Mormon scientists. My personal acquaintances among LDS scientists by now ranged from ultra-orthodox to those who claimed limited belief in the doctrines of the Church but still acknowledged their Mormon heritage, at least conditionally.

The main point of this overlong personal history is to illustrate how I arrived at adulthood with a mind largely devoid of knowledge of Church doctrine or other religious knowledge. Until college my Book of Mormon was essentially unstudied, though much earlier I had concluded that "I Nephi, having been born of goodly parents," was one of the best first lines in all of literature. I had known that there were thirteen articles of faith but could have identified only about five of them. However, both my scientific and personal destiny seemed ineluctably bound up with that of other Mormons. This represented a dramatic shift from my youthful isolation from the Saints. Other than my father's mission to the eastern states without purse or scrip, neither of my parents had held a position in a Church quorum or auxiliary. Therefore, it still had not occurred to me that I might at some point be called to such service. Because of the war, the question of a mission never arose. Accepting Church callings was still outside the boundaries of my personal belief system.

SCIENCE AND RELIGION

When a scientist sets out to record and describe his or her contributions to truth, the process is made to sound very orderly and precise. A hypothesis to be tested is postulated, methodology is explained, results are obtained and interpreted, and only then is it affirmed that the hypothesis is indeed true, as was anticipated (negative results generally are consigned to a bottom drawer, unless they dramatically debunk some highly regarded consensus).

In actuality, the process of finding truth is never that orderly and neat. There is a current movement among some sociologists which asserts that scientific truth exists only in the minds of scientists and is whatever a consensus of scientists says it is. Steven Weinberg answers that fallacy thus: "A party of mountain climbers may argue over the best path to the peak, and those arguments may be conditioned by the history and social structure of the expedition, but in the end either they find a good path to the peak or they do not, and when they do, they know it."

Just as the nonscientist may be confused by the apparent inability of science to agree on what is the truth of a given issue at any given time, the agnostic and atheist may take the same view of religion: i.e., that religious truth seems to be whatever a group of theologians say it is. In the Church we are taught that we learn "line upon line and precept upon precept."[11] However, when we assemble all the lines and all the precepts together in our minds, we often seem to observe a sort of jigsaw puzzle of pieces that don't quite fit. In some regions, gaps loom large, and in others the pieces overlap in mutual conflict. Only here and there do we see regions of order, some quite clear, many more fuzzy and "impressionistic." The human mind does not like disjunctions and will go to great lengths to avoid or eliminate them.

The scientific method provides the means by which scientific truth can be found, and in that method the consensus follows the process rather than leading it. When it comes to religious truth, we are either condemned to the sterile conclusions of endless religious debates about many parts of the religious puzzle which do not appear to fit or we must find a viable religious pathway to truth. Various religious communities resort to differing methods. Some rely upon tradition, others trust in reason, many have holy books, while still others place their hope in charismatic individuals. As Latter-day Saints we believe that a God-given process *exists* and has *always existed* and will *continue to exist*. Joseph Smith found that procedure in the Epistle of James 1:5.[12] It is explained further in the Book of Mormon (see Moroni 10:3–5).[13] As I prepared for various Church assignments, the realization that I could find out the truth for myself and did not have to rely upon the word or authority of another was of critical importance to me. In God's mind confusion does not exist, for he is the author of all truth. If he wants us to know truth, then surely he must provide a pathway by which that truth can be obtained. To understand eternal truths that transcend the bounds of this universe, we must eventually go to the author of that truth, our Creator.

My religious education continued to be very much a matter of chance. In Riverside I accepted a call to teach a Sunday School class of sixteen- and seventeen-year-olds. Since I was scarcely a decade older than the students, it was a much less daunting prospect than it would be today. I accepted, not so much out of a sense of duty, but because the Sunday School president was a friend and colleague. Thus while I was learning to be a scientist I was also forced to undergo a crash course in Mormon doctrine, if only to minimize embarrassment due to my ignorance. This call was followed by a series of Church administrative positions, ranging from Sunday School superintendent to counselor in a bishopric to member of a stake high council and then back to teaching (the Gospel Doctrine class) all within the space of a decade. When given a choice, I adopted a conscious and deliberate use of speaking assignments to select and speak on those religious or philosophical concepts of most immediate concern to me or least understood by me. Interestingly, each new Church assignment seemed to contain elements in common with my baptism. Initially, each call came unexpectedly and left me figuratively "gasping for breath" and wondering why otherwise friendly souls were trying to bring me to grief. Later, as I became wiser in the ways of Churchmanship, I could see some of the calls coming, but this prevision did not alter the sense of lack of preparation nor lessen the feeling of engulfment.

I frequently met Mormon scientific colleagues at professional meetings, in an ever-expanding network. I do not recall that we normally indulged in any significant discussions of the problems of accommodating religious doctrine and scientific "facts," with two exceptions. I had long discussions with two friends who were already on the brink of leaving the Church, and for whom the Pearl of Great Price was a most troublesome document. For them, I think, conflicts between science and religion provided a convenient and "principled" excuse to do what they already wanted to do on other grounds. However, they still accepted many truths of the gospel. From discussions with such disaffected individuals I have learned an important theological principle, since reinforced many times. We are often presented with the choice between two seemingly correct but mutually exclusive principles and must decide which is the higher and the more important. Thus it was with Adam and Eve. I feel that my friends replaced what they considered an error by a more serious error, in that they rejected major truths due to what they perceived to be minor "errors." Such dilemmas are not at all uncommon in science, and they often guide our choice of research subjects.

THE PHILOSOPHIES OF MEN

An opportunity to remedy my ignorance of philosophy occurred early during one of my Riverside years. An evening course on the philosophy of religion was offered at the University of California, where my wife was taking her turn to obtain a higher education. In a class of about twelve other students, we covered subjects ranging from the existence of God, to good and evil, God and human freedom, and immortality. As my wife and I studied for the class, in which we were both enrolled, we read from many of the important philosophers to whom my intense scientific training had given short shrift. On our reading list were names such as Santayana, Alfred North Whitehead, Albert Einstein, Søren Kierkegaard, Blaise Pascal, Thomas Aquinas, St. Augustine, Benedict Spinoza, and many others. By unspoken agreement, none of the participants identified their religious affiliation, if any. Discussions were free-ranging and spirited, with the instructor serving only to keep the discussion moving forward.

The important point which delighted me and surprised me was to learn that every one of the most basic religious questions posed by the distinguished philosophers through the ages was dealt with in the doctrines of the Church. One might or might not accept the answers provided by Joseph Smith, either through modern revelation or through his translations of ancient scriptures, but the issues were addressed, and Joseph Smith (with the essential support of the Book of Mormon) had neither avoided nor sidestepped a single fundamental issue. It would be false to assert that I fully comprehended or accepted all that I read. The important consequence was an affirmation that the Church had a theological basis worthy of investigation and study, deserving a place on the library shelves of all the noted philosophers and theologians. One unexpected point of dissatisfaction I found with the writings of many of the philosophers was the minimal attention paid to the concept of eternal progression, a concept which my Church callings had led me to accept and which my science led me to embrace. Our class had problems with the concept of God's grace as the only means of salvation. In the class members' view, if you followed the arguments of one of the saints of old, you might conclude that you could add greatly to God's grace and glory by sinning as much as possible. Obviously absurd. I had already learned to question scientists who preceded me, but questioning philosophers of world renown was a bold step for me. It was a growing confidence in modern day revelation that emboldened me to reason and ponder things for myself. Looking back, I now realize that I was continuously asking the Lord for confirmation of my reasoning to a much greater extent than I appreciated at the time. Sometimes this confirmation came, sometimes not. It was obvious that much study lay ahead, but this learning experience permanently influenced my approach to religious truth and my approach to correlation of sacred truth with scientific and philosophical truth. I did learn an important concept from the words of St. Augustine. "If you don't believe it, you won't understand it."[14] The scientific analog is the reverse: "If you don't understand it, you can't believe it." I began to appreciate that belief and understanding go hand in hand, both in the religious and the secular spheres of knowledge. Sometimes one comes first, sometimes the other, but they cannot remain very far apart.

SCIENCE AND THE CHURCH

In an attempt to understand LDS doctrine relative to some of the more controversial scientific concepts of the day, I frequently sought help from among those Mormon scientists who have gone before. I have found a particular kinship with Elder John A. Widtsoe, a member of the Quorum of the Twelve from 1921 until his death in 1952. Although I was too young to know him, he was a close colleague of my Uncle Willard Gardner, with whom he published a number of important scientific papers. His early experiments on the water requirements of plants anticipated researches that were to consume three decades of my own career.

Widtsoe wrote at length on science and Mormonism. One helpful passage comes from the volume *In Search of Truth*.[15] In commenting on what he terms "this troublesome squabble about evolution," Widtsoe wrote, "The gospel of Jesus Christ accepts all truth. There is no limitation placed upon that truth that may be accepted by members of the Church. A vast literature sets forth in detail the facts around which the evolution controversy has raged. No one, least of all the Church, objects to those facts *if they are properly verified.* They are to be *accepted, acceptable,* and *welcome.*" Widtsoe goes on to refer to "man-like" forms found in various countries and acknowledges them as "undoubtedly genuine."[16] To me, it is not enough that the scientific community validate the facts and truths of science. I know how difficult that can be, and I have lived long enough to find myself arguing vigorously with colleagues defending interpretations of facts that I myself had promulgated years earlier but now no longer accept. Prayerful study can be an aid to understanding in science as well as in religion.

A significant truth came to me rather suddenly at a time when it was much needed. I had often listened in testimony meetings to those who could assert with obvious sincerity and honesty that they knew the gospel was true, "beyond a shadow of a doubt." I wondered how they could be so certain when my own doubts about certain matters cast dark shadows in the corners of my mind. I had often read Doctrine and Covenants 46:10–26, about the gifts given by the Spirit of God. But during all prior readings I had missed an important point. Verse 13 gives the answer very clearly: "To some it is given by the Holy Ghost to know that Jesus Christ is the Son of God, and that he was crucified for the sins of the world." At that time I did not possess that gift. There was no doubt, however, in my mind that my paternal grandmother, who blessed our home by living with us for three of her 100 years, did have it.

As I became wiser in the ways of God and the gospel, I understood that just as many scientific colleagues knew and understood truths that were yet beyond my comprehension, so it is with the gospel. It is not for me to question what someone else knows nor how they can know it. I must learn for myself as well as hope for the gift described in verse 14, i.e., to believe on the words of those with the gift of knowledge.

From Riverside I went to Madison, Wisconsin, largely to expand my contacts with scientists in other disciplines but also to work with C. B. Tanner, one of the first agricultural scientists to be elected to the National Academy of Sciences and again a very close LDS scientific colleague. This period of fourteen years provided the opportunity to be challenged in my thinking by LDS scholars who had progressed well beyond my own level of understanding. It was an exciting and profitable time, both scientifically and ecclesiastically.

My wife and I also added to our knowledge of the children of Israel through an excellent seminar given by a local rabbi. His insights were extremely illuminating. It also helped us to understand the reasoning of a rabbi who was making a stir in Jewish circles by his book and lectures (one of which we attended) asserting that God was dead. He based his conclusion on the Holocaust and all the other misfortunes visited upon God's supposedly "chosen people." Soon after his lecture in Madison, two items of graffiti appeared on a wall across from the lecture hall: "My God is alive and well, sorry about yours"; and "Nietzsche: 'God is dead.' God: 'Nietzsche is dead.'" As Lord Keynes observed, "In the long run, we're all dead." All humor aside, what happens in the long run may be of eternal importance to us.

SCIENCE AND RELIGION HARMONIZE

Next in my life came seven years as an administrator at the University of Arizona (my previous administrative experience had been derived entirely from Church service). My dean and immediate superior was a Mormon. These were years in which I tried to put into practice both my religious and scientific theory. I also was forced to come to grips with my painful shyness and become more people-oriented. My Church service had taught me that on any given day, many staff and faculty members are probably undergoing serious trauma in their lives and should be dealt with accordingly.

Then came an irresistible opportunity to move to an administrative position with the University of California, the president of which happened to be a Latter-day Saint. My wife and I found a home which turned out to be within the boundaries of the Richmond Ward, just north of Berkeley. After the first visit to our new ward, I was asked to meet with the stake presidency, who were visiting the ward. I interpreted this as a routine interview and courtesy visit designed to let the stake presidency become better acquainted with ward members, and our visit was consistent with this interpretation. I conveyed to the stake presidency the nature of my travel schedule and the time demands and emotional stresses of my new university position. Two or three weeks later, as we were moving into our new home, my wife and I were asked to meet with the stake president in his office in Walnut Creek. I had now been in the Church long enough to know that this was not to be a social visit. One or both of us were about to receive a Church calling. During the forty-five minute drive we succeeded in thinking of many good and sufficient reasons for dissuading the president from issuing any and every conceivable call which might be in his mind. My university assignment was nothing less that the complete restructuring of an entire college. Change is a concept almost foreign to Berkeley, and my abilities and energies were being taxed to the utmost. An appropriate calling might be, say, usher at stake conference or secretary to the high priests group. I was indulging in the self-justification that it is not where you serve but how you serve that is important and that all calls are equal in the eyes of the Lord.

We had overlooked the one calling for which we had no adequate response. When the stake president called me to be bishop of the Richmond Ward, I think my wife was even more shocked than I was. I felt almost as I had when Elder Rose suddenly thrust me under the waters of baptism, except that drowning now appeared almost the better of the two fates. The first thing I discovered was how nearly impossible it is to say no to such a call. I made a feeble *pro forma* attempt to put forth the excuses designed for the anticipated callings, but stake presidents would never find bishops if they accepted protestations of that kind. Thus the week we moved into our new ward I found myself trying to influence a faculty of 150 highly individualistic and independent scholars and at the same time to lead a ward of 740 Mormons, none of whom I knew. No more severe and definitive test of whether I had crossed the chasm from a philosophical belief in God to a sacred theological belief in God and in his organized church could have been devised. When everyone on the ward priesthood executive committee looks at you, the bishop, expectantly awaiting, if not inspiration or a revelation, at least some modicum of wisdom, you know you are dependent on faith and faith alone. No amount of theory or academic training can save you, nor can you fake it. It was at this point that my separate and partially independent searches for truth, religious and scientific, had finally and fully merged into one.

As I look back on my career, I feel that were it not for my interest in science and scientific truth, I would have found it very easy to neglect the search for religious truth. Science is not the only way to God, nor will science lead anyone all of the way to God. Without realizing it, I had been following the admonitions of Bacon and Moroni, quoted above. Science is epitomized by a compelling need to know the truth. This same motivation led me to try to become proficient in both science and religion. In order to do so, I have had to believe in order to understand and to understand in order to believe. I find that my studies of the scriptures are much enriched and more meaningful in the context of my understanding of science, and my understanding and appreciation of science are enlightened by my religious experiences. No longer are they compartmentalized. They are complementary. Together they regulate my conduct. To achieve this state I believe it took a nurturing and understanding environment of family and tolerant church and scientific friends, combined with many hours of study and pondering, driven by a hunger for knowledge and truth.

The promise of a *physical* resurrection tells me that God views both the physical and the spiritual components of the human soul as essential, worthy of careful study, coexistent and harmonized in his sphere of truth. As a physicist I cannot yet begin to imagine how the physical and the spiritual do come together, but as one who has finally overcome the reluctant and feeble faith of my youth and replaced it with stronger, firmer, more willing faith, I have now accepted and try to honor as best I can the baptismal covenant entered into as a bewildered and confused boy so many years ago.

NOTES

1. *Science and Your Faith in God* (Salt Lake City: Bookcraft, Inc., 1958).

2. As cited in John Bartlett, *Familiar Quotations* (New York: Little, Brown and Co., 1968).

3. Will Durant, *The Story of Civilization: Part III, Caesar and Christ* (New York: Simon and Schuster, 1944), p. 554.

4. The National Academy of Sciences has recently published a report entitled *How to Teach About Evolution* (Washington, D.C.: NAS Press, 1998). I was asked to review this report prior to publication because of my known affiliation with the LDS Church. My charge was to ensure that, insofar as possible, the report would not inadvertently appear to denigrate any religion or anyone's religious beliefs.

5. Until early adulthood I knew little of my father's positive feelings about the Church. Having finally, at age forty, found permanent employment in his field of scientific training, he worked seven days a week to ensure his continued employment.

6. This event occurred roughly a week after we had learned of the nuclear bombing of Hirsohima, but prior to our realization that there would be no invasion of Japan. That particular religious service was well attended by troops who were doing their best to try not to think about what might lie ahead for us, and who had taken an uncharacteristic interest in religion.

7. It did not occur to me that I might aspire to be other than a Christian. Ft. Collins appeared to me to be divided into Christians, Mormons, and heathens. I was certain I was not a heathen and my friends seemed unsure that I was a Christian. This misunderstanding still dogs our Church. I have repented of my early opinion of heathens.

8. See Leonard J. Arrington and Davis Bitton, *The Mormon Experience* (New York: Knopf, 1979), chapter 16.

9. I believe it appeared in *Physics Today,* published by the American Institute of Physics, but, regrettably, I did not anticipate a future need for such a citation.

10. Freeman Dyson, *Infinite in all Directions,* The Gifford Lectures, Aberdeen Scotland, April–Nov., 1985 (New York: Harper and Row, 1988).

11. See Isaiah 28:10,13; 2 Nephi 28:30; D&C 98:12.

12. "If any of you lack wisdom, let him ask of God, that giveth to all men liberally, and upbraideth not; and it shall be given him."

13. "And when ye shall receive these things, I would exhort you that ye would ask God . . . if these things are not true; and if ye shall ask with a sincere heart, with real intent, having faith in Christ, he will manifest the truth of it unto you, by the power of the Holy Ghost" (v. 4).

14. *De Libero Arbitrio* 354–430.

15. *In Search of Truth: Comments on the Gospel and Modern Thought* (Salt Lake City: Deseret News Press, 1930).

16. Ibid., pp. 33, 67–88.

RAYMOND L. ETHINGTON *received his formal education at Iowa State University and the University of Iowa. His first position after graduate school was at Arizona State University. In 1962 he accepted a position at the University of Missouri at Columbia, where he has been professor of geology since that time. At Columbia he has taught paleontology and served as chairman of the Department of Geological Sciences. For a number of years he was editor of the prestigious* Journal of Paleontology. *He publishes extensively on Paleozoic paleontology.*

In 1988 Dr. Ethington was elected president of one of the major paleontological societies, the Society of Economic Paleontologists and Mineralogists (SEPM). He was awarded honorary membership in the Society for Sedimentary Geology and now serves that organization as president of the SEPM Foundation. Recently he was awarded the Hartley Visiting Fellowship at the University of Southampton.

A convert to the LDS Church during his graduate student days, Dr. Ethington married Leslie Nielsen and has two daughters. His many church callings have included serving as a high councilor in the Columbia Missouri Stake and serving as elders quorum president, high priests group leader, and bishop of the Columbia Missouri First Ward.

CHAPTER 5

"Oh Say, What Is Truth?"

RAYMOND L. ETHINGTON

A n estimated date for Earth's origin, based on events reported in the Old Testament, was published in 1658 in the name of James Ussher (1581–1656), Archbishop of Armagh and Primate of Ireland. He summarized as follows: "In the Beginning, God created Heaven and Earth, Gen. I.V.I., Which beginning of time, according to our chronology, fell upon the entrance of the night preceding the twenty third day of October in the year of the Julian calendar, 710."[1] Transposing that date to the Gregorian calendar, which has been used to record time since 1752, provides 4004 B.C. as the year when Earth was said to have joined the other planets in the solar system.

William Lloyd, then Bishop of Winchester, entered this chronology prominently in the English Bible in 1701. Since that time, the year 4004 B.C. has been cited frequently, although the method by which it was determined is probably unknown to many who quote it. This figure for the age of Earth is in marked contrast to the estimate that has been assembled by persons who based their conclusions on careful examination of Earth itself.

In the last half of the eighteenth century, a Scottish intellectual named James Hutton (1726–1797) made numerous observations about the spatial relations of the rocks of Scotland and thought deeply about how they had come to be. He noted that the kinds of raw materials needed to form the rocks could still be found along the coasts and in the mountains and valleys of Scotland, and he believed that similar raw materials of the past had been transformed into the present-day rocks through the action of natural processes that still operate. Hutton summarized his ideas in 1795 as a small book entitled *Theory of the Earth*.[2] The substance of this volume was that Earth had undergone constant change during its history, and the author remarked that he saw no indication recorded in the rocks as to how or when these changes began and no suggestion of when they might end.

Baron Georges Cuvier (1769–1832), a man best known for his contributions to the development of the biological sciences, and his colleagues studied the layers of rocks in the region surrounding Paris. They noted that these rocks occurred in a specific vertical succession of layers and that the fossil animals they contained changed through the sequence. Some of these fossils represented marine animals, and others were of typical land dwellers. None of the fossils had living counterparts, and the farther down in the succession they were found, the more they differed from anything known to be living at that time.

Cuvier's group reported discovery of evidence at some levels within the succession of rapid elevation of the sea floor to a subaerial position and at other levels of quick submergence of a land area. They noted that such events were marked by the disappearance of the animals whose fossils characterized older rocks and that new populations of fossils were present in rocks formed after the events. Cuvier concluded that these relationships indicate a series of episodic cataclysmic events during Earth's history that caused near instantaneous extinction of the entire population of living things, after which a new creation led to repopulation with a different set of organisms. It is not surprising that his published discussions of his ideas in 1811 and 1812 referred to these events as "Revolutions of the Surface of the Globe," a comparison no doubt to the political and sociological turmoil that dominated his native France while he was a young man. Cuvier's paradigm was widely accepted in the Western world during the first half of the nineteenth century and is generally identified by the word *catastrophism*.

William Smith (1769–1839), a contemporary of Cuvier, worked as what we would call a civil engineer, making surveys, planning construction projects, and especially building canals, an important activity in England at the start of the industrial revolution. His observations of the spatial distributions of rocks and fossils in Britain largely duplicated those made by Cuvier in France. Whereas Cuvier was an analytical intellectual, Smith was a pragmatic person who did not draw upon his experience to provide insight into the deep meaning of things. He learned to use the orderly distribution of rocks and fossils to anticipate what he would encounter in the course of his construction projects and thereby enhance their planning and execution. Smith adopted the practice of recording his data graphically on maps, and in 1815 he published a map showing the rocks immediately beneath the soil cover of England, Wales, and part of Scotland, thereby pioneering a fundamental format for reporting data that is used by all geologists. His other major contribution was to note the order of succession of fossils in the rocks and then use this succession as a key for the identification of individual layers found in isolation and out of the context of a continuous succession of strata.

SCIENCE TODAY

These pioneering efforts, together with those of less well-known persons of the late eighteenth and early nineteenth centuries, laid the theoretical as well as the practical bases for geology and paleontology. They also are situated centrally in a debate that has waxed and waned in intensity over the past century and a half. On one side of this debate are those who recognize the history of Earth as a dynamic succession of events expressed over an extremely long period of time measured in billions of years, with a population of organisms that has displayed near constant change. The opposing view, commonly supported by citations of scripture, envisions Earth's history as brief, measured in thousands of years and essentially static, with no significant changes in its physical or biological configurations. A dramatization of some twenty years ago represented the issues in this debate in the format of a famous trial in the first half of this century. One of the protagonists, a witness under oath, advocates an age for Earth consistent with the ideas of Bishop Ussher. The other, in the role of a cross-examining attorney, responds by asking him if the calculated age was according to eastern or central standard time. Unfortunately, public discussion often has been in this vein, with each side seeking to trivialize the arguments of the other and to demonize those who advanced them, thus discrediting the opposition without coming to grips with either position.

Most of us can take a passive position with regard to this long-standing concern about the history of Earth, for we can accept it as an accomplished fact and devote our time to the everyday problems that are our lot and whose outcomes are not directly influenced by the specifics of history. My experience and day-to-day activities deny me this comfortable option. I am a geologist, and more specifically a paleontologist, which means that I have devoted my adult life to seeking knowledge and understanding of Earth, its materials, its population in the broadest sense, and its history. Space does not permit me to summarize what I have observed in forty years of examination of rocks and fossils from many parts of this country, and readers likely would find it tedious were I able to review it. My experience demonstrates to me that two things are inescapable. First, Earth is much older than six thousand years (the current estimate is that Earth, like the moon and the rest of the solar system, is of the order of 4.5 billion years old). Second, Earth had no population at the time it was created, the things that lived on it have changed continuously since it was populated, and the present population is the most recent phase of a dynamic history of the living things that have inhabited this planet.

RELIGION

In modern scriptures we find the account of Moses, who went into a high mountain and there experienced a vision whereby he saw many earths and their populations. He implored God, saying, "Tell me, I pray thee, why these things are so, and by what thou madest them?" (Moses 1:30). After giving Moses an answer that does not contain the requested details but rather emphasizes God's purpose, control, and influence in the process, God provides the ultimate justification for the existence of this and other earths: "For behold, this is my work and my glory—to bring to pass the immortality and eternal life of man" (Moses 1:39). The second chapter of the Book of Moses is an explication of the beginning of Earth as reported in the Bible in the first chapter of the book of Genesis.

Does my professional experience negate the scriptural treatment of Earth history? Do the scriptures render my experience false? That dilemma has persisted for those who deal with Earth history from both religious and secular perspectives for several hundred years at least and perhaps longer. It still is before us today. The words that follow may not reconcile these conflicting perspectives; rather, they are intended to convey my understanding.

Examine a picture printed in a newspaper. What does it represent? A photograph depicting a person or events at some time and some place. But what is actually shown in the newspaper? Not the original event and not the photograph that was made to record the event. Instead it is a collection of dots—big dots, small dots, widely spaced dots, crowded dots. If we get close enough to it we see only a single dot, and what it represents is lost to us. But the newspaper representation also is flawed when we view it from a distance. The rendering is achieved by photographing the original picture through a screen in order to produce the pattern of dots. The finer the screen, the greater the detail that is retained from the original photo, and newspapers use relatively coarse screens in their reproductions. When the pattern of dots is printed, the image is not recorded accurately on the newsprint because the ink tends to blot and flow on the fibrous surface, producing an irregular outline rather than a well-defined circle. As a result, illustrations in newspapers often lack definition, the contrast often presents problems in interpretation, and they not uncommonly display less-than-perfect definition of the objects that are pictured.

I liken the scriptures to the illustration on the newspaper page and the geologic evidence that I have examined over my forty years to the dots. Together they provide me with independent representations of the reality of something that I did not experience personally. We seek to understand what is before us by considering it from both perspectives, although admittedly many of us feel more comfortable and informed about one approach than the other. Perhaps that is where our difficulty in resolving the issue arises.

TRUTH

We have two ways of establishing what is true. We observe things about us through our physical senses, and we integrate those experiences over our lifetime to produce our view of the physical world. This aspect of our life is easy for us to comprehend and to define, and it allows us to convey this kind of learning and knowledge to others in a way they will comprehend. They in turn can, if they choose, replicate our observations and, if they are consistent with their own experiences, obtain the same insights. We also experience things spiritually, and this brings us personal understanding and conviction about the world around us. Our spiritually obtained insights cannot be shared except by testifying of them to other people. These people then may accept them or reject them, but they cannot reproduce them.

My professional career has been devoted to physical observations of Earth—to increasing the number of dots that make up the picture and to define them ever more rigorously in order to produce the best possible image. Were my life limited to those professional observations, I would have a strongly secular outlook on the world around me. My outlook is tempered by the spiritual experiences that have accompanied my professional experience. I want to share one of these because it exerted a profound influence on my thinking and will remain with me forever.

More than a decade ago, our first grandson was born. My companion and I and his parents eagerly awaited his arrival, anticipating the joy we would experience as we welcomed another generation into our family. Everything was judged to be normal as the projected date of his birth approached. We were delighted to receive a telephone message early one morning that informed us of his birth and that he and our daughter were doing well. Our joy turned to dismay when our son-in-law phoned us some twelve hours later to say that unexpected complications had arisen and our grandson was experiencing seizures whose cause had not been determined. The medical treatment he received over the next several days was to no avail. The seizures increased in frequency, duration, and intensity, and at one point our grandson had to be resuscitated. We began to despair.

Specialists were consulted to review the situation. After a few more days with no progress, the physicians met with the child's parents and grandmother to summarize their findings. They presented a grim prognosis, concluding that his chance of survival was slight and that even if he lived, he would require institutional care throughout his life. Our daughter asked that I give her son a blessing, her only hope for him in the face of this crisis. Our stake president and a close personal friend of our family went with me to the hospital to perform the ordinance. It was heart wrenching to see his tiny body encased in instruments that continuously monitored his bodily functions, an intravenous drip entering through a needle implanted in his scalp, and the baby lying encased in a transparent plastic capsule. We placed our hands on him and offered our prayer in his behalf, then solemnly departed with heavy hearts, leaving him behind in the technological jungle that was all he had known in his brief life and that was projected to be his future.

He was transferred to the medical center at the local university where he could receive continuing attention from the experienced physicians on the staff. The prognosis remained the same. But then, after about a week without any change in treatment, his condition began to improve. The seizures were less frequent, of briefer duration and intensity, and then they just faded away. In another week he was discharged to join his parents in their home for the first time. The physicians who attended him could offer no reason why he had suffered the difficulties that beset him, and they could not account for why he had overcome them. None of the tests and measurements that are part of normal medical procedures gave any insights into these questions. I suppose they assumed that they had been fortunate to recommend a treatment that eventually resolved the unde-

termined difficulty that afflicted him. I know that he was the benefi-
ciary of a more powerful intervention in his behalf, one not limited
by human knowledge. That experience convinces me that we cannot
develop a full understanding of Earth merely by measuring, weigh-
ing, and analyzing it.

The gospel tells us that all things have a spiritual component,
and it emphasizes the physical component as well. We cannot come
to a complete knowledge of ourselves or of the universe unless we
consider fully both the physical and spiritual nature of things.
Unfortunately, as we seek to do so we see through a glass darkly.
Some of us are most comfortable with a spiritual perspective; others
are preoccupied by the physical nature of the world. Too frequently
in our pursuit of reality we have aligned ourselves on opposite sides
of a perceived dividing line and shouted past each other rather than
engaging in a discussion. We focus our attention on the imperfect
picture, or we concentrate on the individual dots. Whatever our perspective, the more we learn, the more the mystery remains and new
questions appear.

SUMMARY

Within the last year an announcement was circulated in the press
that those who are concerned with the ultimate structure of matter
had found the top quark after a long search. Probably a typical
reader's reaction was a statement like "I didn't know it was lost." As
scientists, including geologists and paleontologists, have probed in
search of ever more fundamental attributes of the natural world, the
field of investigation has become increasingly abstract and far from
what we can see, smell, hear, and feel with our senses. Scientific
investigation, a work of the mind, seems to me to often converge
with revelation and the world of the spirit. I am impressed by how
closely my thinking comes to words written over a century ago by
W. W. Phelps:

> The works of God continue, and worlds and lives abound;
> Improvement and progression have one eternal round.
> There is no end to matter; there is no end to space;
> There is no end to spirit; there is no end to race.

There is no end to virtue; there is no end to might;
There is no end to wisdom; there is no end to light.
There is no end to union; there is no end to youth;
There is no end to priesthood; there is no end to truth.
("If You Could Hie to Kolob," *Hymns,* 1985, no. 284)

I wish I could complete this essay with a grand conclusion that would unify the spiritual and physical insights about Earth and man that my life has provided me, but to my regret I cannot. Just as Einstein was frustrated in his aspiration to formulate a unified field theory that would provide a set of equations that could account for all of the fundamental forces recognized by physicists, so a complete theory of Earth has eluded me. But I take heart in my conviction that continued efforts to understand our planet and each other as physical and spiritual entities will bring to me and you insights that we now lack. To achieve this end, we cannot concentrate on either the dots or the fuzzy pictures that collectively constitute our experiences, for they force us to define personal limits to ultimate truth, which has no boundary.

NOTES

1. James Ussher, *The Annals of the World* (London: E. Tyler, 1658), p. 54.
2. James Hutton, *Theory of the Earth with Proofs and Illustrations* (London: Caldwell & Davies, 1795).

H O L L I S   R .   J O H N S O N received his bachelor's and master's degrees in physics from Brigham Young University and his Ph.D. in astrogeophysics from the University of Colorado. He did postdoctoral work at Yale University and at the Paris Observatory in Meudon, France, before joining the faculty at Indiana University, where he has been professor of astronomy since 1963 and has served as chairman of the Department of Astronomy twice. He has specialized in solar and planetary physics and has published more than eighty papers and co-authored three books related to his specialties. He has held a National Academy of Science–National Research Council Fellowship at the NASA Ames Research Center in California and was the F. C. Donders Visiting Professor at the University of Utrecht, the Netherlands, and a guest professor at the Niels Bohr Institute at the University of Copenhagen. Dr. Johnson has been an active member of a number of commissions of the International Astronomical Union and a member of the board of directors of the Association of Universities for Research in Astronomy.

He and his wife, Grete Margit Leed, have six children and seventeen grandchildren. The Johnsons recently returned from service as Church Educational System missionaries in Copenhagen. Hollis served as a missionary for the Church in Denmark (1948–51) and has held many Church callings, including bishop of the Bloomington Indiana Ward, president of the Indianapolis Indiana Stake and of the Bloomington Indiana Stake, stake mission president, and ordinance worker in the Chicago Temple.

CHAPTER 6

ATOMS, STARS, AND US

HOLLIS R. JOHNSON

Gazing at the heavens from our wondrous blue planet, we humans can be excused if we marvel at the beauty and ponder the meaning of our spectacular view. What is our place, we ask, in this grandeur?

As we marvel and ponder, we are aware that we do so, for we are sentient, conscious, intelligent beings. According to both ancient and modern revelation, we humans also are composite beings—spirits clothed in bodies of flesh and bones. Our spirits existed before our bodies were created (see Abraham 3:18–23). Moreover, a distinctive teaching of The Church of Jesus Christ of Latter-day Saints is that we are literally spirit children of God, our Heavenly Father. Our perspectives and lives are enormously enriched, we believe, by the knowledge that our spirits are eternal and that, through our divine heritage, we have unlimited potential in the eternal realm.

Like all material objects, our marvelous bodies are subject to senescence and decay. In the end each of us must die. In theological terms, our bodies will be laid in the grave and our spirits will return to the spirit world. However, that is not the end of us; a glorious future awaits each human being in the resurrection, for spirit and body will be reunited, never again to be separated.

Let's consider the heap of atoms so marvelously arranged into our incredibly lovely and useful bodies. Where did the constituent building materials of our bodies—molecules and atoms—originate? Have they always existed? If not, they must have been made. But where? when? how? of what? Behind these questions lies a fascinating story of stars and stardust.

Atoms are the fundamental building blocks of the universe and everything within it. A million atoms strung in a line would barely reach across the period at the end of this sentence. Atoms are composed of protons, neutrons, and electrons; these in turn are composed of quarks, which might even be composed of something more fundamental. Our bodies, like all animals and plants, are composed of atoms of hydrogen, carbon, nitrogen, oxygen, and other trace elements.

If asked where a particular carbon atom in our body came from, we might reply that it came from the hamburger we ate at lunch. So where was it before that? It was part of the cow or steer from where the hamburger came. Before that? It was in the grass the animal ate. Before that? It was a part of the soil. Before that it was a part of Earth, and before that it must have been a part of the cloud of gas and dust from which Earth and the entire solar system were assembled. Where was that carbon atom before the solar system existed? That must be a fascinating story. Can we find out? Where are the clues? Let's discover this remarkable connection between atoms and stars and us.

In searching for clues to the origin of atoms, we are struck by the fact that the two simplest and lightest atoms, hydrogen and helium, represent the two most abundant elements in the universe.[1] In that vast expanse there are, for every one million atoms of hydrogen, about one hundred thousand atoms of helium; about one thousand atoms of oxygen; a few hundred atoms of carbon and neon and a few less of nitrogen; a few dozen atoms of magnesium, silicon, sulfur, and iron; and even fewer atoms of all other elements.[2] How did the universe's chemical composition come to be arranged this way? Furthermore, there is a surprising odd-even effect in the elemental abundances of lighter elements: elements with even atom numbers (carbon, oxygen, neon, and magnesium) are relatively more abundant than those with odd atomic numbers (nitrogen, fluorine, and sodium). Why? Finally, we might inquire into the physical conditions necessary to produce atoms. What values of temperature and density are needed? Where are these conditions to be found? These clues will lead us far.[3]

MY BACKGROUND

A farm is a great place to grow up, for there are so many interesting things to see and do. Of necessity farmers live close to nature. That closeness is very helpful if one is interested in science, the study of nature, and in God, the Governor of nature.

On warm evenings after the day's chores were done, while Arcturus and Vega wheeled slowly overhead, I could be found outdoors at the edge of the hay, grain, or sugar beet fields watching the friendly stars and talking to the God of nature. Where did it all come from? How did it get to be this way? Where does our Heavenly Father live? What are we humans doing here on Earth? Are there other people out there? It seemed crystal clear to me that God must be the ultimate Scientist.

Garland, Utah, where our family lived, is a typical Mormon community with deep pioneer roots. It was settled largely after 1902 when the canals were dug and the sugar factory opened. E. Lewis and Ida Johnson and their seven children, with me in the middle, lived with Lewis's parents, Lewis O. and Celine Johnson, who had originally built the house. Our Mormon pioneer heritage was still close at hand. We worked the land with horses as did our pioneer forefathers. Houses in town had indoor plumbing, but many farms, including ours, did not. The Johnsons were an ordinary, hardworking Mormon farm family who made their way only because they, like their neighbors, worked hard and worked together.

The Johnsons knew that God had raised up a prophet, Joseph Smith, in our day and through him had restored the true gospel and Church of Jesus Christ. Evil-disposed people had driven the Mormons (including some of their Watkins ancestors) from their homes in Missouri and Illinois. Other ancestors from New England, Denmark, and England had worked and sacrificed for the restored church. Now the Johnsons were privileged to help build Zion in the mountain wilderness. From Zion the gospel was being taken to all nations, kindreds, tongues, and peoples. And the Johnson family, on their little farm in Bear River Valley, were part of that divine venture.

As a youth, I enjoyed the outdoors and the satisfaction that comes from hard work. All the time, whether milking cows by hand or thinning beets or pitching hay, I contemplated the mysteries of nature: How do plants (and weeds!) grow? How do they suck nourishment from the dry soil? On a certain day I examined a pear tree on a neighbor's farm. Where did the stem stop and the pear start? How does a cell know whether to become a leaf or a limb or a lemon? What about rocks? My older sisters said that the banks along the Bear River, where their pasture was and where they spent many tiresome hours working and many happy hours exploring, would someday become rock. Now, these banks had been there for thousands of years, I reasoned, yet they were still clay, not rock; it would take eons for them to become rock. But the mountains around were rocky, so Earth had to be old enough for them to have become rocks. Indeed, Earth must be very, very old.

What about weather? Like every other kid, I loved snow, even though it made chores more tedious. Is there a way to make it snow more? What made the wind blow, so refreshing in summer and so bitter cold in winter? What made the spectacular and occasionally frightening thunderstorms that formed over the Great Salt Lake and marched up along the western mountains? So much to learn and understand!

What about the stars? What are they? Freshmen English students at Bear River High School in the winter of 1943–44 were assigned a reading project in which they were to read and write a review of a number of books. Having chosen astronomy as a topic, I quickly devoured the few astronomy books in the high school library. A whole new universe opened to my view! Stars are very far away from us, and they are not eternal. They are formed, they live, they change, and they fade away. We live in the Milky Way galaxy. Galaxies are enormous systems. The universe was much larger and much older and much more complex than I had ever imagined! Because there were not enough astronomy books either to satisfy my reading appetite or to help me earn an A grade on my class project, I also read chemistry books. (Chemistry ran in my family. My father was a chemist at the sugar factory, and so was my mother during several war years. As for me, I had a wonderful chemistry set.)

As a freshman at BYU, I naturally concentrated on chemistry. To say I devoted myself to this study would be to exaggerate, however. Rooming across the street from the men's gym on the lower campus, two high school buddies and I developed our basketball skills at least as fast as our academic skills. Then came a mission for the Church. When my call to Denmark came, my mother was delighted, my father, as usual, said little, I was a bit frightened, and everyone else was pleased. But off I went, of course. A mission is a great opportunity to learn while serving: to learn to teach the gospel, to learn the conversion process firsthand, and to learn to value the brotherhood and sisterhood of the Saints. Principles taught since one's youth become more meaningful for a missionary. By personal experience I learned the reality of spiritual things and began to make these an integral part of my life.

Returning from my mission during the Korean War, I was soon drafted into the army. After basic training, I was sent to Aschaffenburg, Germany. On a furlough I met Grete Margit Leed in Horsens, Denmark, and remembered her from my mission. The two of us began to write; then to visit, and we finally decided to make a team of it. Back from the army, I pursued studies in physics at BYU.

Grete came to the United States the next summer, and we were married in the Salt Lake Temple. Our goal was to serve the Lord and to create a bond of love strong enough to provide a loving home atmosphere for a family. Our hope was that our children would be good friends and happy, devoted servants of the Lord Jesus Christ. Blessed with three sons and three daughters, our marriage has brought much happiness.

At some moment I realized that people were actually paid to study and teach about the stars, and that realization made my career decision easy. After earning a bachelor's and a master's degree in physics at BYU, I went on to earn a Ph.D. in astrogeophysics from the University of Colorado. Then came postdoctoral stints at the Paris Observatory and at Yale. Finally, my family settled in Bloomington,

Indiana, where I took a position on the faculty in the astronomy department of Indiana University in 1963.

My wife and I have had the privilege of serving in a variety of Church positions. Such important experiences of serving the Lord through callings should not be lightly skipped over, for they leave a clear mark on one's character and outlook. To be a servant of the living God is not a light load. Having made sacred covenants with God, Latter-day Saints strive to obey His word and serve Him even when doing so might be inconvenient or even dangerous. Yet the compensation is great because, like virtue, obedience and service are their own rewards. Moreover, God pours down on us transcendent blessings such as increased faith, hope, peace of mind, inspiration and guidance, enlightenment, and the refreshing of body and mind, to name a few. As King Benjamin so nicely put it, we can never repay our Heavenly Father for the bounties he shares with us (see Mosiah 2:20–21). Among other blessings, occasional insights into the plans and purposes of God are worthy of mention here because of their relation to the exhilaration of scientific discoveries. Those who have felt the power of the Spirit of God will forever view the world and people and God in a different and more spiritual way.

As members of the Church, we expect much, perhaps too much, of our leaders. It is amazing that we expect a person, an ordinary elder one day and a bishop the next, to know everything about everything. As all bishops, I faced questions ranging from marriage (the roles of men and women and their treatment of each other) to financial affairs (tithing, credit cards), interpretation of obscure biblical passages (there are lots of them), justification for war (the Vietnam War was a hot topic, and members and nonmembers alike wanted clear answers regarding the morality of the U.S. involvement), scientific questions (age of Earth, distances in the universe, evolution), and a wild array of other questions, mundane and esoteric.

This expectation on the part of members is, of course, unrealistic. Church leaders are men and women chosen by the Lord for qualities he sees. It is not necessary that they be knowledgeable in other fields. A Church leader might have beliefs, for example, about the creation or age of Earth, dinosaurs, light, meteorites, UFOs, black holes, relativity, or life itself that are not in accord with the facts of nature. What then? Obviously, we should support that person as a leader chosen by the Lord. A person who believes the world to be flat, for example, might still be a prophet if the Lord chose to call him as such.

Differences of opinion over scientific facts and theories sometimes arise in the Church. Whatever the reasons for controversy (there may be many), our discussions (outside the meetinghouse) ought to be carried on in the spirit of love so they do not distract from the unity our mission as a church requires. Sometimes science is used simply as a vehicle to carry on arguments between members who like to argue. Some members use the latest scientific discoveries to display their superior knowledge. Occasionally members seize upon unusual or outlandish stories from friends or the media that seem to support some tenet of our faith without investigating the evidence behind the story, and sometimes in spite of well-established facts to the contrary. (Everyone should understand that many stories in the media and in books are flatly incorrect in one or more ways and are often exaggerated simply to be sensational.).

To preserve unity, we often do not discuss disagreements over scientific matters.[4] Worse yet, some Church members appear to take the position that science and religion are intrinsically antagonistic. They may even further emphasize the superiority of revealed religion to the ideas of men. But what does this tactic accomplish? Surely it will not slow scientific progress nor change the facts of nature! Because scientific discoveries may influence the way we perceive Earth and the universe, in the long run such new information must be taken into account in our world view. We members ought to make the effort to differentiate between scientific facts and theories as do scientists themselves.

Believing as we do in a revealed religion, we Latter-day Saints are used to having questions answered in black and white. Unsettled matters make some of us nervous. On the other hand, controversies are common in the world of scholarly research as scientists try to figure out how things (atoms and life and planets and stars and the universe) got to be the way they are. Puzzles and controversy lead to progress. Settled questions (facts and neat explanations) are written in textbooks; unsettled questions attract our research efforts. Furthermore, scientists are willing to suspend judgment when necessary. Controversies over science and Mormonism may mean the answers are not completely understood, and we must await further revelation or further scientific discoveries for clear resolution. Both science and Mormonism are struggling to learn truth—the laws of nature and the laws of God. In addition, Church members are struggling to apply in their lives the laws of God. There are common points, and I believe we might gain by an increased awareness of them.

I have deliberately used the term *discoveries* to emphasize the task of the scientist to describe nature. Yet one should understand that scientists describe not nature itself, but some picture or model of nature we have in our mind. The phenomena of nature are extremely complex, while our descriptions of them are generally quite simple. It is remarkable that in many cases science has seen amazing success in describing incredibly complex things such as natural objects, phenomena, and processes with such simple ideas and mathematics.

The believer in God must accept that God is the Creator of Earth and the heavens. From this point of view, a scientist studying nature is perforce studying the handiwork of God (see Psalm 19:1). The Scientist God, who lovingly creates worlds for his children, and the Father God, who lovingly reveals commandments to his children, are one and the same being! With this understanding of God, it is very difficult to imagine a contradiction between the discoveries of science and the revelations from God. If disagreements over these arise, it must be because someone does not properly understand scientific discoveries or someone does not properly understand divine revelations, or both.

As we understand better the facts of nature and the revelations of God, we can expect to find less disagreement between science and Mormonism. We should be warned, however, that some characteristics of the universe are very strange (e.g., protons and electrons are waves as well as particles, black holes exist, and we are made of stardust), and some aspects of the gospel are very strange (e.g., Jesus

Christ atoned for past and future sins, all spirit is made of ultrafine and ultrapure matter that "can only be discerned by purer eyes" (D&C 131:7), and we must learn to love people we don't like). As with everything else of value, learning is an ongoing process, and increased knowledge will occasionally force us to change some of our ideas, sometimes even our religious ideas.

STARS AND ATOMS

Who would believe that Earth and the pile of atoms that constitutes our body are made of stardust? As we explore the magnificent universe about us—especially stars, stardust, and atoms—we will surely find some surprises! This short summary will at best whet the appetite.[5]

Why are there such things as stars? Some people might say stars exist because they are so beautiful. Some might say stars exist because God created them. Some might say a star exists because it has the right mass for a gas so that its internal temperatures and pressures are high enough that the outward force of hot gas and radiation perfectly balances the enormous inward force of gravitation throughout the star. Otherwise, stars simply could not exist. Our sun lies somewhere in the middle of that mass range. It so happens that the high central temperatures of most stars lie in a favorable range for many nuclear reactions, especially among the lighter elements, including the fusion of hydrogen to helium. This fusion and the resultant conversion of mass to energy provide the energy that allows stars to shine so brightly for so long. In that sense a star is similar to a giant hydrogen bomb, except that its powerful gravity holds it together against even this fierce outward push.

Stars change slowly over enormous periods of time. In a sense the life story of a star is the tale of its losing battle against gravity. Gravity never relaxes its grip, but the pressure of gas and radiation depends on temperature, and a high temperature depends on the presence of an energy source. However great the energy store of a star is, it is finite and will eventually be used up. Gravity then gains its final victory. But what a story is that battle!

In trying to deduce the life story of a star, scientists must be detectives. They first find the facts, as far as possible, and then try to construct a plausible scenario (a theory or several theories) to account for these facts. They try to answer this question: What happened to cause the things (facts) we observe? The more facts scientists can discover, the more tightly constrained is the scenario they can construct. Put another way, scientists proceed by constructing theories or making hypotheses (ideas of all kinds) and then trying to test these theories against observations or experiments (facts). A good theory is one that makes testable predictions and stimulates thought and research even if in the end it is disproved. Moreover, theories may be changed several times along the way, or new scenarios may be constructed in light of new facts. Often scientists have grand discussions and arguments over such matters. Laymen sometimes misinterpret what is happening and form the idea the scientists often change their minds. (Actually, it is often very difficult to get scientists to change their minds!) If scientists as a group change their minds, it is likely in response to new facts that cast doubt on their initial theories or hypotheses.

Eventually, if enough facts can be discovered, the main points of some theory may become sufficiently well attested (meaning that enough of its predictions are verified and it is not contradicted by any empirical fact) that scientists will regard it as more or less certain. But one should always be wary of saying science has proven something. Scientists search for facts. In this search they may disprove a theory, but it is extremely difficult to prove a theory. Thus science does not so much prove statements or theories or scenarios as it disproves them. Theories that stand the test of repeated experiments come to be regarded as more or less correct. Scientists are trained to keep facts separate from theories, and others should do so as well. Evidence for and against every theory or point of view should be cited so that each person can make his or her own decision regarding the likelihood that a statement is true or false.

GALAXIES AND STARS

Like all galaxies, our Milky Way galaxy consists of gas, dust, and stars along with a massive outer halo of more or less unknown stuff.

The gas and dust are not spread evenly throughout the galaxy but are often clumped into clouds. Recall that our rotating Milky Way galaxy is about one hundred thousand light-years across and contains about 150 billion stars. Our sun, some twenty-five thousand light-years from the galactic center, drags its planets along with it at a speed of 250 kilometers per second in an orbit so huge that it takes us 200 million years to go around![6]

Far out in galactic space, these gigantic clouds are extremely cold, and their atoms are often associated as molecules, sometimes complex ones.[7] Like clouds in Earth's atmosphere, these interstellar clouds form and dissipate over and over again. Once in a while, however, part or all of a cloud may be compressed so that it begins to contract gravitationally because every particle attracts every other particle. This contraction speeds up as the cloud collapses, and it also fragments into a spray of cloudlets. Cloudlets of the right size will become stars. Do astronomers actually see "starbirth"? In a way. They see young stars in regions of dense gas clouds. These are stars that are just beginning to burn (fuse) hydrogen and have not had time to dissipate the placental gas and dust from which they were formed.[8]

Because spectra of the oldest stars show extremely small amounts of any elements besides hydrogen and helium but stars formed later show increasing amounts of these elements, we must accept that atoms of heavier elements were not present in the early stages of our galaxy; rather, they gradually appeared during the lifetime of the galaxy and universe.[9] Where were these atoms formed? Other sites with sufficient energy are excluded for one reason or another, leaving the interior of stars as the likely site. This idea is supported by the fact that scientists have also shown over the years how heavier atoms could in fact be manufactured from hydrogen and helium in stellar interiors. The whole argument has been nicely set forth quantitatively.[10]

STARS AND ATOMS

As a cloudlet contracts and its volume decreases, its density, temperature, and energy density increase rapidly. At first this increasing energy is radiated away, but as the density increases so does the opacity, and the radiation becomes trapped in the gas, further heating it. Eventually, the outward force of gas and radiation balances the inward force of gravity, and the cloudlet becomes stable.[11] However, if this were the entire story, a gas cloud with the mass of the sun would have enough gravitational energy to shine at its present energy output for about 100 million years. Unfortunately, this is far less than the length of time life has existed on Earth,[12] and we must look for other, larger sources of energy. Fortunately, our sun has enough nuclear energy stores to keep shining for at least 10 billion years!

Our sun is a good, average star. Some stars have less mass (but a star must have about 0.06–0.08 solar masses in order to burn hydrogen and be a real star), some have more mass (up to about 60 solar masses, but these huge stars are very short-lived), and some are older and younger, brighter and dimmer. But the sun, with its long lifetime, is an ideal furnace to warm and light a planetary system. The more massive a star is the shorter is its lifetime. It is also true that high-mass stars are relatively rare, while tiny (low-mass) stars are much more abundant.

What will happen when hydrogen in the core has been burned (fused to helium)? Hydrogen continues to burn in a narrow shell around the now almost inert helium core, but gravity compresses the inert core, and the enormous energy released by this compression increases the luminosity and puffs out the star. As the star becomes larger, its temperature falls and it becomes a cool (red) giant star. Although the star has grown to more than fifty times its original diameter, its mass has not changed and its outer density must be as low as a good vacuum on Earth. As the core contracts, its central temperature increases until it is high enough (about 100 million degrees for the sun) for a new reaction: helium burns (fuses) to carbon with the emission of a great deal of energy.

Our story now gets more complicated, and the outcome depends more and more on the mass of the star. As the concentration of carbon in the core rises, helium can burn only in a shell around the carbon core. In this double-shell phase of a red giant's life, hydrogen burns (to helium) in an outer shell, and helium burns (to carbon) in a slightly smaller shell. The carbon or carbon-oxygen core (some carbon captures helium and becomes oxygen) is now extremely compact. As time passes, the thin helium-burning shell begins to flicker, and some of the burned material is churned into the envelope (the deep gaseous layer overlying the core) and eventually to the surface of the red giant. This burned (nuclearly processed) material, enriched in carbon and often in heavier elements (by neutron-capture), changes the chemical composition of the surface.[13] Fascinating as it is, the red-giant phase is relatively short, partly because these giants are blowing themselves apart. As a red-giant star grows in size and its temperature falls, gas starts flowing away from the surface with speeds of about ten kilometers per second. The rate of mass loss can be very large, rising to values of 10^{-6} or even 10^{-4} solar masses per year. At this high rate, a star would lose lots of its mass in one hundred thousand years.

"Stardeath"—to use a sensational term for the natural end of a star—occurs in one of three ways, depending sensitively on the star's mass. Ordinary stars like the sun, and all stars with masses up to about eight solar masses, blow away their outer envelope so that only the compact core remains. For a few thousand years, this expelled shell glows in exotic forms and colors before it finally fades away. The hot core cools rapidly at first and then more slowly. Amazingly, this core (a *white dwarf* star) is only slightly larger than Earth, but it must be about a million times as dense as water. White dwarfs are supported against gravity by the resistive pressure of their electrons, which are so squashed together that their motions are severely restricted. Although there is a maximum limit of 1.4 solar masses in order for a white dwarf to support itself against gravitation, stars up to about eight solar masses may shed enough mass (this is serious weight reduction!) during the red-giant stage to end as white dwarfs. There is no known way by which a white dwarf star can be revitalized.

If a star's mass exceeds about eight solar masses on the main sequence, its evolution is faster and different. It blazes forth as a super-giant star and burns (fuses) elements, one after the other, in sort of an onionlike chemical structure, up to iron. In addition, such a huge star, in its final collapse, forms the heaviest of the elements by neutron capture.[14] For reasons explained below, its energy supply suddenly ends there, and the outward force of gas and radiation abruptly decreases, initiating a catastrophic collapse of the star. In the stellar core the enormous gravitational force crushes free electrons and protons into neutrons and pushes these neutrons tightly together until they form a hard core and abruptly halt the collapse. The infalling material then rebounds, and a strong shock blasts most of the envelope into space in a supernova explosion. Only a neutron star remains, a star composed of hard-packed neutrons. Its mass may be as large as that of the sun, but it will be only ten or twenty kilometers across. Its density is stupendous. Neutron stars are actually seen as rapidly rotating objects whose radiation is channeled by extremely strong magnetic fields along the magnetic poles. As the object spins (on an axis different from the magnetic axis), whenever its magnetic pole happens to point in our direction we receive a pulse of radiation, and the objects are called *pulsars*. Often these remarkable stars pulse hundreds or thousands of times each second.

Perhaps the most incredible part of our story is still ahead. As with white dwarfs, there is also an upper limit of a few solar masses for neutron stars. Imagine now a star with, say, fifty solar masses. Although the star may lose much of its mass along the way, when it finally collapses and rebounds as a supernova, gravity may compress the core beyond the resistive capacity even of hard-packed neutrons. When this occurs, the star becomes a *black hole*—an object so compressed that the escape velocity at the surface exceeds the velocity of light.[15]

Why do atoms or ions of some elements combine (burn or fuse) to produce atoms of other elements? Natural processes "run downhill"; that is, they take the easiest path to the easiest destination. As free particles are bound in an atomic nucleus, some energy is given up. For example, a helium nucleus (two protons and two neutrons to give a mass of four) is more tightly bound than two free protons and two neutrons, and a nucleus of carbon is more tightly bound than are three helium nuclei. In fact, atomic nuclei are more tightly bound (and therefore yield energy by fusion) along the periodic chart of the elements up to iron. Iron is the most tightly bound of all elements, and no energy can be extracted from it. In a sense, then, iron is the ultimate ash of the universe.

Stellar evolution, the life story of stars, presents us with an interesting opportunity to combine theory and observation. Of necessity, the calculations are theoretical. How much confidence can we have in the results? Whenever possible, comparison is made with observations. For example, theoretical models have been constructed for the sun, for which the chemical composition is well known. To be acceptable, such a model must predict the correct radius, temperature, and luminosity for the sun at its current age.[16] The age for the sun is estimated to be 4.6 billion years—a value measured from radioactive dating of Earth[17] and meteorites.[18]

Different requirements can be set for models of stars in star clusters, where all stars have the same age and are formed of the same materials but differ in mass. Repeated, exhaustive comparisons of brightness (luminosity) and color (temperature) of the predictions of model calculations to real star clusters assure us that the basic results of stellar evolutionary theory are correct.[19] However, there is still much to be learned about binary stars, novae, supernovae, variable stars, convection, stellar seismology, solar and stellar activity, stellar dynamos, stellar winds, molecules, grain formation, mass loss, and evolution of the biggest and tiniest stars—just about everything! Although for simplicity we describe the evolution of single stars only, most stars are in binary systems, and these systems, especially interacting binary systems, are important to galactic evolution and the formation of the elements. Describing these systems would fill a whole book.

This is the time to note that fuel reactions often involve nuclei of ^{4}He. That is, the addition of ^{4}He to ^{12}C produces ^{16}O, and further addition of ^{4}He nuclei produces in order ^{20}Ne, ^{24}Mg, ^{28}Si, and so on up to iron. As the astute reader may have noticed, this series of elements with even atomic numbers are exactly those elements whose abundance in the universe is greatest. Clearly, the stellar atom factories have left their fingerprints in the abundance of the elements (and isotopes), and this fact neatly explains the odd-even effect noted earlier (and much more). Such heavier elements as mercury, gold, and uranium can also be manufactured in stellar cores when iron or other elements capture neutrons, but their production consumes energy rather than yields it. There are two processes: one process operates in red-giant stars (remember, these are the very abundant, low-mass stars like the sun) to fabricate the medium-heavy elements such as carbon, nitrogen, and oxygen; and the other process operates in supernovae (the rare, high-mass stars) to fabricate a different set of heavy elements. Detailed comparisons between the predictions of stellar evolutionary theory and spectra of real stars is a fascinating story that continues today.

Exotic as are stellar lives and evolution, the important point for our purpose here is that most of the material of the star, be it a red giant or a supernova, is blown outward into the galaxy. This material is rich in nuclearly processed material—heavier atoms created from hydrogen and helium deep within the star. As the ejected matter mixes with the gas of the galaxy, it enriches the material from which the next generation of stars and planets will be formed.[20]

There is, of course, a limit to starbirth. When all the raw material in a galaxy has been used up in stars, no new stars can be produced. Indeed, there are such galaxies. Most of the material in the Milky Way has already been used in stars. Gradually, in the distant future, no new stars will be formed, and the existing stars will gradually age and die.

REFLECTIVE SUMMARY

Let's now step back and view the entire sweep of the history of a galaxy of stars. Several lines of evidence point to the origin of most galaxies, including the Milky Way, as a huge cloud of hydrogen and helium some 15 billion years ago.[21] Spectra of the oldest stars, some of which appear to have been shining for 12 to15 billion years, show only extremely weak traces of any elements except hydrogen and helium. Apparently, when these old stars were formed, the galaxy consisted essentially of these two elements. They are notably the lightest and most abundant elements and the two that are believed to have been formed early in the expansion phase of the universe,[22] lightheartedly called the "Big Bang."

Soon after the galaxies formed, the first stars formed. Any planets that might have circled these early stars were also composed mainly of hydrogen and helium, and these planets would have been sterile. Life as we know it is based on the chemistry of carbon, and its appearance had to await the formation of heavier elements.

As these early stars, composed of hydrogen and helium, went through the evolutionary stages described above, they formed heavier elements in their interiors, which are literally atom factories. The most massive stars formed quickly, raced through their lives, and exploded as supernovae. In doing so they blew out into space newly created heavy elements—those ranging from carbon through iron and used as fuel, and those heavier elements formed by neutron capture.[23] Now imagine countless generations of massive stars forming and quickly dying, each contributing a load of heavier elements to the galactic gas. The far more numerous stars of solar mass evolved more slowly, but eventually these became red giants and blew away their newly formed heavier elements into space as well.

As time passed and generation after generation of stars formed and died (see Moses 1:35, 38), the Milky Way and all galaxies gradually became rich in heavier elements. After an enormous amount of time had passed, perhaps as long as 10 billion years after the Big Bang, our solar system formed. By that time—some 4.6 billion years ago—atoms of carbon, nitrogen, and oxygen and other heavier elements were available as described above. The stage was finally set for the appearance of planets like Earth, with the chemical elements necessary for life.

Are there other planets with life? That is an exciting question. On the one hand, it seems that if our solar system, with its life-bearing planet, is an ordinary natural product, there ought to be many other life-bearing planets (and this agrees with Moses 1:33). On the other hand, in spite of thorough searches, astronomers have found no evidence whatever of any other life-bearing planet. It is a puzzle, but even an elementary discussion would require at least another book. However, recent reports of possible fossils in a meteorite from Mars might be evidence for at least fossil life on other planets.[24] In addition, astronomers have recently discovered a few planets in orbit around other stars, but these are huge planets, bigger than Jupiter. Finding an Earth-sized planet is a daunting challenge, but it is perhaps imaginable in our lifetime. We must wait for more answers from this exciting search.

A voyage over the entire universe, even if limited essentially to facts, would fill many books, and the universe is so remarkable as to be almost beyond our capacity to imagine. The descriptions we humans give, marvelously ingenious and complex as they are, may be poor representations of reality. Were any of us to write a science fiction story about a universe of our own imagining, it is highly doubtful that our imagined universe would be as remarkable as the real one!

One of the greatest accomplishments of mankind has been the discovery of the universe, and that voyage of discovery constitutes a grand adventure of the human mind and spirit. To be even a small part of that adventure is exciting for me. Those magnificent, sparkling stars are the atom factories, where heavier elements are created out of hydrogen and helium. Our bodies are made of these elements. We are literally made of stardust!

And what is the place of mankind—our spirits and bodies—in this vast, cold, dark universe? What are we humans doing here? Are we a chance product of remarkable biochemistry, or are we the result of careful design?

Consider the incredible panorama of our universe, one that is billions of light years in extent and has been billions of years in the making! Giant clouds of hydrogen and helium (proto-galaxies) formed within a billion years after the Big Bang. Stars then formed in these clouds, and as they lit up the heavens, the stars also fabricated heavier atoms from the original hydrogen and helium. When the stars died in mild or titanic explosions, they dispersed these atoms into galactic space. Thus, the Milky Way Galaxy and all galaxies became slowly enriched in heavier elements with time, and this has been our focus in this brief article. Atoms of these heavier elements became associated into molecules, as are seen in abundance in interstellar space. When newer stellar systems, such as the Solar System, were later formed (about 4.6 billion years ago), they contained a load of these heavier elements, which formed complex molecules. From these complex molecules, living cells and then larger plants and animals, including man, could be created.

Where does God fit into this remarkable picture? The nonbeliever might say this spectacular caravan of events happened by chance or by the action of natural processes and laws. Every step is describable by mathematical equations. Some might even say the equations themselves are the Final Answer. The believer might maintain that when one views the whole picture, a pattern clearly emerges. There is a direction and a goal indicative of design and intelligence. The discussion will likely go on for a long time!

We humans are conscious of our own existence. We appreciate beauty and logic. We remember and decide and think. We worship. We know the difference between right and wrong. We could ask many questions here that would be wonderfully difficult to answer completely. It is clear, however, that humans are distinct from other animals intellectually and spiritually. From that point of view, one might say we are most human, in the best sense, when we develop and use to the fullest our great intellectual and spiritual powers.

According to the gospel, we human beings are much more than a pile of atoms, however wonderfully arranged. We are composite beings. We are composed of body and spirit. Our spirits existed before our bodies were created and will exist beyond the grave and beyond the resurrection.

Remarkable as our marvelous world and solar system and galaxy and universe are, and exciting as our search for further knowledge about them is, this kind of knowledge is not of paramount importance. Some knowledge has greater significance than other knowledge. What is of greatest importance to us? Both in our daily lives and in the long term, we are most concerned with our relationship with our Heavenly Father, with one another, and with our environment, and we must be if we and civilization are to survive. Spiritual truths and values take precedence over all else.

How do we learn the ethical and moral values that govern our lives? How do we know what is right or best? How do we know we should serve others? In particular, how do we learn the will of God? From science? Hardly. Powerful as it is in the discovery of facts about the universe and in attempting to put these facts into an understandable picture, science can tell us little about how we ought to live. Science can say little about ethics, morals, ideals, and values, and it can say next to nothing about God. For this knowledge we must look to experience, both of our own and others, and directly to the revelations of God.

Although to the prophet Alma, Earth and all the planets witness of a "Supreme Creator" (Alma 30:44), others may or may not accept the wonders of nature as proving the existence of God, and they will likely continue to argue about it for a long time. Only God, not nature, can tell us of himself and his plans. We Mormons believe God has revealed himself and his plans anew in our day, and we benefit from that knowledge. To me it is of the greatest importance to know and follow that plan. It is the plan of exaltation and happiness.

Truly the universe is remarkable and the gospel is wonderful. Each human being is precious to our Heavenly Father, and we should be to each other. Life is great. Our task is to learn to live a Christlike life, to build a righteous society, to serve one another, and to enjoy the work!

NOTES

1. Hydrogen and helium are not the most abundant elements on the earth, however, where atoms of oxygen, silicon, iron, and magnesium are more numerous. How the composition of the earth came to be so different from that of the universe at large is another interesting story, but far outside the scope of this essay. For information on this topic, see C. J. Allegre and S. H. Schneider, "The Evolution of the Earth," *Scientific American* 271, no. 4 (October 1994): 44–51; R. P. Kirschner, 1994, "The Earth's Elements," *Scientific American* 271, no. 4 (October 1994): 58–65.

2. See E. Anders and N. Grevesse, in *Geochim. et Cosmochim. Acta* 53 (1994): 191–214; N. Grevesse, A. Noels, and A. J. Sauval, "Standard Abundances," in Stephen S. Holt and George Sonneborn, eds., *Cosmic Abundances,* Astronomical Society of the Pacific Conference Series, vol. 99 (San Francisco: n.p., 1996), pp. 117–26; N. Prantzos, E. Vangioni-Flam, and M. Casse, *Origin and Evolution of the Elements* (Cambridge, England: Cambridge University Press, 1993).

3. See D. N. Schramm, "Primordial Nucleosynthesis," in Holt and Sonneborn, eds., *Cosmic Abundances,* pp. 36–47; and R. P. Kirschner, "The Earth's Elements," *Scientific American* 271, no. 4 (October 1994): 58–65.

4. See E. R. Paul, *Science, Religion, and Mormon Cosmology* (Urbana: University of Illinois Press, 1992), which may well be the best current book on science and Mormonism.

5. See W. Kaufman, *Discovery of the Universe* (San Francisco: Freeman, 1996); J. Kaler, *Astronomy!* (New York: HarperCollins, 1994); J. Kaler, *Stars* (New York: Scientific American Library, 1991); R. Kippenhahn, *100 Billion Suns* (New York: Basic Books, Inc., 1983); M. Zeilik, *Astronomy: The Evolving Universe* (New York: Wiley, 1996). .

6. See S. van den Bergh and J. E. Hesser, "How the Milky Way Formed," *Scientific American* 268, no. 1 (January 1993): 72–78. See also sources listed in n. 5.

7. See G. L. Verschuur, "Interstellar Molecules," *Sky and Telescope* 83, no. 4 (April 1992): 269–384.

8. See S. Parker, "The Eagle's Nest," *Sky and Telescope* 91, no. 2 (February 1992): 32–34; R. Naeye, "The Story of Starbirth," *Astronomy* 26, no. 2 (February 1998): 50–55; F. H. Shu, F. C. Adams, and S. Lizano, "Star Formation in Molecular Clouds: Observation and Theory," *Annual Reviews of Astronomy and Astrophysics* 25 (1987): 23–81.

9. See F. X. Timmes, "Chemical Evolution of Galaxies," in Holt and Sonneborn, eds., *Cosmic Abundances,* pp. 298–306; and N. C. Rana, "Chemical Evolution of the Galaxy," *Annual Reviews of Astronomy and Astrophysics* 29 (1991): 129–62.

10. D. N. Schramm, "Primordial Nucleosynthesis," in Holt and Sonneborn, eds., *Cosmic Abundances,* pp. 36–47; I. Iben, Jr., "Asymptotic Giant Branch Stars: Thermal Pulses, Carbon Production, and Dredge Up; Neutron Sources and s-process Nucleosynthesis," *Stellar Evolution: The Photospheric Abundance Connection,* ed. G. Michaud and A. Tutukov (Dordrecht, Netherlands: Kluwer Academic Publications, 1991), pp. 257–74; R. Kippenhahn and A. Weigert, *Stellar Structure and Evolution* (New York: Springer-Verlag, 1990), pp. 308–62.

11. See S. W. Stahler, "The Early Life of Stars," *Scientific American* 264, no. 1 (July 1991): 48–55; 28–35.

12. See D. York, "The Earliest History of the Earth," *Scientific American* 269, no. 1 (January 1993): 72–81.

13. I. Iben, Jr., and A. V. Tutakov, "The Lives of Stars: From Birth to Death and Beyond," *Sky and Telescope* 74, no. 2 (December 1997): 36–43.

14. J. C. Hayes and A. Burrows, "A New Dimension to Supernovae," *Sky and Telescope* 90, no. 2 (August 1995):30–34.

15. Everyone seems to be fascinated by black holes, and there are several accounts of these remarkable objects. See, for example, S. W. Hawking, *A Brief History of Time* (Toronto: Bantam Books, 1988); K. S. Thorne, *Black Holes and Time Warps* (New York: Norton, 1994).

16. D. A. Vandenberg, "The Status of Stellar Evolutionary Models," in K. Janes, ed., *The Formation and Evolution of Star Clusters,* Astronomical Society of the Pacific Conference Series, vol. 13 (San Francisco: n.p., 1991), pp. 183–99.

17. See D. York, "The Earliest History of the Earth," *Scientific American* 269, no. 1 (January 1993): 72–81.

18. See C. J. Allegre, and S. H. Schneider, "The Evolution of the Earth," *Scientific American* 271, no. 4 (October 1994): 44–51; J. J. Cowan, F.-K. Thielemann, and J. W. Truran, "Radioactive Dating of the Elements," *Annual Reviews of Astronomy and Astrophysics* 29 (1991): 447–97.

19. See, for example, R. Kippenhahn and A. Weigert, *Stellar Structure and Evolution* (New York: Springer-Verlag, 1990), pp. 308–62; A. Renzini and F. Fusi Pecci, "Tests of Evolutionary Sequences Using Color-Magnitude Diagrams of Globular Clusters," *Annual Reviews of Astronomy and Astrophysics* 26 (1991): 199–244.

20. See N. C. Rana, "Chemical Evolution of the Galaxy," *Annual Reviews of Astronomy and Astrophysics* 29 (1991): 129–62; G. L. Verschuur, "Interstellar Molecules," *Sky and Telescope* 83, no. 4 (April 1992): 269–384.

21. See A. Dressler, "Observing Galaxies Through Time," *Sky and Telescope* 82, no. 2 (August 1991): 126–32; M. S. Longair, "Outside the Stars," in W. W. Weiss and A. Baglin, eds., *Inside the Stars,* Astronomical Society of the Pacific Conference Series, vol. 40 (San Francisco: n.p., 1993), pp. 1–24.

22. See P. J. E. Peebles et al., "The Evolution of the Universe," *Scientific American* 271, no. 4 (October 1994): 28–35; N. Prantzos, E. Vangioni-Flam, and M. Casse, *Origin and Evolution of the Elements* (Cambridge, England: Cambridge University Press, 1993).

23. See I. Iben, Jr., and A. V. Tutakov, "The Lives of Stars . . . ," pp. 36–43; J. C. Hayes and A. Burrows, "A New Dimension to Supernovae," pp. 30–34.

24. See D. S. McKay et al., "Search for Past Life on Mars: Possible Relic Biogenic Activity in Martian Meteorite ALH84001," *Science* 273 (16 August 1996): 924–30.

D A V I D   L .   C L A R K   *studied at Brigham Young University and Columbia University and received his Ph.D. from the University of Iowa. He taught at Southern Methodist University in Dallas and at Brigham Young University before joining the Department of Geology and Geophysics at the University of Wisconsin in 1963. He was chairman of that department from 1971 to 1974 and associate dean for natural science in the university's College of Letters and Science from 1986 to 1991. Dr. Clark was a Senior Fulbright Fellow and visiting professor at the Institute for Paleontology at the University of Bonn and has conducted paleontologic research in Europe and western North America. During the past twenty-five years, his principal research has been focused on marine geology and paleoclimatology of the Arctic Ocean. In addition, he teaches paleontology and oceanography and has published more than 150 articles concerned with these specialties. Currently the W. H. Twenhofel Professor of Geology and Geophysics at the University of Wisconsin, he serves as the chairman of the U.S. national committees for both the Antarctic and the Arctic in his position as chairman of the Polar Research Board of the National Academy of Sciences.*

Dr. Clark is married to Louise Boley, and they are the parents of four children and sixteen grandchildren. His service in The Church of Jesus Christ of Latter-day Saints has included callings as elders quorum president, Sunday School president, Young Men president, branch president, bishop, stake high councilor, and, for nine years, counselor in the Madison Wisconsin Stake presidency.

CHAPTER 7

EARTH HISTORY AND HUMAN HISTORY: RANDOM EVENTS OR ORDERED SEQUENCES?

DAVID L. CLARK

S cience has successfully interpreted the major factors involved in the history of Earth as well as the history of its inhabitants. Putting together the sequence of events for the past four to five billion years has not been an easy task, but in spite of the idiosyncrasies of the fossil record, what has been interpreted as the "big picture" is remarkably complete. While these facts do not imply that everything is known concerning either Earth or its inhabitants, or even that all of the scientific interpretations are correct, some future historian will record these scientific accomplishments as among the greatest achievements of the nineteenth and twentieth centuries. Similarly, a future historian will conclude that during this same time interval the restoration of the gospel and the growth of the restored church of Christ were the most important religious accomplishments. In spite of these separate accomplishments in what are generally considered to be quite diverse areas of life's activities, the fact remains that science progresses without much regard for any religious principles, and most religions move on with only minor regard for scientific progress. There are areas of harmony and areas of discord, but as the essays in this volume testify, the truth of both must converge at some level.

My personal life experiences, professional and religious, have focused on the harmony that should exist between religion and science because the gospel is true and, similarly, many scientific endeavors have eternal value. However, this fact raises a host of questions related to which part of science correlates with which part of theology, and which part of theology is in conflict with some area of science. Most important is the question concerning which scientific interpretation is in the most apparent conflict with theological understanding. While most of the possibilities identified for this last question center on organic evolution and the age of Earth, its solar system, and the universe, I am convinced that reduced to its most fundamental level, the question, as the title of this essay suggests, may really be thus: Are events of Earth history random, ordered, or some combination of the two? Randomness in both earthly and biological events is accepted as fact and can be taken as evidence against any grand design, while indications of an ordering of events can be used to support purpose and direction. So, are events of Earth history and organic evolution ordered or random? In order to examine this idea, I turn first to my own professional specialty, the Arctic Ocean.

EVOLUTION OF AN OCEAN

The modern Arctic Ocean is the least studied of Earth's oceans because of its north polar location and the logistical problems of working in an ocean with a permanent ice cover. Probably less is known concerning the Arctic Ocean than is known concerning any other of Earth's major features. For example, the largest unknown geologic feature on Earth, the Alpha Ridge (larger in areal extent than the Alps), is a prominent structure of the Arctic Ocean. In addition, only a few of the events associated with either the major crustal movements that were responsible for the ocean's origin or the climatic changes that have produced its inhospitable environment are understood. Because one of the objectives of geology, a historical science, is to reconstruct the sequence of events that produced Earth's present structure, for more than thirty years, I, along with a number of students from many countries, have tried to figure out the sequence of events that has resulted in the modern ice-covered Arctic Ocean and its organisms.

It is believed that most of the western half of the Arctic Ocean basin formed when a fracture in one of Earth's major crustal plates rotated a large part of present Alaska from its preexisting location against the present region of the Canadian Arctic Islands counterclockwise to its present position. And there is fairly good evidence from paleomagnetic and geochemical dating of rocks that were involved in this movement that this event occurred at rates of a few centimeters a year beginning more than 100 million years ago.[1] As the rotation progressed, the gap that was created by separating the original Alaskan-Arctic Island complex was filled with magma that moved up from the lower part of Earth's crust along a rifting axis, and this became the floor of the modern deep Arctic Ocean basin.[2]

The eastern part of the Arctic Ocean formed in a similar manner but not until approximately fifty million years ago when the Nansen Ridge, an extension of the Mid-Atlantic Ridge, which includes Iceland, began the sea-floor spreading that enlarged the Arctic basin to its present size.[3] We know a few more details of this "big picture" of the ocean's formation, but not much.

Perhaps the most distinctive feature of the modern Arctic Ocean is its ice cover. This layer of frozen seawater is a product of Earth's changing climate, probably initiated at least forty-five million years ago and attributable to both the tectonic forces that partially isolated the ocean as well as to profound changes in Earth's atmosphere.[4] There were changes in Earth's ocean-current heat-transporting systems from low to high latitudes as well. The exact timing of the formation of the Arctic Ocean's permanent ice cover is unknown, but the consequences of a large, frozen seawater ice cap around the North Pole have been profound for Earth's climate. Of course, also important for Earth's climate has been the formation of ice around the south rotational pole in the Antarctic continent, and this may have occurred at about the same time the north polar ice cap developed. All of these activities enhanced the general cooling of Earth from warmer conditions about forty-five million years ago to the present climate.

In addition to its effect on Earth's climate, the Arctic's ice cover has played a role in biologic changes in the polar areas. In the Arctic the polar bear, among a number of other mammals, is a product of the climatic change that produced the ice cover; similarly, in the Antarctic the evolution of the penguins has been directly linked to the development of the south polar ice mass.[5]

Thus, the modern Arctic ecosystem owes its origin to the energy of Earth's interior as well as to solar energy that drives the atmosphere. Earth's residual energy produced the rifting of its crust, and some variation in the amount of the sun's energy available for the Arctic produced the ice cover. And as is true for the Arctic Ocean, the geographic modification of all of Earth's surface began with crustal plate movement originating with forces deep beneath the surface of Earth. These forces ultimately are linked to heat generated deep in Earth, and this is related to the chemical structure of Earth at the time of its origin. This, in turn, was a result of sequences of events that began with the origin of our solar system and our galaxy.

There is little argument concerning cause and effect in what actually happened to produce Earth's modern configuration. There has been a sequence of events, each step of which has been a prerequisite for the succeeding step. This series of interdependent steps produced the modern Arctic Ocean just as different sequences of events produced others of Earth's structures. If any of the steps had involved different processes than those that actually occurred, we would be living on a different kind of Earth surface. While it is fun to think about alternative events, my professional objective has been to understand what actually happened, not what might have been. And this brings us to one of the fundamental questions in science, one already answered by most religions: Was the sequence of events that has resulted in Earth and its inhabitants a series of random events, a series of ordered events, or some combination of the two?

EARTH'S OTHER STRUCTURES

Before addressing that question, we need a few definitions. The Arctic Ocean is designated as one of Earth's "minor" ocean basins. The Pacific, Atlantic, Indian, and Antarctic Oceans are all larger in water volume and area than the Arctic, and each has an origin distinctive from the others yet involving the same kind of sequences of events that account for the Arctic Ocean. In contrast, Earth's continental areas have histories that include different kinds of events than those of the major modern ocean basins, and together the story of the origin of each of Earth's oceanic and continental features comprise the history of Earth. Some parts of this history are better understood than are other parts, and Earth scientists are constantly reminded of the place of humility in their studies because they realize that today's dogma may become tomorrow's discarded theory. During the past thirty years, fuzzy ideas concerning the long-term stability of Earth's major features, oceans, and continents have been replaced with the testable theory that Earth has a mobile crust. The concept of a mobile crust has forced scientists to think differently about Earth and its inhabitants. Yet humility does not necessary indicate ambiguity, and many of the basic theories of Earth science developed in the last few years are as sound as are some of the basic laws of physics. The important point is that Earth's structure, climate, and inhabitants are understood as the result of sequences of events that extend uninterrupted back 4.5 billion years or more.

SEQUENCES OF EVENTS AND MODERN EARTH

For the faithful who pay any attention to science, sequences of naturally occurring events represent God's method of creation, and the end product of scientific endeavors simply is an understanding of this creation process. While the implications of God's hand in a perfectly ordered and predictable sequence of events is obvious, science insists that we cannot preclude the existence of randomness in Earth's systems. Indeed, random events are well documented and apparently are an important part of many physical and biological processes.

All of this introduces the major unresolved problem for religion and science: Are God's fingerprints apparent in Earth and human history? Is there evidence of ordering or progress in the sequence of events that resulted in the inhabitable Earth with human beings?

According to a prevalent scientific idea, if one could rewind (as if with a tape recorder) the history of the solar system and Earth and then push the "record" button and record what would happen the second time around, the randomness of the entire process would be evident and the next playing of the tape would show a different Earth perhaps with different dominant kinds of inhabitants than was recorded the first time. According to this idea, the random events that are involved in crustal processes in the Arctic 100 million years ago could have produced a different kind of ocean basin if a second "recording" were possible, a basin whose waters may not be so isolated from the warmer lower latitudes. If this happened, a different sequence of events would have been initiated, an ice cover may not have formed, and the evolutionary processes would not have produced a polar bear but possibly some other kind of organism. Because there are good reasons for considering that this could be true, we must consider the role of random processes in Earth history and how this could affect the idea of ordered sequences or direction.

SCIENTIFIC THEORY AND REALITY:
4.5 BILLION YEARS OF HISTORY

There is compelling evidence of randomness in many of Earth's natural processes. The argument is made that just because certain events happened as they did does not alter the fact that they might have occurred differently. While it is important to acknowledge this possibility of randomness in a number of systems, progress, the opposite of randomness, has been argued for several generations and must also be acknowledged as a scientific possibility. Moreover, there is the disturbing thought that at least some of those who argue against progress in evolution, for example, are more interested in eliminating the touch of a Creator from everything than in acknowledging the truth.

For the believer, good arguments can be made that what has

actually happened in Earth and human history is the inevitable result of celestial mechanics under the direction of a higher power and that the apparent progress is not random. Is this argument as scientifically tenable as the argument that everything that has happened during the past 4.5 or 10 billion years is the result of random, non-repeatable processes with no hint of direction or progress?

The history of Earth, as suggested by the Arctic Ocean analogy, indicates that its surface features were produced by a combination of internal and external forces whose interactions might have resulted in different kinds of things if certain conditions that were involved during Earth's evolution were different. There is no real argument against this idea. However, magma is not released from deep crustal areas of Earth randomly, but only following the buildup of sufficient heat and pressure that occurs only in specific geographic areas. These internal factors are themselves the product of a different sequence of events that are, in turn, dependent on yet another series of events. Similarly, earthquakes are not random but have specific causes only partly understood yet certainly representative of crustal activity that is the result of a sequence of events that also is dependent on other sequences ultimately reflecting differential energy derived from Earth's interior. The sculpturing of Earth's external structures by atmospheric activity represents predictable results based on climate and rock chemistry. So altering any of the factors involved in the events would certainly change the final structure that is produced. But it is reasonable to assume that this kind of randomness in Earth systems occurs only within certain limits imposed by sets of chemical, physical, and biologic variables, and there could be progress or direction in this.

It seems that many features of modern Earth are the result of sequences of events that could have happened in different ways if conditions and timing events were different. Yet what has happened during the past 4.5 billion years only happened in the way it happened! The external and internal forces of Earth produced what has been produced, not something else, and the result is an Earth suitable for an enormous cargo of humans, and the human condition is accepted by a number of scientists (but certainly not by all) as good evidence for progress in evolution.

Perhaps most important for the whole argument for the Creator is the idea of progress in human evolution. If humans represent the end product of creation, it is logical to suppose there must have been direction along the way. Yet this basic concept is not widely accepted among biological scientists. Let's consider the kind of questions they ask: Is progress in evolution identifiable? Where is the evidence?

Of course, this kind of question is not new. Scholars still argue about the significance of Charles Darwin's concept of progress as part of his revolutionary nineteenth-century theory. Herbert Spencer's later ideas of social evolution, because they definitely included the idea of progress, receive little respect among some modern philosophers. For them the problem is this: If progress is acknowledged for human evolution, then this points toward a Creator. On the other hand, if all events that produced the human body are random and no progress or direction is obvious, then philosophers and scientists who reject God's role in creation have scored in a big way. Addressing the history of thought on the question of progress is important for resolution of the dilemma.

A recent review of thought on directionality or progress in evolution traces the idea of progress and direction in human evolution from the Greeks and the Romans through the early Christian era.[6] Evidently, the idea of humans representing progress first became suspect only during the Renaissance.[7] The fact that Darwin and other advocates of evolution, such as Spencer and Huxley, argued for progress is dismissed by some modern students. To them Huxley's idea that "humans are the pinnacle of evolutionary progress" is evidence only that nineteenth-century cultural values were superimposed on the facts of evolution.[8]

The ideas of recent students of evolution who see the hand of God in creation, such as Teilhard de Chardin and geneticist Theo Dobzhansky, are similarly dismissed.[9] The strong antitheistic bias of William B. Provine leads him to the conclusion that even the

National Academy of Sciences is intellectually dishonest because its actions can be interpreted as being in defense of progress in evolution. According to Provine, the idea of progress is perpetuated by the academy in order to secure support from the U.S. Congress, most members of which have similar "cultural bias" as did Huxley and de Chardin.[10] While the implications of this charge are silly at best and insidious at worst, they are interesting to consider.

According to Robert J. Richards, both Darwin and Spencer had visions of moral and intellectual progress that were "sharpened by the Christianity of their youth; and when the vision dimmed, so that the Creator seemed to recede into the vague interstices of nature, the moral aspects of the vision were retained."[11] Evidently, an important threshold was crossed in progressive evolutionary thought in 1966 when George Williams pointed out features of the evolutionary process that were in conflict with the possibility of long-term progress in evolution, something that is necessary if God was involved.[12] We cannot ignore the fact that there are arguments against evolutionary progress.

In spite of these proclamations, the idea of progress in evolution is not dismissed by all in spite of (or because of) cultural basis. For example, there is widespread agreement that evolutionary progress is difficult to define because the "criteria for its recognition are subject to an extreme diversity of opinions."[13] Thus Michael Ruse argues that in spite of the difficulty of agreeing on the concept of progress, "if one equates progress with cellular DNA content, then it is indeed true—that humans come out well ahead of bacteria."[14] Maynard Smith adds that if complexity is the measure of progress, then it is obvious that both oak trees and elephants show progress over anything that existed a billion years ago.[15] However, Smith concludes his essay with doubts concerning the inevitable consequences of evolution by natural selection.[16]

Much of the discussion on progress in evolution is, of course, related to the acceptance of the "nondirectional" nature of the source of evolutionary change—mutation. How could characteristics that are produced randomly and then are "selected" by whatever proper environmental processes exist at that time show real progress when the starting point is a random event? If we rewind the tape recorder, the next time it will probably record the production of a different character potential, and a different organism eventually will emerge. As far as Huxley's idea of humans being at the "pinnacle of the evolutionary process" is concerned, the fact is that Huxley recognized that it did happen in a particular way, and humans with the potential to be morally and intellectually superior to all other products of evolution did indeed appear. The apparent randomness of some things does not mean that all things are random. Still the argument continues:

> The direction of evolution is the direction of increasing entropy and increasing organization. The thermodynamic arrow of time and the biological arrow of time point in the same direction and suggest a common law of entropy increase that is shared between thermodynamic systems and physical information systems. However, the increase in organization that is observed in evolutionary systems is not due to increasing tendency to perfection, nor does it signal progress. It is a byproduct of the historical constraints placed on species by past history.[17]

Others who have entered the debate do not proclaim victory as emphatically. According to David M. Raup, "It is unclear whether the presence or absence of evolutionary progress can be demonstrated rigorously."[18] Raup uses his statistical background to demonstrate that at least some parts of the fossil record that seem to indicate progress are really the result of Markovian processes that really are random, without any driving forces.[19] Raup does not deny the existence of progress in evolution (in fact, he concludes that the history of life on Earth observed from a great distance and only at a few points in the continuum shows directionality), but he is ever alert to the problem of firmly separating apparent evolutionary trends from those that may appear to be directional but actually may have resulted from random processes.[20]

Probably the most conspicuous and eloquent modern critic of the concept of progress in evolution is Stephen J. Gould. While his attempt at neutrality in the believer-versus-nonbeliever arguments is obscured behind the smoke screen of "culturally conditioned responses," it is very difficult for Gould to be neutral on any subject: "Progress is a noxious, culturally embedded, untestable, nonoperational, intractable idea that must be replaced."[21] Even as he expounds on the untestable component of the idea, he simultaneously dismisses any notion of its validity with the dogmatic conclusion that humans are the afterthought rather than the goal of all creation.[22] While there are not many who have the privilege to be so positive in testing an untestable theory, Gould also confesses that the fossil record does contain legitimate cases of progress.[23] However, to superimpose any theistic interpretation on such cases would be contrary to Gould's thesis that progress is the human response and defense to real scientific discoveries.

Science has little patience with untestable hypotheses, yet the argument against progress in evolution may be a splendid example of just such a thing. Earth evolved and humans appeared, and few disagree with this. To argue that it could have happened in a different way than it actually happened is an argument that is difficult to win, because it did not happen in a different way. It is an untestable hypothesis, a thing shunned by most scientists. The fact that a different sequence of events could have happened is factual, but it is stretching the point to use this as evidence against progress in evolution. It might be just as reasonable to argue that the polar bear would have appeared if no Arctic Ocean ice cover appeared. But either argument is untestable and is not good science.

SUMMARY

Henry Eyring was fond of reminding people that they only need to believe the truth. The truth is that Earth structures *could* have had a different history, but they did not. Also, given the idiosyncrasies of genetics and the environment, humans, without direction, might not have appeared. But humans are around, and they have distinct biologic features that suggest considerable progress. Certainly, compared to the animals that surround us, we have a better brain, the most distinctive biological organ we possess. While the accomplishments of civilizations have been erratic and slow, the accomplishments also include the ability to define the fact that if the tape recorder analogy is valid, another Earth could have evolved with different organisms. This we should acknowledge. But we should also acknowledge that there has been progress in evolution and humans are at the top of the heap.

As far as I am concerned, this interpretation is viable, and it has sustained me through a variety of Church callings that have involved dialogue with equally serious students of religion who would ignore science and take the easier road of "true believers." It has not been easy to deal with such people, in spite of their sincerity. However, attempting to deal with them has taught me the important Christian principle of tolerance. Except for a few years of teaching at BYU, I have tried to keep my religious convictions personal, out of the secular classroom, especially not wanting to exercise unrighteous dominion over those dependent on me for a grade. From time to time, students have approached me after class to ask how the subject matter of the course might be reconciled with their own religious beliefs. I have interpreted that as the necessary invitation to explain my own reconciliation of science and religion and the proper time to suggest how they might reach a similar, comfortable philosophy of life. While I have no quantitative measurement of the success of this approach, it has kept me free from any charge of teaching theology instead of geology in a secular university and has provided a comfortable lifestyle. I know of at least one student who was impressed enough with my own reconciliation that he later joined the Church. Many others, I think, are less critical of Christianity in general and LDS theology in particular than they otherwise might have been. More important, it should be apparent that regardless of which approach to a reconciliation is taken, reconciliation is possible. In my own case it has been a necessary ingredient for intellectual honesty, professional responsibility, and serious religious conviction in my life.

NOTES

1. See David L. Clark, "Early History of the Arctic Ocean," *Paleoceanography* 3 (1988): 539–50.

2. See J. (Hans) R. Weber and Jack F. Sweeney, "Ridges and Basins in the Central Arctic Ocean," in A. Grant, L. Johnson, and J. F. Sweeney, eds., *The Arctic Ocean Region*, vol. L of *The Geology of North America* (Boulder, Colo.: Geological Society of America, 1990), pp. 305–36.

3. See David L. Clark et al., "Late Neogene Climate Evolution of the Central Arctic Ocean," *Marine Geology* 93 (1990): 69–94; D. L. Clark, "The Pliocene Record in the Central Arctic Ocean," *Marine Micropaleontology* 27 (1996): 157–64.

4. See David L. Clark, "Arctic Ocean Ice-Cover: Geologic History and Climatic Significance," in Grant, Johnson, and Sweeney, eds., *Arctic Ocean Region*, pp. 53–62.

5. See George G. Simpson, "Fossil Penguins," *Bulletin of the American Museum of Natural History*, no. 87 (1946): 99.

6. See Matthew H. Nitecki, ed., *Evolutionary Progress* (Chicago: University of Chicago Press, 1988), p. 354.

7. See David L. Hull, "Progress in Ideas of Progress," in ibid., pp. 27–48.

8. See William B. Provine, "Progress in Evolution and Meaning in Life," in Nitecki, ed., *Evolutionary Progress*, p. 49.

9. See ibid., pp. 51, 62.

10. See ibid., p. 69.

11. Robert J. Richards, "The Moral Foundations of the Idea of Evolutionary Progress," in Nitecki, ed., *Evolutionary Progress*, p. 147.

12. See ibid., p. 129.

13. See Adam Urbanek, "Morpho-Physiological Progress," in Nitecki, ed., *Evolutionary Progress*, pp. 195–96.

14. Michael Ruse, "Molecules to Men: Evolutionary Biology and Thoughts of Progress," in Nitecki, ed., *Evolutionary Progress*, p. 98.

15. See J. Maynard Smith, "Evolutionary Progress and Levels of Selection," in Nitecki, ed., *Evolutionary Progress*, p. 219.

16. See ibid., p. 229.

17. Edward O. Wiley, "Evolution, Progress and Entropy," in Nitecki, ed., *Evolutionary Progress*, p. 290.

18. David M. Raup, "Testing the Fossil Record for Evolutionary Progress," in Nitecki, ed., *Evolutionary Progress*, p. 293.

19. See ibid., p. 297.

20. See ibid., pp. 298–301.

21. Stephen J. Gould, "On Replacing the Idea of Progress with an Operational Notion of Directionality," in Nitecki, ed., *Evolutionary Progress*, p. 319.

22. See ibid.

23. See ibid., p. 234.

W ILLIAM L EE S TOKES *received undergraduate and graduate degrees at Brigham Young University and earned his Ph.D. from Princeton University. After seven years with the U.S. Geological Survey, he began a career of teaching and research in 1947 at the University of Utah, where he was professor of geology and, for thirteen years, chairman of the Department of Geology. He received many honors, including the Governor's Medal for Science and Technology. He was one of Utah's earliest dinosaur enthusiasts, and as a result of his interest and guidance, more than forty natural history museums throughout the world exhibit Utah dinosaurs, many of which he excavated. He published extensively on the paleontology and geology of Utah. His text for historical geology, published by Prentice Hall, was the leading U.S. book for introductory geology for a number of years. He authored or coauthored thirteen other books and, with colleagues Lehi Hintze and James Madsen, was responsible for the first comprehensive geologic maps of Utah.*

Dr. Stokes married Betty Curtis, and five children were born to them. He held a number of positions as teacher and officer in Church auxiliary and priesthood units, including high priest group leader and service as a stake missionary.

Dr. Stokes published six books that address his personal reconciliation of science and LDS theology. The essay included in this volume is reprinted with permission of Betty Stokes. Dr. Stokes was emeritus professor of geology at the University of Utah when he died in 1994. The following essay is adapted from his book Joseph Smith and the Creation.[1]

If There Be Bounds

WILLIAM LEE STOKES

J oseph Smith left behind a great prophecy of events that will take
place in the Space Age:

If there be bounds set to the heavens or to the seas, or to the
dry land, or to the sun, moon, or stars—

All the times of their revolutions, all the appointed days,
months, and years, and all the days of their days, months, and
years, and all their glories, laws, and set times, shall be revealed
in the days of the dispensation of the fulness of times—

According to that which was ordained in the midst of the
Council of the Eternal God of all other gods before this world
was. (Doctrine and Covenants 121:30–32)

The Prophet recorded this while he was a prisoner in Liberty Jail,
in Missouri, on March 20, 1839. In this prophecy specific future
events are described that will be revealed in a certain time period,
namely, "in the days of the dispensation of the fulness of times." This
dispensation, which began with the organization of The Church of
Jesus Christ of Latter-day Saints by Joseph Smith in 1830, is still in
effect and is the last we shall receive or experience. Each of us, indi-
vidually, is participating in the fulfillment of the events of this great
prediction. Some of it has already been fulfilled, some is in process
of fulfillment, and some is yet to be fulfilled as the Space Age

unfolds. Nowhere else in religious literature can one find a prediction about specific objectives, events, and attainments so inclusive and far-reaching as this. Think of the cost, energy, and technology applied to explorations of our total surroundings in the interval since 1839 when the Prophet made this prediction.

There is something intriguing about the wording of this prophecy. Note that everything listed is to be revealed in the "*days* of the dispensation of the fulness of time." By not using the word *day* or the word *year,* this statement avoids any possible confusion with the so-called God's day of one thousand years or any other identifiable time period. Might it not be that the revelations mentioned are not to come forth all at once, but rather in a step-by-step manner? Truly, as one learns by reading the daily news, great astronomical discoveries are being made and reported on almost a daily basis. We are experiencing the fulfillment of the Prophet's words almost without realizing it.

THE BOUNDS OF LANDS AND SEAS

Man has a continuing urge to explore his surroundings. Ancient man wandered aimlessly or made daring voyages over unknown seas. In time, a need to record past travels was recognized. Beginning with crude charts, the making of maps has progressed to the point where any spot on the globe can be located from space-based satellites with an accuracy of within only a few feet.

Early advances in mapmaking include the standardization of units of measurement, the adaptation of the compass, invention of the sextant, and steady improvement of clocks. A major advance was the establishment of the worldwide latitude-longitude system to unify and standardize all mapping.

The application of electronic technology brought further refinements. Radar, an invention of World War II, utilizes radio waves not only to locate stationary features such as coastlines but also to track moving objects such as ships and aircraft. With the drilling for oil in shallow water out of sight of land, the need for establishing and reestablishing specific spots and tracts became very important. This is now done with the aid of satellites far above Earth.

The waters of Earth are found in three-dimensional bodies; in other words, they have depth as well as length and breadth. Although surface configurations were well known at the time of Joseph Smith, it is only within the past few decades that much has been learned about the depths of the world's lakes, seas, and oceans. During World War II, submarine warfare motivated several nations to study the ocean floors. In determining water depths, what had once been a laborious process of lowering weights became immeasurably easier with the invention of sonar, basically a process of bouncing sound waves off the ocean floor. This process enables a ship to make continuous recordings of water depths wherever desired. Now, with multiple records of numerous traverses, the configuration of the major ocean basins is well known.

An unexpected result of underwater surveys was the discovery of a continuous 24,000-mile mountain chain totally unlike anything on dry land. The best-known segment bisects the Atlantic Ocean and is known as the Mid-Atlantic Ridge. A deep trench follows the crest of the ridge, and evidence is clear that this is a zone of separation constantly filled with lava from below as the sides move apart. This process, called seafloor spreading, is known to be operating in all the oceans.

Of course, the ocean floors cannot expand without forcibly colliding with bordering continents. The fact is that they are colliding, with the result that the ocean bottoms slide downward beneath the continents and are remelted at deeper and hotter levels of Earth. Deep trenches called subduction zones mark places where the crust is descending. Thus the deepest spots of the ocean are in trenches near continental borders; the deepest spot known, 36,198 feet (almost seven miles), is in the western Pacific near the island of Guam.

Following World War II, exploration of the ocean bottom was continued as a cooperative international project known as the Deep Sea Drilling Project. Vessels equipped for drilling holes under deep water were built and sent out on separate expeditions to investigate specific patches of sea or ocean bottom. As of 1990, most of the world's oceans have been charted and sampled in a systematic way.

For the first time, the major physical features of Earth are understandable in a comprehensive, unified framework. The great moving plates, bearing both continents and oceans, encase Earth and interact as an interlocking, dynamic system. The geologic expression of this system is called global plate tectonics. All aspects of present structure and past history of Earth seem compatible with tectonic theory in an eminently satisfactory way. As far as Earth is concerned, the "bounds" of its oceans and dry lands seem to have been determined in a comprehensive way.

HEAVENLY BOUNDS

Turning to the sun, moon, and stars, we find equally startling discoveries. To refer to individual celestial bodies as having bounds may seem illogical, but they do have invisible force fields of various kinds that are boundaries under permissible meanings of the word. We have landed on the moon and have sent space vehicles past other planets and around the sun. We know their distances and dimensions and have measured the invisible electrical, magnetic, and gravitational fields that accompany them through space.

Before the invention of the telescope, five planets were known and named—Mercury, Venus, Mars, Jupiter, and Saturn. These were known to be different from other stars only because they moved constantly across the heavens. Adding Earth to the above list gives the six planets known to Copernicus, who correctly described the solar system as a flattened disk with multiple bodies circling a central sun. Using telescopes, astronomers eventually discovered three additional planets: Neptune, Uranus, and Pluto. Uranus was discovered more or less accidentally in 1781 by William Herschel, who initially mistook it for a comet. Neptune was located in 1846, mostly because of the gravitational effects of Uranus. Several astronomers aided in the search, but chief credit goes to the Frenchman Leverrier.

Pluto, named for the god of the underworld, was discovered in 1930 by the American astronomer Clyde Tombaugh. The mean distance from the sun to Pluto's orbit is 33,656,000,000 miles. The corresponding figure for Earth is 93,000,000 miles. A popular textbook view is that Pluto's orbit marks the outer limit of the solar system. At the time of its discovery, each of the planets was considered to be the ultimate or outermost member of the solar system. The possibility of a tenth planet is seriously discussed, and surveys have been made in the hope of finding it.

Regardless of whether or not there is a tenth planet beyond Pluto, a large amount of solid matter is in orbit within and beyond the fringes of the planetary system. This is in the form of relatively small icy bodies, technically called inactive comets, that seem to be leftover remnants of the cloud from which the solar system condensed some 4.6 billion years ago.

The inactive comets are calculated to exist in several clouds or swarms, the densest of which is near the orbit of Neptune. The inactive clouds surround the sun in a sort of elliptical cocoon and are not in a flattened disk like the planets. The total number of comets is estimated in the billions, but their average size is measured in feet or yards, and they are widely separated in space. Adding them all together might give a mass equal to only several Earths. If we define the solar system as all matter circling the sun, and there is something out there two light-years away moving under the sun's influence, then that must be the bounds of the system.

A galaxy is defined as an extensive system in space consisting of millions to billions of luminous stars with great quantities of gas, dust, and fine invisible matter. In order of size, galaxies stand next above the stars. There is nothing of intermediate magnitude—nothing between pennies and dollars as it were. For some much-debated and little-understood reason, the galaxies are of roughly the same size and are so widely distributed that only by accident do they come close to or collide with each other.

Photographs of galaxies reveal that the majority have a striking two-armed spiral shape. If their spiral shape tells us anything, it is that galaxies are rotating around their dense central cores. The rotational motion has been verified in a number of ways. Our home, the Milky Way galaxy, is revolving along a path and at a speed that carries the solar system completely around its center in about 250 million years. When astronomers studied entire galaxies as rotating gravitational systems, they discovered an unexpected thing. At their calculated speeds they should be flying apart, and yet they maintain their compact shapes.

It is amazing how long it took us to find out enough about the Milky Way to know that it has boundaries and is one of a numerous company of similar entities that seem to extend outward to infinity. It is a long story that could be told in terms of a steady belittlement of the status of man and his home planet.

For centuries, everyone regarded Earth as flat and the center of the universe. The first big adjustment came when the sun proved to be our master and governor instead of the other way around. We adjusted to this reduced position but maintained a belief that the solar system is the center of the galaxy and possibly of the universe as well. In the early 1900s, astronomers demonstrated that the solar system occupies an obscure corner of one average-looking galaxy, and our sun is a superficially undistinguished member of a group of billions of other shining stars.

The only force able to hold a galaxy together is the gravitational pull of a large mass of invisible matter, most of it out beyond the limits of the luminous stars. The total mass of this invisible matter must be many times that of the visible component. The nature and distribution of dark matter is one of the major unsolved problems of cosmologists.

Considering all galaxies, the average distance between them is about one thousand light-years, far enough to ensure that galaxies are not touching each other—each is distinctly separate and apart. In other words, each has its own distant boundaries. Even the dark matter of one galaxy does not seem to mingle with that of its neighbors. The Andromeda Galaxy and our Milky Way are hurtling toward each other at a rate of three hundred miles per second. We need not be alarmed. So great is the distance between us that we will not actually meet for millions of years.

As with the solar system, we cannot yet say that we have discovered the bounds of our galaxy. We know there are bounds, but where are they? There is something about matter that has caused it to clump together in roughly equal masses that may separate into stars, but these stars do not fly apart to fill surrounding space. Stars are not like an endless field of closely packed daisies; they are most like blossoms on neatly but irregularly spaced celestial rosebushes. Furthermore, they are so far apart that bees from one bush are not likely to visit their neighbors. Why galaxies are distributed the way they are is one of the great unsolved mysteries of astronomy.

This brings us to a final great question: Are there bounds to the great universe itself? We are fairly sure that it is at least ten to fifteen billion light-years across, but everything looks the same in all directions. With no boundaries anywhere, can we safely define the boundary as that nothingness beyond which there are no galaxies?

Would that we could understand the great revelation that reads: "And there are many kingdoms; for there is no space in the which there is no kingdom; and there is no kingdom in which there is no space, either a greater or a lesser kingdom" (Doctrine and Covenants 88:37).

A FINAL QUESTION

Joseph Smith's predictions may be tested by how we answer these questions:

* Have geologists and geographers completely mapped the lands and water bodies of the planet? *Almost, but not completely.*

* Have astronomers located the bounds of the solar system? *Approximately.*

* Have astronomers located the limits of the Milky Way or any other galaxy? *Again, only approximately.*

* Have cosmologists found an edge to the universe? *Definitely no, not even a hint of it.*

At this point, let it be understood that I accept divine revelation, not science, as the standard of truth. One must indeed confirm the other; truth cannot exist in conflict with itself.

NOTE

1. William Lee Stokes, *Joseph Smith and the Creation* (Salt Lake City: Starstone Publishers, 1991), pp. 50–63, 35.

B. KENT HARRISON was valedictorian of his Brigham Young University class when he graduated with a B.S. in physics in 1955. He received his Ph.D. in theoretical physics from Princeton University in 1959 and worked at Los Alamos Scientific Laboratory following post-doctoral work. In 1964 he joined the Department of Physics and Astronomy at BYU and has been a full professor in that department since 1971 as well as its chairman from 1972 to 1979. Dr. Harrison spent two years at the Jet Propulsion Lab in Pasadena, California. He has served as a member of the editorial board for the Journal of Nonlinear Mathematical Physics and the Journal of Mathematical Physics. He has published extensively on physics and is coauthor of a book on gravitational theory and gravitational collapse. In addition, he is coeditor of a book related to social welfare problems.

Dr. Harrison is married to Janyce Maxfield, and they are the parents of three sons and a daughter. He has served in the LDS Church as stake clerk, stake high councilor, counselor in a branch presidency, and bishop of a BYU ward.

CHAPTER 9

TRUTH, THE SUM OF EXISTENCE

B. KENT HARRISON

In The Church of Jesus Christ of Latter-day Saints,[1] members generally understand the word *truth* to mean an all-encompassing system of knowledge. Truth is defined by the statement found in Doctrine and Covenants 93:24: "Truth is knowledge of things as they are, and as they were, and as they are to come"—surely an all-encompassing statement. This view of truth is supported by the general tone of other scriptures, for example, "truth abideth forever and ever" (Doctrine and Covenants 1:39), "truth abideth and hath no end" (Doctrine and Covenants 88:66), and "the glory of God is intelligence, or, in other words, light and truth" (Doctrine and Covenants 93:36). Implicit in these statements is the idea that truth is absolute, unified, and self-consistent.

C. Terry Warner goes further than the above definition[2] by noting that Doctrine and Covenants 93:24 is usually taken out of context and that a broader and more correct LDS view is that the word *truth* signifies an entire way of life. (He also comments that many current philosophers have abandoned the search for absolute truth and have settled for a relative, or personal, view of truth.) I am entirely in agreement with these remarks, but for purposes of this essay I will regard truth in the narrower sense as an absolute system of knowledge. Whether truth is "increasing"—particularly as regards God's comprehension—is another question, one I will touch on later.

B. H. Roberts makes a distinction between personal truth, as suggested by Doctrine and Covenants 93:24, and the broader sense of truth as an impersonal, broad statement of the "way things are" (my terminology)—of which any one individual can comprehend only a tiny part.[3]

For Latter-day Saints, it is desirable and ultimately necessary to learn all truth. A famous statement is that from Doctrine and Covenants 88:78–79: "Teach ye diligently and my grace shall attend you, that you may be instructed more perfectly in theory, in principle, in doctrine, in the law of the gospel, in all things that pertain unto the kingdom of God, that are expedient for you to understand; of things both in heaven and in the earth, and under the earth; things which have been, things which are, things which must shortly come to pass; things which are at home, things which are abroad; the wars and the perplexities of the nations, and the judgments which are on the land; and a knowledge also of countries and of kingdoms."

Brigham Young made many statements supporting the learning of all truth. Two brief examples will suffice: "Every art and science known and studied by the children of men is comprised within the Gospel," and "The more I learn the more I discern an eternity of knowledge to improve upon."[4] Indeed, implicit in the concept of eternal progression, held dear by Latter-day Saints, is the idea that all truth will become available to those faithful men and women who are able to progress without limit.

DEFINITIONS

From such a foundation follows the conclusion that all truth is acceptable, no matter what its source. There is no distinction among types of truth. All things are to come within our purview. There should be no distinction between sacred and secular knowledge.[5] President Brigham Young taught that all truth will ultimately be self-consistent: "Our religion will not clash with or contradict the facts of science in any particular."[6] However, sometimes a distinction is made between sacred and secular knowledge. Why is this? The differences lie in the fact that there are various sources of knowledge or methods of obtaining knowledge, and different sources are emphasized in gaining these two types of knowledge. This essay will often speak of these two types of knowledge. However, I believe that ultimately all truth will be unified.

Grant W. Mason and his colleagues identify four sources of knowledge: authority, intuition, reason, and sensation.[7] (The term *experience* is quite general and perhaps would include all of these.) Drawing from Mason's work, I offer the following definitions of these terms, including my own comments on their limitations.

Authority. Authoritative knowledge is obtained from recognized authorities in an area (teachers, prophets, etc.) and their teachings presented in books, lectures, scriptures, and so on. Obtaining such knowledge means that one does not have to repeat the investigation; on the other hand, it is recognized that authorities may be wrong and that sometimes one needs to find out for oneself.

Intuition. This includes information obtained from one's own mind. Self-generated ideas or hunches fall into this category. Mason and his colleagues also place inspiration and revelation here, which of course are taken much more seriously by LDS people (and some others) than are such things as hunches. The point is that this is individual knowledge, obtained by oneself. The oft-quoted example that one cannot describe a testimony, just as one cannot describe the taste of salt, illustrates this aspect of individuality.

Reason. Well-established rules for logical, correct reasoning have been known for millennia, beginning with Aristotle. Modern philosophers, logicians, and semanticists have developed and extended these methods. Great reasoning power results from these systems, such as in inductive and deductive procedures in modern science and mathematics. The truth of logical deductions depends, however, on the truth of the premises and on the validity of the reasoning, both of which are always subject to question.

Sensation. A huge amount of information about the world around us has been gathered by the senses. This is more "community" knowledge than the intuitive knowledge discussed above. However, we recognize, first, that such knowledge can be wrong (as in optical illusions), and second, that it is incomplete. For example, our senses do not tell us directly about atoms, although observation of results of various experiments may be interpreted to imply their existence.

What sources or methods of knowledge are used by religion and science? Why, all of them! Sacred knowledge is gained from authoritative pronouncements of inspired Church leaders, by one's own inspiration, through reasoning about gospel truths—"come . . . let us reason together, that ye may understand" (Doctrine and Covenants 50:10)—and by sensation and simple observation—"by their fruits ye shall know them" (Matthew 7:20). Scientific knowledge also comes through authorities in the field (published results in scientific journals), self-generated ideas (perhaps from inspiration; Latter-day Saints believe that the scientific and technological progress of our day is inspired by the Lord),[8] reasoning, and observation. Through experimentation, an essential part of the scientific method, we can make our own observations and compare them with those of others; experimentation is also part of religious understanding, as Alma 32 makes clear (though the counsel therein is to experiment in the development of one's faith, part of intuitive knowledge rather than sensation).

There may be great differences in the *importance* to us of various types of knowledge. Joseph Smith taught, "It is impossible for a man to be saved in ignorance" (Doctrine and Covenants 131:6). This statement is often interpreted to mean that we cannot be saved in ignorance of the saving ordinances of the gospel.[9] However, some of the Prophet Joseph Smith's original comments may be construed as encouraging the gaining of all types of knowledge.[10]

SCIENCE AND RELIGION

Thus searches for truth in science and in religion use all these methods, but the emphases are very different. Religious truth depends heavily on revelation, which is not subject to criticism but is subject to clarification and refinement as the Lord sees fit. Latter-day Saints rely on their own inspiration as well as instructions from Church leaders at general conferences and in Church publications like the *Ensign*. Scientific truth, however, relies on sensation, reason, and experimentation. Experiments are controlled and repeated, and results are published in the community literature, a vehicle not available for private knowledge. Scientific knowledge is always regarded as tentative and is subject to criticism by others. Thus interpretations of information by scientists and religionists, even when they purport to describe the same situation, often differ. Disagreements inevitably occur.[11]

In cases of disagreement it is absolutely essential to remember that the canons of knowledge of both science and religion are incomplete. Science has an enormous amount of information that has been compiled over centuries, yet much of this becomes outdated and is superseded year after year. It is an article of faith in science that there is much more yet to learn. For example, it is not yet known how to combine gravitation—as expressed in Einstein's theory of relativity—with quantum mechanics, a topic discussed later in this essay. There even has been some debate about whether a successful unification of scientific knowledge will ever be achieved, partly because we lack the enormous experimental resources to do that. On the other hand, there has been some talk lately about the possibility of soon achieving unification and completing the basic frontiers in physics.[12]

It is similarly an article of faith (literally!) in religion that our information is incomplete: " . . . we believe that He [God] will yet reveal many great and important things pertaining to the kingdom of God" (Articles of Faith 1:9). Further enlightenment will come. For example, the scriptures speak of great visions, to such people as the brother of Jared (Ether 3:25–26) and Moses (Moses 1:8, 27–38), which contain many things yet unknown to most persons. Mormon said he could not write a hundredth part of the information he had available, and other records are yet to be found and translated. The Lord told Joseph Smith, "As well might man stretch forth his puny arm to stop the Missouri river in its decreed course . . . as to hinder the Almighty from pouring down knowledge from heaven upon the heads of the Latter-day Saints" (Doctrine and Covenants 121:33). How this is to be done is, of course, not known.

So disagreements are inevitable because our knowledge is incomplete. But we believe in a unified truth and so we eventually expect agreement. It is tempting to seek agreement now. *However, it is inappropriate, and often dangerous, to attempt a premature reconciliation of conflicting ideas where there is a lack of complete knowledge.* If a scientist concludes that there is no God—based on inadequate evidence!—and thereby casts doubt on those who believe in God, he does them a disservice. For example, it is inappropriate for a scientist who accepts organic evolution to claim that there is no God. (However, many scientists do indeed take the position that they cannot comment on religious truth because they have little or no information on it.)

Similarly, if an ecclesiastic states that such and such a scientific idea is not true—based on inadequate evidence!—then he does a disservice to the scientist who has carefully explored that idea. As a hypothetical example, it would be inappropriate for a church authority to make a flat statement that special relativity is invalid because it limits information transmission such as prayer to the very slow (!) speed of electromagnetic waves. It may later turn out to be invalid in some sense, but current experimental and other considerations support it strongly.

The proper stance, it seems, is to withhold judgment on such questions until we have more information—but also to take advantage of what knowledge we do have. A closely related point is that one's view of what is "true" depends on one's interpretation of one's (always incomplete) data. The provision of more data may lead one to change one's mind. But one is always expected to gather as much knowledge as can be found currently before making further conclusions. One must do one's homework.

Disagreements sometimes result because of pride. Jacob (2 Nephi 9:28–29) criticizes the learned who think they are wise, but goes on to say that learning is good if one hearkens to God; the problem is clearly not learning, but pride.

Are there limits on the scientific search for truth that should be imposed because of our religious beliefs? In some areas of science such a question may never arise, because the perceived overlap, as discussed later, is small. In other areas, where overlap is perceived as considerable, there may be strong feeling against some types or methods of research. It is not hard to think of examples. Research in human sexual response, such as the research carried out by Masters and Johnson and involving mechanical aids for sexual stimulation and measurement of that stimulation,[13] would almost certainly be proscribed at Brigham Young University. Research attempting to prove that the Book of Mormon is not historical would also be clearly forbidden at that institution, and attempts to create life in a test tube might be discouraged. Yet the general feeling among Latter-day Saints, as noted at the beginning of this discussion, is that all truth is acceptable. Whatever is found must be compatible with other truth, be it religious or scientific. Ultimately it reduces to a matter of faith in truth's universality.

R E S O L U T I O N

Religious and Scientific Truth

In view of our belief that religious and scientific truth will eventually agree as we gain enough information, it is somewhat surprising that there is as little overlap between the two as currently exists. To see this lack of overlap, one needs only, for example, to attend any science course and any religion course at BYU. Despite attempts to achieve some interaction, there is little the two curricula have in common. Of course, we need to put this fact into perspective; there is likely not much in common between any two courses, from different disciplines, taught at BYU or anywhere else. Yet science and religion both claim to search for fundamental, basic truth despite some difference in approach. Why is there not more overlap?

I will attempt to explain some reasons for this lack of common ground. In doing so I make no attempt to be complete in surveying the vast literature dealing with the comparison of science and religion.[14] Rather, the present discussion is meant to be a treatment of how I view the two areas in my own life and reconcile them where possible.

First, as noted earlier, it seems clear that despite the enormous progress in science of the last few centuries, and despite the considerable spiritual information obtained in this last and final dispensation, there is still a huge amount of knowledge yet to come forth. We are still babes in the woods. Also, each individual knows very little of the knowledge that is already available. This realization is clear enough to anyone who has worked in research and is presumably clear to other people as well. The ultimate statement of this ignorance is exemplified by Moses, who, upon beholding (only!) our world and its inhabitants, said, "Now, for this cause I know that man is nothing, which thing I never had supposed" (Moses 1:10).

It is helpful to note that progress in both areas has served to dispel some previous misconceptions. For Latter-day Saints, the true gospel of Jesus Christ has been restored; misconceptions of spiritual truth have been erased and replaced by the coming forth of the Book of Mormon and by modern revelation, although the primary statement of new doctrine was made by Joseph Smith. In science, many early misunderstandings have been replaced after the rise of modern science around the 1600s. For example, basic ideas in astronomy and in the science of force and motion were totally changed by such developments as Copernicus' realization that Earth went around the sun, not vice versa; Kepler's insistence, in his study of planetary orbits, that theory had to be consistent with observation; and the contributions of Galileo and Newton to our understanding of motion and gravitation. The modernization of biology began later but progressed substantially in the nineteenth and twentieth centuries. Assumed overlaps between science and religion have been investigated, sometimes paradoxically seeming to further the distance between them. For example, the old idea that angels were needed to push planets in order to keep them moving has been abandoned in view of Newton's first law of motion, which states that no such agent is needed for uniform motion to persist.

This last remark illustrates an important point: if science shows that some particular religious explanation is faulty or unnecessary—such as the planet-pushing angels—that does not necessarily mean that science is antireligion. In this example the lack of need for angels for this purpose simply means that alone; it does not prove or even suggest that angels do not exist. As I am fond of pointing out to students, angels have better things to do. The French astronomer and mathematician Laplace is often quoted as saying, when asked where God was in his description of the solar system, that he had no need for that hypothesis. Laplace may have been exhibiting proud atheism, but it is true that the equations and science describing solar system astronomy can be written down and processed without explicitly invoking God. That does not say that God does not exist. The common view of many scientists, including many LDS scientists, is to say that God set up laws for physical and astronomical operation and then simply let them "work," allowing nature to progress consistently with them.

Latter-day Saints believe that God himself is subject to law. Spiritually, he is bound by his own covenants and integrity: "I, the Lord, am bound when ye do what I say; but when ye do not what I say, ye have no promise" (Doctrine and Covenants 82:10). However, which physical laws constrain him we do not know. We also believe that God does intervene in human affairs, particularly in response to prayer; but when or why he allows us to manage and muddle through our own affairs by ourselves (in other words, when his answer to prayer is "wait") is not entirely clear.[15]

In contrast to Laplace, some other scientists were pleased to invoke God in their science. Isaac Newton is a prominent example. A long section in the *Principia* speaks of God: "This most beautiful system of the sun, planets, and comets, could only proceed from the counsel and dominion of an intelligent and powerful Being. . . . This Being governs all things, not as the soul of the world, but as Lord over all. . . . He is eternal and infinite, omnipotent and omniscient. . . . He governs all things, and knows all things that are or can be done."[16]

Another example is Thomas Wright, discoverer of galaxies: "Since as the Creation is, so is the Creator also magnified, we may conclude in consequence of an infinity, and an infinite all-active power, that as the visible creation is supposed to be full of siderial [sic] systems and planetary worlds, so on, in life similar manner, the endless immensity is an unlimited plenum of creations not unlike the known."[17] Others, more contemporary, suggest or imply the existence of a supreme intelligence but do not say much about it.[18] Many take an unabashedly agnostic, pessimistic, or atheistic point of view. Freeman Dyson, a well-known physicist and science writer, quotes

Nobel Prize winner Steven Weinberg: "The more the universe seems comprehensible, the more it also seems pointless."[19] Eugene Wigner, another Nobel Prize winner, also waxed somewhat pessimistic about whether we would ever achieve full understanding of nature: "We have no right to expect that our intellect can formulate perfect concepts for the full understanding of inanimate nature's phenomena."[20]

Second, as a kind of corollary to the first reason why science and religion lack common ground, researchers in the areas of science and religion often investigate disparate areas and may have different aims. As already noted, their methods differ substantially. Religious studies do not investigate equations of motion; astronomers do not study the first principles of the gospel. The *purposes* of the two types of study are different. As Galileo said (quoting another person and here slightly paraphrased), the one seeks to find out how to go to heaven, the other to find out how the heavens go.[21] Overlaps may be somewhat accidental. Where these occur, there may be disagreements, but not always. (In the story of the Creation, there is lack of agreement as to the time scale and other great gaps in knowledge, but the order of creation as briefly given in Genesis, Moses, and Abraham is roughly the same as astronomers, physicists, geologists, and biologists suppose.[22])

A clear statement that science and religion must be viewed differently is found in a National Academy of Sciences paper on creationism: "Religion and science are separate and mutually exclusive realms of human thought whose presentation in the same context leads to misunderstanding of both scientific theory and religious belief."[23]

In the following discussion I examine areas in which science and religion both have something to say and compare their tentative conclusions.

Creation of the Universe

Jesus Christ is a Creator; so there must have been a creation. What form did it take, and when did it happen? Genesis 1:1 suggests a moment of creation—but this presumably refers only to Earth. To find religious texts referring to larger assemblies than that, such as the entire universe, we must refer to other scriptures.[24] Doctrine and Covenants 76:24 speaks of creation, by the Only Begotten, of "the worlds" and their inhabitants. Is this the entire universe as we know it from astronomy and theory? No time scale is given in that scripture.

Moses 1:33 speaks of the creation of "worlds without number," and verse 35 says that many worlds have already passed away and that innumerable worlds yet remain. Joseph Smith's King Follett sermon and his sermon of 16 June 1844, both suggest an infinite extension of gods, although there is no agreement on exactly what his statements mean.[25]

Incidentally, when Joseph suggests in the King Follett sermon that matter can neither be created nor destroyed,[26] he is essentially stating the law of conservation of mass-energy, a law currently and universally accepted in science but not known in his time. The Creation was an organization of preexisting matter. That this is our LDS belief—contrary to the theory of *ex nihilo* creation (out of nothing) of traditional Christianity and of creationism—has been clearly pointed out by numerous authors.[27]

The currently accepted scientific view of the origin of the universe is the "Big Bang" theory. According to this view, the universe—including the space and time in it—is presumed to have begun at some definite moment in the past, expanding from an initially extremely small and extremely dense clump of matter to its present size. How long ago this took place is still very uncertain but is commonly estimated at 12–15 billion years. If there is enough gravitating matter in the universe, then it will eventually recollapse—fall back on itself. Then it may reexpand, perhaps many times (in which case it is said to "oscillate"). If there is not enough matter to make it fall back, the universe will expand forever. Within this theory, which of the two scenarios will take place is not known.

A number of persons, scientists as well as nonscientists, who are uncomfortable with the Big Bang's postulate of sudden initial expansion of matter and other features have sought alternative explanations of the universe's existence. For example, a rival theory called the "Steady State" universe competed for acceptance for a quarter of a century. It was abandoned because it could not explain the observed "microwave background radiation"—a constant radiation coming from all parts of the sky and apparently a result of the Big Bang.

Such observational evidence for the Big Bang indicates that that theory is in fairly good shape. However, many cosmologists currently believe—in order to explain some awkward features of the Big Bang—that after the initial event there was a tiny period of tremendous expansion called "inflation." There is also a new alternative explanation, one based on the idea of a recollapsing universe.[28] For the interested reader, there are several good popular accounts of the current status of our scientific understanding of the creation of the universe.[29]

It is clear from the above comments that religion and science have little information in common regarding the Creation, except for the fact that (and this is in itself highly significant) there does seem to have been a specific creation. Whether our religious understanding of the creation of the universe is consistent with the scientific belief in the Big Bang is unclear. Ernan McMullin, speaking from the Roman Catholic point of view, observed, "What one cannot say is, first, that the Christian doctrine of creation 'supports' the Big Bang model, or second, that the Big Bang model 'supports' the doctrine of creation."[30]

In some versions of the "inflation" model, it is suggested that many additional universes could have come into being during inflation.[31] Might these be new universes, awaiting the advent of those faithful individuals who inherit exaltation in the celestial kingdom?

The Big Bang's postulation that the universe suddenly comes into being sounds suspiciously like creation *ex nihilo*. Keith E. Norman raises the question whether modern cosmology in this sense might contradict LDS doctrine on the Creation as stated by Joseph Smith in the King Follett sermon and as noted earlier.[32] My point of view is simply that, in the absence of information about a prior state, we cannot really say that the universe was indeed created out of nothing. (Incidentally, this "nothing," the vacuum, seems to be remarkably active in modern physics, because particles, maybe even universes, can come into or out of existence from the vacuum.) Our future prospects for gathering further scientific information on the

Big Bang—despite the Hubble telescope—are quite limited, and so the problem seems to be unanswerable for the foreseeable future.

A useful idea discussed recently among cosmologists is the "weak anthropic principle" (WAP), which states that only those creations consistent with the existence of human life (ours in particular) can have taken place.[33] In other words, we exist and so the universe must be consistent with that fact (obviously). However, a number of other possible "principles" have been suggested that are not so obvious; for example, the "strong anthropic principle" (SAP), which states that the universe must have those properties that allow life to develop within it at some stage in its history. This principle is somewhat similar to the older "argument from design," which argues that the design apparent in the universe is evidence for the existence of a designer (just as the existence of a watch argues for the existence of a watchmaker, to use an old metaphor). John Barrow and Frank Tipler state the argument from design as follows: "There exists one possible Universe 'designed' with the goal of generating and sustaining 'observers.'"[34]

It has been noted that only certain conditions could have existed in order to make life possible (which can be taken as support for either the argument from design or the anthropic principle). For example, the noted British astronomer Fred Hoyle pointed out that a particular nuclear energy level occurs in carbon 12 at a position where a "resonance" (along with other features) makes the production of carbon in stellar interiors possible; a slight change in its placement would make carbon formation impossible, which in turn would mean that carbon-based life would be impossible.[35] (The source of terrestrial carbon, and indeed of all elements beyond helium, is understood to be the interior of stars, generations earlier than our sun.)

The anthropic principle and the argument from design suggest to the mind a teleology—a purpose in creation—which in turn suggests the existence of God. Thus the existence of the favorable carbon energy level can be seen as an evidence for the existence of God, in particular a God who was interested in forming human life. Hoyle does *not* say this, but instead attributes the situation to more or less random accidents. True enough, it is not necessary to assume that this energy level was created by a supreme being, because if any of the processes favorable to our existence had failed, we would not be here anyway. Our existence demonstrates only that conditions were right for life formation in our own universe; there could have been billions of other universes that formed, existed, and passed away in which there was no life developed at all.

An interesting form of the anthropic principle is the "participatory universe" suggested by Princeton physicist John Archibald Wheeler, in which, perhaps in a quantum mechanics context of an observer-dependent reality, the creation of the universe is bound up with our ability to observe it. As Barrow and Tipler state this idea, "Observers are necessary to bring the Universe into being."[36] They note that this idea is closely related to another possibility: "An ensemble of other different universes is necessary for the existence of our Universe."[37] This is intriguing, although it is not clear how observers formed after the creation of the universe could have affected its initial creation.[38] Barrow and Tipler suggest that this might be related to Hugh Everett's "many-worlds" interpretation of quantum mechanics, in which an infinitely branching set of possible worlds really exists.[39] (A short story suggestive of the many-worlds approach was published in 1941—*before* Everett's work—by the Argentine author Jorge Luis Borges.)[40]

While the argument from design is not a proof of the existence of God, it suggests to us that God exists. Scriptures support this view: "The heavens declare the glory of God; and the firmament sheweth his handywork" (Psalm 19:1); "The earth rolls upon her wings. . . . Behold, all these are kingdoms, and any man who hath seen any or the least of these hath seen God moving in his majesty and power" (Doctrine and Covenants 88:45, 47); "All things denote there is a God; yea, even the earth, and all things that are upon the face of it, yea, and its motion, yea, and also all the planets which move in their regular form do witness that there is a Supreme Creator" (Alma 30:44). Such scriptures may be read not as an attempt by the writer to prove the existence of God (although the latter passage *was* such an attempt), but simply as an expression of worship and awe in the presence of a God already presumed to exist.

It should be noted that the SAP, as currently understood, indicates that the universe was created only to give rise to our own existence. Thus it implies that there are no other human civilizations in the universe, a view certainly contrary to LDS scriptures and thought (see Doctrine and Covenants 76:24).[41]

The Nature of Space and Time

Despite considerable progress in the twentieth century, our understanding of space and time still seems to be rudimentary. Numerous tantalizing scriptures refer to space and time: "All is as one day with God, and time only is measured unto men" (Alma 40:8); "Listen to the voice of the Lord your God, . . . whose course is one eternal round, the same today as yesterday, and forever" (Doctrine and Covenants 35:1); "The light which shineth . . . proceedeth forth from the presence of God to fill the immensity of space" (Doctrine and Covenants 88:11–12); "There are many kingdoms; for there is no space in the which there is no kingdom; and there is no kingdom in which there is no space" (Doctrine and Covenants 88:37); "Kolob was after the manner of the Lord, according to its times and seasons in the revolutions thereof; that one revolution was a day unto the Lord, after his manner of reckoning, it being one thousand years according to the time appointed unto that whereon thou standest" (Abraham 3:4); "We will go down, for there is space there, . . . and we will make an earth" (Abraham 3:24); "One day is with the Lord as a thousand years, and a thousand years as one day" (2 Peter 3:8).

It is interesting to consider these statements in the context of Albert Einstein's relativistic view of time and space.[42] As understood from his theory of special relativity set forth in 1905, measurements of time duration and space extent may range from one frame of reference to another, depending on the exact experiment performed and on the frames' relative motion. In addition, one's speed through space is limited to speeds lower than the speed of light, rapid for Earth life but incredibly slow if one wants to travel in space. Thus, special relativity seems to be inconsistent with the existence of prayer and of travel possible for celestial beings, both of which seem to be extremely rapid.

Special relativity was revolutionary when it was proposed, but it is hardly cosmic in the sense of the scriptural quotes above. (Many people have asked me what special relativity has to say about theology; I usually answer that I don't know.) The apparent numerical correspondence between God's time and man's time indicated by Abraham 3:4 (one day for the Lord equals a thousand years for man) is sometimes taken as a definite ratio of time scales, perhaps arising in special relativity. However, according to relativity, that ratio would require the Lord and man to be traveling at nearly the speed of light—for a long period of time—relative to each other. This sort of thing seems preposterous.

A better interpretation is suggested by 2 Peter 3:8, which speaks of the ratio of a thousand years to a day operating in *both* ways. I regard that simply as indicating that time, as perceived or controlled by God, is very different from our perception. This suggests that it would be premature to force the meaning of these scriptures beyond that point and avoids the temptation to try to work out some sort of definite numerical correspondence of the two scales (as has often been tried by LDS people). Relativity may still play a role, but we do not know as yet what that role might be.

In the extension of Einstein's theory called general relativity (1916), space time is viewed as "curved," allowing gravitation to be explained as a natural effect of that curvature. (Imagine the sun creating some sort of depression or funnel in space, around which planets are forced to travel. Thus the planets move in orbits.) This allows a very nice view of the creation and operation of the universe, in that it extends into more than three spatial dimensions, allowing all kinds of interesting phenomena—and, of course, the Creator would be able to comprehend and use all dimensions although we cannot. Travel of celestial beings—as we understand it from events such as Moroni's appearances to Joseph Smith in his bedroom—might easily be explained by postulating extra dimensions.

Such kinds of travel through "hyperspace" have indeed been considered in science fiction. This sort of thing is often based on ideas from general relativity. For example, in the 1950s John Wheeler suggested such routes through curved space with complex topology and called them "wormholes."[43] (Imagine folding a rectangular piece of paper in half widthwise and allowing travel from one end to another across the gap between the ends instead of being required to follow the paper lengthwise.) As noted by Kip Thorne, the possibility of such things was first discovered right after the genesis of general relativity in 1916.[44] Wormholes could conceivably provide routes alternate to, and possibly shorter than, normal routes. One can also imagine wormholes through time, or "closed timelike curves" (CTCs), that would allow time travel to the future or the past.

A similar development in the 1950s and 1960s led to our modern understanding of "black holes," regions in space from which nothing can escape. One could never get into a nonrotating black hole and back out again; however, exit did appear possible in an electrically charged or rotating black hole, leading to different times and places (although one's exit point was not guaranteed even to be in one's own universe!).[45]

Kip Thorne, some of his students at Caltech, and other physicists elsewhere have made thorough, serious studies of such models of space or time travel—wormholes or CTCs—asking how consistent with known classical and quantum physics they would be. Although neither space nor time travel has been entirely ruled out, either one would appear to be highly difficult to achieve. For example, an object or individual making such transport would likely be required to be made of exotic matter of a type not available to us on Earth.[46] The answer is not known, however, and papers continue to appear on this subject.[47]

Nevertheless, such space travel or time communication appears possible, even required, from spiritual experiences as stated in scripture and elsewhere. How does God know the end from the beginning? (see Abraham 2:8). How did he know, thousands of years in advance, that Joseph Smith would lose the 116 pages of manuscript and that an alternate set of records would be needed? (see Words of Mormon 1:6–7). Again, how was it possible for Moroni to travel through space, to appear, in a boy's bedroom, standing in the air, having control over gravity as well as space and time? (see Joseph Smith—History 1:30). In what sense is God above time? (see Alma 40:8).

Scientists associate time duration with causality—the idea that causes precede effects. Surely there is still cause and effect in the eternities; that is simply the law of the harvest. (It has also been commented that time is God's way of preventing everything from happening all at once!) Is time simply a sequence of events, without a quantitative label? And how is God able to answer prayer almost instantaneously? If he is at any distance at all from Earth—a few light-years perhaps—transmission of such information at the speed of light or less would be impossibly slow. And if he is close to us and yet has other worlds he cares about (see Doctrine and Covenants 76:24; Moses 1:33, 35), how could he communicate with them? (Perhaps spirit matter or resurrected matter is the exotic matter needed in order to traverse wormholes or CTCs!)

As noted earlier, the usual view among cosmologists, especially general relativists, is that space and time "began" at the Big Bang—in other words, that it makes no sense to speak of their existence "before" the Big Bang. From the standpoint that we have absolutely no information about such a prior existence, that is a reasonable position. On the other hand, as noted earlier, because we have no such information, we cannot conclude that there was no existence then! If we truly believe that our entire universe was created by God, then one naturally assumes that he existed prior to that creation,[48] outside our perceived universe, implying that his time is different from our time. Alma 40:8—"all is as one day with God, and time only is measured unto men"—makes the dichotomy clear, although it does not help us understand God's time. Presumably, in God's universe cause precedes effect and there is eternal progression, which would suggest some sort of time order—but beyond that we cannot go. We can only ask whether God's understanding applies just to our universe or to the (possibly) more extensive space and time in which he dwells.

Nature of Matter and Spirit

The current scientific explanation of matter is that it is made up of a number of elementary particles occurring in a number of families. These interact by means of four known forces, or interactions: gravitational forces, electromagnetic forces, and strong and weak nuclear forces. The families are "quarks" (out of which protons, neutrons, and other particles are made), "leptons" (electrons, neutrinos, and such), and "interacting bosons" (particles that are interchanged between other particles and that give rise to the forces). These forces work together in the framework of quantum mechanics, the theory that explains the behavior of such elementary particles in terms of waves and probability. These particles come together to build the matter familiar to our eyes.

In recent years the existence of a number of undiscovered elementary particles has been proposed. In addition to theoretical motivations for such proposals, another motivation has been the evidence of so-called missing matter (commonly called "dark matter") in the universe—nonluminous matter that seems to be present because of its gravitational effect on its surroundings. However, we may never be able to detect such particles because of limitations on our experiments.

How is matter described in a religious context? It seems to have constant, real existence, as suggested earlier from the King Follett sermon. But in addition to the solid matter we are accustomed to, there appears to be spirit matter. Along this line Joseph Smith taught: "There is no such thing as immaterial matter. All spirit is matter, but it is more fine or pure, and can only be discerned by purer eyes; we cannot see it; but when our bodies are purified we shall see that it is all matter" (Doctrine and Covenants 131:7–8).

It is clear enough that, despite its invisibility, spirit matter can interact with ordinary matter, as witness the violent effect on individuals of evil spirit possession (see, for example, Matthew 8:28–32; Mark 9:25–26). Yet there do not appear to be significant immediate physical changes in the body as a person dies, beyond the cessation of activity. The interaction must be of some rather delicate nature, strong only on occasion. Science has no information about such a thing. It seems to me that that interaction would constitute at least a fifth interaction, beyond the four currently known to physics.

What of mind-to-mind communication? We commonly call this telepathy, one of other such mental abilities termed psychic phenomena. These abilities are viewed with skepticism among most scientists, who are unable to demonstrate their operation with any degree of certainty or consistency. Yet many LDS people believe such things are possible under unusual conditions. Could this phenomena result from the interaction of spirit matter with ordinary matter or other spirit matter?

In Doctrine and Covenants 93:23, 29, and 33, and in the King Follett sermon, the Prophet Joseph spoke of intelligence and of its being "co-equal" (corrected by B. H. Roberts to "co-eternal" in the footnote)[49] with God. Intelligence appears to be even more ethereal than spirit. In what form was it? If intelligence existed as embryo individuals in the infinite past, then one wonders how it is possible to have so much structure (as intelligent individuals). But if intelligence existed only as some amorphous substance and individuals came into being, say, as God created spirits (this seems to be supported by Abraham 3:22), then one is faced with some old philosophical problems. There is the concern with the idea of the "contingent" existence of man (as opposed to "necessary" existence)—that we are created by God and our very existence is contingent upon him—and with the feelings of instability and insecurity that idea engenders. There is also the question of the existence of evil; if God is good, how could he create men who have the possibility of sin? This idea is discussed further later on.

The question of the nature of preexistent matter is a long-standing one in the Church. The question of whether intelligence is really co-eternal with God is not settled. Some Church members seem to prefer a contingent existence for intelligences rather than a necessary existence, despite Doctrine and Covenants 93.

Chance, Statistics, and Quantum Theory

The idea that there is an element of chance in the operation of nature occurs in a number of places. First, we recognize that material things are made up of atoms and molecules that are generally all moving very rapidly—the molecular model, or kinetic theory, of matter. It is convenient to treat such assemblies of particles statistically; the number of particles is so large that it is far beyond our abilities to calculate their individual behavior, even with the best computers, actual or contemplated. However, the particles are still presumed to obey classically deterministic laws (such as Newton's laws of motion and the electromagnetic and gravitational force laws). If one knows the particles' situation at one time, then one can in principle determine all future situations.

To complicate matters, modern chaos theory has demonstrated that many systems exhibit extreme sensitivity to initial conditions. This means that one cannot calculate and predict the future in such systems, to any reasonable extent, unless one knows the present conditions to very high accuracy—to many decimal places. (This is one reason that weather predictions cannot be made precise, even for a few days.) Systems need not be very complex in order to show this behavior, and of course our universe is extremely complex.

So we are faced with having the Creator understand many particles and their characteristics to high accuracy. The scriptures do speak of his omniscience, and so we can accept on faith the idea that he can determine, or observe, the behavior of the huge number of particles in the universe, although it is difficult for our finite minds to see how.

Quantum mechanics is the twentieth-century view of matter at the atomic level and smaller. Our present understanding of matter (termed the "Copenhagen interpretation") postulates an uncertainty that translates into a fundamental inability to determine the complete description (in terms of position and velocity) of a system of particles. Exact determination of the future becomes impossible; such matters are seemingly governed by chance, probability, and statistics.

Quantum mechanics is a two-edged sword. On the one hand, the lack of certainty in the behavior of matter seems to allow real freedom of action to individual intelligence. This freedom seemed illusory under the older (Newtonian) determinism, which suggested that all our actions were irrevocably determined by the beginning state of things. On the other hand, because of its dependence on chance, quantum mechanics seems to imply a limit on God's ability to know the future. A number of physicists from Albert Einstein and Erwin Schrodinger onward have been distressed by the probability/chance aspect of the Copenhagen interpretation (which gave rise to Einstein's famous saying that God does not play dice with the universe). Several of these physicists have postulated an underlying structure (referred to as "hidden variables") to try to remedy the theory's perceived incompleteness.

Such efforts have not succeeded to date. In fact, things have become more bizarre than before. Recent experimental results even suggest the possibility of "nonlocality"—the idea that an action at one place can influence results elsewhere, at apparent instantaneous speeds. There are even experiments in which the experimenter can affect the results by changing his mind in the middle of the experiment or even afterward.[50] Physics at the quantum level is stranger than we can imagine; there is no possibility at present of unifying it with religion.

So we are left with the question of how God deals with, acts in, or controls a world that seems to be highly dependent on chance in several important ways. It may be that he is actually able to exert control—on the spot as needed—to direct the universe and its structure and inhabitants in the way he desires. On the other hand, there appears to be an uncreated, individualistic part to each of us that is beyond God's control, for "man was also in the beginning with God. Intelligence, or the light of truth, was not created or made, neither indeed can be" (Doctrine and Covenants 93:29).

That partially solves the problem of the existence of evil in the world, but it leaves open the question of how God is able to perceive the future so well. For instance, how did the Father know in the premortal existence that Jehovah could and would serve as his Only Begotten Son, eventually to become the Redeemer and to be so obedient that—despite the terrible requirements of the Atonement—he would finish the work? (see Doctrine and Covenants 19:16–19). How did God foreknow the details of the loss of the 116 manuscript pages?

Despite the seeming success of science and rational thinking in other areas, our present state of scientific knowledge cannot begin to answer such questions about God, the eternal world, and matters of faith and revelation with any degree of confidence.

Holism and Reductionism

Scientists and others have asked for millennia, "What is life?" A basic assumption among many scientists has been, and continues to be, that life is simply an effect resulting from the combination of basic structural elements of matter—atoms and molecules and the physicochemical interactions by which they are held together (reductionism).[51] Opposed to this view has been the view of holism, or "vitalism," in which some sort of essence or life force is proposed in order to explain life. In the latter view it would presumably be impossible to reduce the explanation of life to mere matter interactions. This would suggest that ultimate scientific explanation of life by scientific methods would be impossible. It would also suggest that creation of life in a test tube is impossible. On the other hand, one could perhaps argue that if one created exactly the right assembly and conditions for life to exist, a spirit from the spirit world might be allowed to enter that assembly. (Clearly LDS people would find this difficult to accept.)

One can also note the rather intriguing view in some current mathematics that total reduction sometimes fails, that sometimes one must consider a complex system as a unit.[52] Whether this can be viewed as an argument for holism in the biological sense is not clear.

In the last few decades the question about what life is has been sharpened to, or replaced by, the question, "What is consciousness?" This has often been assumed to be related to presumed freedom available through the looser predictions of quantum mechanics, as opposed to rigid determinism; however, this is a greatly simplified view. The topic of consciousness has been explored extensively in the last few decades from many aspects; it even has been the subject of recent conferences. In his recent book, Francis Crick discusses the reductionist view of consciousness and concludes that each of us is really just a vast, complex network of neurons. At the end of the book he suggests that the seat of the will is near the anterior cingulate sulcus (an area in the human brain).[53] On first inspection it is likely that most Latter-day Saints would oppose such a reduction. On the other hand, it could be that physical operations relating to the will are located there, while there could still be a spirit, made of spirit matter, resident in our brains and controlling those physical operations. (That this is not Crick's view is clear from his opening remarks in chapter one of his book.)

Another recent treatise, opposing simple reductionism, is set forth in a notable book by Frank Tipler,[54] in which he claims that modern physics—including quantum theory, general relativity, and ultimately quantum cosmology (for which a complete theory does not exist, as noted earlier)—actually demonstrates the existence of God, called in his book the "Omega Point" (a term originally coined by the paleontologist/Jesuit priest Teilhard de Chardin). The Omega Point is to have a pointlike structure in the ultimate future. Needless to say, this view is substantially different from the LDS anthropomorphic God.

The Ability to Create and Entropy

We know from the second law of thermodynamics that the universe has a tendency to "run down"—to approach a state in which energy is unavailable, even though it has not been destroyed. The final such state is sometimes called the "heat death"; it seems to portray an inexorable, even if very far distant, end to organization and intelligence.

The essence of creation would seem to be the ability to circumvent this law (see Isaiah 65:17; Doctrine and Covenants 29:22–25; 88:18–27). Indeed, we speak of creation as "organizing." This seems clearly recognized by scientists concerned with the question.[55]

I remember a remark from my graduate-school days, attributed to Professor Valentine Bargmann, that there is one area in physics that seems not to be subject to that law—general relativity. We can imagine that if the universe recollapsed after the Big Bang, that would wind things up again, providing the needed order. There is no guarantee that the recollapse would yield enough order to really recreate a universe like ours. And what happens to God in this recollapse? Hopefully he stands outside the universe and is not caught in the crunch! Furthermore, what happens if the universe does not recollapse, but continues to expand forever, as would seem to be indicated by current measurements of the density of matter in the universe or by inflationary models? Freeman Dyson notes that life could perhaps go on indefinitely in an open, continuously expanding universe by reducing the rates of processes,[56] but this seems to be an unsatisfactory, passive, ungodlike way of prolonging existence or progression.

Such matters relate to questions of the direction of time. The second law of thermodynamics is often spoken of as "time's arrow," a law that actually points time's direction (in the sense that things become more disordered as time goes on). There are other time's arrows: the fact that radiation from a source expands outward; the expansion of the universe; the collapse of the wave function in quantum mechanics, in which, for example, an observation suddenly makes the position of an electron definite (in place of its formerly uncertain location). Extensive discussions about the possible relationships of these arrows have taken place, with no certain conclusions forthcoming.[57]

Scriptural Items with Seemingly No Scientific Counterpart

There are many occurrences mentioned in scripture that we cannot fully understand by either science or religion. I will briefly mention a few here and also note that many such instances have been treated in the excellent earlier work by LDS scholars, *Science and Religion: Toward a More Useful Dialogue.*[58] Readers may also wish to consult the writings of Henry Eyring.[59]

The Noachian flood. We see no evidence of a worldwide flood. In fact, we see overwhelming evidence that there was *not* such a (recent) event. Geologists know the geologic effects of flooding, as for example in the scablands in the state of Washington that resulted from the emptying of Lake Missoula. No such topography is seen on large scale. A possible explanation is that the Flood was a relatively local event.

The sun standing still. (See Joshua 10:12–13.) It is clear from

Helaman 12:15 that the sun does not move; rather, Earth does. This raises the problem that the sudden stopping of Earth's rotation would have produced huge cataclysms on Earth, of which there is neither geological nor scriptural evidence. So was Earth stopped gradually? How much time would it take to stop it so gradually that cataclysms would not happen? How did the Lord do it? We don't know.

The destruction in America at the time of Christ's crucifixion. The events described in 3 Nephi 8 seem extreme. However, they can quite easily be explained by assuming that a very large earthquake or volcanic eruption, with its attendant disasters, took place.[60] This would then be a fairly local catastrophe; it would not explain geologic changes elsewhere, as is sometimes supposed.

The division of Earth. This division mentioned in Genesis 10:25 is, of course, suggestive of continental drift, but the time scales are all wrong. The division of Earth may simply mean an earthquake.[61] It has also been suggested that the splitting is only political.

The seven thousand years of Earth's temporal existence. The question of the age of Earth has been a prominent one, both in LDS and in traditional Christian thought. It is probably fairly well understood now that the "days" of creation can be viewed as indefinite, long periods; yet Doctrine and Covenants 77:6 sounds quite definite. Presumably the reconciliation is to be found in the definition of "temporal existence." Scientifically, the age of Earth is considered to be 4.5 billion years, a figure borne out by many measurements, using various forms of dating. In particular, these include a number of methods of radioactive or fission-track dating, which give reasonably consistent figures. In addition, this age is consistent with stellar ages and the (rough) age of the universe as determined by astrophysics and cosmology.[62]

Astronomical significance of Facsimile No. 2 and related comments in Abraham 3. The caption to Facsimile No. 2 in the Pearl of Great Price mentions the thousand-years-to-one-day ratio mentioned earlier. What is meant by the statement that the sun borrows its light from Kolob? The scientific explanation for the sun's light is that it comes from nuclear fusion proceeding in the sun's interior, never from some external source. And where is Kolob? How does it govern fifteen (only fifteen?) other planets or stars? Probably this caption, which contains the wording "called by the Egyptians" and "called in Egyptian," is to be viewed only as relating to the Egyptian world view.

Origin of man. My father, Bertrand F. Harrison, taught botany at BYU for many years. I grew up with the idea that more complex forms of life evolved from simpler forms. I had no problem, religiously or otherwise, with it and was surprised to find there were people who were horrified by the idea. It still seems reasonable to me that organic evolution could occur and, in particular, that man's body could have been formed that way by our Heavenly Father. All life is his creation, and just because we may not identify with lower creatures does not mean that the Creator did not use them in this process. Certainly at some point—no matter what process was used!—God had to make the bodies of Adam and Eve perfect—presumably making them potentially divine by putting into them their spirits.

A good (and unusual) reference on this topic is an article written for the *Instructor* by my father when he served on the General Sunday School Board. He wrote the article at the invitation of Lorin Wheelwright, who was the managing editor of the magazine at the time.[63] While this article does not go into detail about the possibility of organic evolution or its being the source of man's body, it makes that idea plausible and points out that a person can believe in evolution and still be a faithful member of the Church.

An example of a strong argument for the possibility of the organization of man's body by development from lower forms of life is the existence of vestigial organs—organs that exist in the human body yet have no clear function and presumably are remnants from some earlier form of life. Some of these organs are evident in the embryo stage, and others exist in the adult form—including the appendix, hair on the body, and the male nipple (see Revelation 1:13).

CONCLUSION

Through the years it has been my experience that many persons are concerned about the interaction and seeming conflicts between science and religion.[64] It is natural that there should be this concern, given people's interest in these two areas. It is also natural that people should try to reconcile them whenever possible. However, it seems clear that we are a long way from the possibility of reconciliation and synthesis. Despite the advances of knowledge, both religious and scientific, of our modern age, we still are but children in understanding. Once such a stance of humility is adopted, it is easier to be comfortable with apparent differences between the two areas, especially if one has a faith that all truth will eventually be unified. We can look forward to that unification.

I am comfortable with this stance. I recognize that there are many seeming disagreements between scientific and religious truth, even some so disparate as to cause one to wonder how reconciliation can ever be possible. However, it may be that reconciliation will be easier than supposed; perhaps even simple redefinitions (of what is meant by the "earth's temporal existence," for example) will aid that synthesis. To some observers this attitude may be disdainfully viewed as compartmentalized thinking; however, to me, it appears to be the only safe approach, one that does not do violence to either type of truth by prematurely forcing agreement.

Many people anticipate much knowledge to come forth when the sealed part of the Book of Mormon is unsealed (see 3 Nephi 26:6–11). That will indeed be a glorious revelation; however, I believe it will still contain only a relatively small, albeit important, amount of knowledge (contrast what we know about the size of the sealed part with the millions of volumes of printed information in the libraries of the world). Perhaps the description of the white stone available to each of us (mentioned in Doctrine and Covenants 130:10–11) provides some indication of the manner of receiving knowledge in the hereafter, for inhabitants of the celestial kingdom. (Another indication of the later provision of knowledge to us is found in Doctrine and Covenants 101:32–34: "in that day when the Lord shall come, he shall reveal all things. . . .")

In any case it seems reasonable to assume that considerable effort is needed to gain such knowledge. Our model for learning is this mortal life, which does require effort. At the same time, however, the acquisition of truth must be associated with not just learning but with living right, as suggested by Terry Warner in his definition referred to at the beginning of this essay. Our complete appreciation of truth will come only in the eternities, when we finally understand and live the full meaning of Jesus' statement to the Twelve Apostles, as recorded in John 14:6: "I am the way, the truth, and the life: no man cometh unto the Father, but by me."

NOTES

1. I appreciate helpful discussions and criticism by Professors William E. Dibble and William E. Evenson of BYU's physics and astronomy department and by Professor Duane E. Jeffery of the university's Zoology department.

2. See C. Terry Warner, "Truth," in Daniel H. Ludlow, ed., *Encyclopedia of Mormonism,* 5 vols. (New York: Macmillan, 1992), 4:1489.

3. See B. H. Roberts, *The Truth, The Way, The Life,* ed. John W. Welch (Provo, Utah: BYU Studies, 1994), pp. 19–28.

4. *Discourses of Brigham Young,* sel. John A. Widtsoe (Salt Lake City: Deseret Book Co., 1969), pp. 246, 250. For similar comments, see Stephen L. Richards, "An Open Letter to College Students," *Improvement Era,* June 1933, pp. 451–53, 484–85.

5. For an excellent discussion on the unity of truth, see Jae R. Ballif, *In Search of Truth and Love* (Salt Lake City: Bookcraft, 1986).

6. *Discourses of Brigham Young,* p. 264; Jae R. Ballif, *In Search of Truth and Love* (Salt Lake City: Bookcraft, 1986).

7. See Grant W. Mason et al., *Physical Science Concepts* (Provo, Utah: Soundprint, 1989), pp. 1–2.

8. As an example, I note the following: "We affirm that all wisdom is of God, that the halo of His glory is intelligence, and that man has not yet learned all there is to learn of Him and His ways. We hold that the doctrine of continued revelation from God is not less philosophical and scientific than scriptural" (James E. Talmage, "The Philosophy of 'Mormonism,'" in *The Story and Philosophy of "Mormonism"* (Salt Lake City: Deseret News, 1914), p. 116.

9. For example, see Bruce R. McConkie, *Mormon Doctrine,* 2nd ed. (Salt Lake City: Bookcraft, 1966), preface and pp. 425–28.

10. See *Teachings of the Prophet Joseph Smith,* comp. Joseph Fielding Smith (Salt Lake City: Deseret Book Co., 1965), pp. 217, 297.

11. For a more extensive treatment of these topics, see the remarks on method in Richard F. Haglund Jr., "Science and Religion: A Symbiosis," *Dialogue* 8 (autumn/winter 1974): 23–40.

12. This possibility is discussed in chapter 10 of Stephen W. Hawking, *A Brief History of Time* (Toronto: Bantam Books, 1988). See also Steven Weinberg, *Dreams of a Final Theory* (New York: Pantheon Books, 1992). For a skeptical view, see David Lindley, *The End of Physics* (New York: Basic Books, 1993).

13. See William H. Masters and Virginia E. Johnson, *Human Sexual Response* (Boston: Little, Brown, 1966).

14. However, I will refer to two excellent sources: the comprehensive book by Erich Robert Paul (*Science, Religion, and Mormon Cosmology* [Urbana: University of Illinois Press, 1992]) and the extensive bibliographic study by Richard F. Haglund Jr. and Erich Robert Paul, "Resources for the Study of Science, Technology, and Mormon Culture," in *Mormon*

Americana: A Guide to Sources and Collections in the United States, ed. David J. Whittaker (Provo, Utah: BYU Studies, 1995), pp. 559–606.

15. See Richard G. Scott, "Learning to Recognize Answers to Prayer," *Ensign,* November 1989, pp. 30–32.

16. Isaac Newton, *Mathematical Principles of Natural Philosophy* (Chicago: Encyclopaedia Britannica, 1952), pp. 369–71.

17. Quoted in Freeman J. Dyson, "Time without End: Physics and Biology in an Open Universe," *Reviews of Modern Physics* 51 (1979): 447–60; also in Freeman J. Dyson, *Infinite in All Directions* (New York: Harper & Row, 1988), 115–18. Henry Eyring, in *Science and Your Faith in God* (comp. Paul R. Green [Salt Lake City: Bookcraft, 1958], p. 33), cites a survey of twelve scientists in 1957 in which all twelve said they believed in a supreme being.

18. I take the liberty here of interpreting the remarks of E. P. Wigner, in "The Unreasonable Effectiveness of Mathematics in the Natural Sciences," *Communications on Pure and Applied Mathematics* 13 (1960): 1–14. Wigner expresses wonder at the topic of his title, and while he does not specifically mention a higher power, the reader may feel that such a belief does underlie his words.

19. Quoted in Freeman J. Dyson, *Time Without End,* p. 447.

20. Eugene P. Wigner, "The Limits of Science," *Proceedings of the American Philosophical Society* 94 (1950): 422–27.

21. See Stillman Drake, *Discoveries and Opinions of Galileo* (Garden City, NY: Doubleday, 1957), p. 186.

22. For an extensive treatment of LDS creation narratives, see Anthony Hutchinson, "A Mormon Midrash? LDS Creation Narratives Reconsidered," *Dialogue* 21 (winter 1988): 11–74.

23. Committee on Science and Creationism, National Academy of Sciences, *Science and Creationism* (Washington, D.C.: National Academy Press, 1984), p. 6.

24. Hugh W. Nibley has an excellent discussion of creation accounts found in early manuscripts. See his "Treasures in the Heavens: Some Early Christian Insights into the Organizing of Worlds," *Dialogue* 8 (autumn/winter 1974): 76–98; reprinted in his book *Nibley on the Timely and the Timeless* (Salt Lake City: Bookcraft, 1978), 49–84.

25. See *Teachings of the Prophet Joseph Smith,* pp. 345–47, 369–73.

26. See ibid., pp. 350–52.

27. See, for example, Duane E. Jeffery, "Seers, Savants, and Evolution: The Uncomfortable Interface," *Dialogue* 8 (autumn/winter 1974): 43–75; and Keith Norman, "Ex Nihilo: The Development of the Doctrines of God and Creation in Early Christianity," *BYU Studies* 17 (spring 1977): 291–318.

28. See Ruth Durrer and Joachim Laukenmann, "The Oscillating Universe: An Alternative to Inflation," *Classical and Quantum Gravity* 13 (May 1996): 1069–87.

29. See, for example, James S. Trefil, *The Moment of Creation* (New York: Scribner's, 1983); and *The Dark Side of the Universe* (New York: Scribner's, 1988). Norris S. Hetherington (*Cosmology* [New York: Garland, 1993]) presents a broad description of various perspectives—historical, cultural, scientific, religious—on cosmology. A recent popular article is John Horgan, "Universal Truths," *Scientific American* 263 (October 1990): 108–17.

30. Quoted in Paul Davies, *God and the New Physics* (New York: Simon & Schuster, 1983), p. 20.

31. See Andrei Linde, "The Self-Reproducing Inflationary Universe," *Scientific American* 271 (November 1994): 48–55.

32. See Keith E. Norman, "Mormon Cosmology: Can It Survive the Big Bang?" *Sunstone* 10 (1985): 19–23.

33. A popular article on the anthropic principle and its various versions is Tony

Rothman, "A 'What You See Is What You Beget' Theory," *Discover* (May 1987): 90–99. A comprehensive treatment is given in John D. Barrow and Frank J. Tipler, *The Anthropic Cosmological Principle* (Oxford: Oxford University Press, 1988), especially pp. 15–22.

34. Barrow and Tipler, *The Anthropic Cosmological Principle,* p. 22.

35. See Fred Hoyle, *Galaxies, Nuclei, and Quasars* (New York: Harper & Row, 1965), pp. 147–50.

36. Barrow and Tipler, *The Anthropic Cosmological Principle,* p. 22.

37. Ibid.

38. See also remarks about the participatory universe in Davies, *God and the New Physics,* pp. 39–40.

39. Barrow and Tipler, *The Anthropic Cosmological Principle,* p. 22. See Hugh Everett III, "'Relative State' Formulation of Quantum Mechanics," *Reviews of Modern Physics* 29 (July 1957): 454–62.

40. See Jorge Luis Borges, "The Garden of Forking Paths," in *The Norton Anthology of World Masterpieces,* ed. Maynard Mack, 6th ed. (New York: Norton, 1992), 2:1919–26.

41. See Erich Robert Paul, *Science, Religion, and Mormon Cosmology;* and Erich Robert Paul, "Joseph Smith and the Plurality of Worlds Idea," *Dialogue* 19 (summer 1986): 12–36.

42. See, for example, Albert Einstein, *The Meaning of Relativity,* 4th ed. (Princeton: Princeton University Press, 1953).

43. This concept is discussed extensively in John Archibald Wheeler, *Geometrodynamics* (New York: Academic Press, 1962), a collection of earlier papers by Wheeler and others.

44. See Charles W. Misner, Kip S. Thorne, and John A. Wheeler, *Gravitation* (New York: Freeman, 1973), p. 921.

45. See ibid., p. 921 diagram; see also Stephen W. Hawking and G. F. R. Ellis, *The Large Scale Structure of Space-Time* (Cambridge: Cambridge University Press, 1974), p. 165, fig. 28; W. Misner et al., *Gravitation,* p. 490.

46. See Kip S. Thorne, *Black Holes and Time Warps: Einstein's Outrageous Legacy* (New York: Norton, 1994), chapter 14.

47. A popular account is given in Paul Halpern, *Cosmic Wormholes* (New York: Penguin Books, 1992).

48. See Joseph Smith's King Follett sermon, in *Teachings of the Prophet Joseph Smith,* pp. 345, 347.

49. See *Teachings of the Prophet Joseph Smith,* p. 353n.

50. See John Horgan, "Quantum Philosophy," *Scientific American* 267 (July 1992): 94–104.

51. A good discussion of reductionism is found in Davies, *God and the New Physics,* pp. 58–71.

52. See Ian Stewart, *Nature's Numbers* (New York: Basic Books, 1995), chap. 9.

53. Francis Crick, *The Astonishing Hypothesis: The Scientific Search for the Soul* (New York: Scribner's, 1994).

54. See Frank J. Tipler, *The Physics of Immortality* (New York: Anchor Books, 1995).

55. See, for example, Paul R. Green, comp., *Science and Your Faith in God* (Salt Lake City: Bookcraft, 1958), with remarks by Henry Eyring on p. 35 and by Harvey Fletcher on p. 51.

56. See Freeman J. Dyson, "Time Without End," pp. 447–60; see also Tipler, *The Physics of Immortality.*

57. See, for example, H. D. Zeh, *The Physical Basis of the Direction of Time,* 2nd ed. (Berlin: Springer, 1992).

58. Wilford M. Hess and Raymond T. Matheny (and Donlu D. Thayer for vol. 2), *Science and Religion: Toward a More Useful Dialogue* (Geneva, Illinois: Paladin House, 1979), vols. 1 and 2.

59. Henry Eyring, *The Faith of a Scientist* (Salt Lake City: Bookcraft, 1967); and *Reflections of a Scientist* (Salt Lake City: Deseret Book Co., 1983).

60. See Hugh W. Nibley, *Since Cumorah*, 2nd ed. (Salt Lake City and Provo, Utah: Deseret Book Co. and FARMS, 1988), 231–38; James L. Baer, "The Third Nephi Disaster: A Geological View," *Dialogue* 19 (spring 1986): 129–32.

61. The word *Peleg* may mean "earthquake" (personal communication to author from William E. Dibble).

62. An excellent discussion of this matter as it relates to creationism is found in Paul, *Science, Religion, and Mormon Cosmology;* and in Nibley, "Treasures in the Heavens."

63. See Bertrand F. Harrison, "The Relatedness of Living Things," *Instructor,* July 1965, pp. 272–76. President David O. McKay, who was the editor of the *Instructor* at the time, suggested removal of one illustration but approved the text of this article without changing a word.

64. See, for example, Andrew D. White, *A History of the Warfare of Science with Theology in Christendom* (New York: D. Appleton, 1897); issued in several editions up to the middle of the twentieth century. See also the writings of Ian G. Barbour, Ernan McMullin, and F. S. C. Northrop. There is also a journal, *Zygon,* devoted to science and religion questions.

DE VERLE P. HARRIS studied at Brigham Young University and received his Ph.D. from Pennsylvania State University in 1965. He has worked with Geophoto Services in Denver and Calgary and with Union Oil in California. He was professor of mineral economics at Pennsylvania State University, and currently he is a professor in the Department of Geoscience at the University of Arizona. His research has resulted in more than sixty papers and three books related to mineral resource exploration. In 1993 Dr. Harris was awarded the Krumbein Medal by the International Association for Mathematical Geology, and in 1996 he received Pennsylvania State University's Charles L. Hosler Alumni Scholar Medal in recognition of his outstanding academic and research achievements. He has served as consultant for a number of government agencies, both U.S. and foreign, and on a number of National Research Council committees.

Dr. Harris married Sandra Ellen Hall, and they are the parents of six children. He has served in many capacities in the LDS Church, including bishop of a ward in the Tucson Arizona Stake.

CHAPTER 10

RELIGION AND SCIENCE OF MINERAL

AND ENVIRONMENTAL RESOURCES

DE VERLE P. HARRIS

I am pleased with the opportunity to contribute to this book but am humbled by its mission. My participation is not based on cutting-edge geoscience or new insights into the mysteries but on the following three reasons. First, I am grateful for the opportunity to bear witness of Jesus Christ. Second, because earlier in my life I struggled to resolve for myself apparent conflicts of science and religion, perhaps my experience may be helpful for others facing the same challenge. Third, man's need for and use of mineral and environmental resources entails religion- and science-related dimensions that may be of general interest. Before commenting on these issues, however, I provide a brief description of my professional interests, followed by an account of some of my personal struggles with religion, science, and testimony of the restored gospel.

A GEOLOGIST CONTAMINATED

Although initially I was educated to be a geologist, after a few years of professional experience I developed an interest in the optimum use of geoscience information in decision making and in the formalization of those decisions. Especially intriguing to me was the relevance of probability theory to uncertain geologically based decisions and prognostications. The principle of multiple working hypotheses, for example, has an analogue in Bayesian probability theory, in which at the completion of each successive stage of investigation the geologist revises his previous *a priori* probabilities for each hypothesis to new *a posterior* probabilities, based on his geoscience (expressed as conditional probabilities for geologic features, given each hypothesis) and on the existing and newest geologic information. Similarly, mineral exploration decisions, which typically are made under great uncertainty, can be viewed as special cases of statistical decision theory in which the explorer wishes to minimize the combined losses of incorrectly continuing exploration and prematurely abandoning the area.[1]

Some decisions that involve geologic phenomena require more than qualitative geologic descriptions. For example, the finding that the geologic terrain of an area is favorable for the occurrence of massive sulfide deposits is important scientifically, but it is of limited utility in selecting the greatest-value land use from competing alternatives until that science-based favorableness is recast in relevant quantitative terms—for example, magnitude (numbers of deposits, total metal, deposit tonnages and grades) and uncertainties (probabilities).[2] Much of my research has been directed to developing new quantitative methodologies that better use geoscience information to estimate the magnitude, quality, and economic value of undiscovered mineral and fuel resources.[3] The use of geoscience information to support land-use decisions is indicative of a current general trend of greater involvement of all kinds of scientists in societal decisions.

Among important issues that impact society are mineral resource adequacy and environmental preservation. I will briefly examine some aspects of these two issues. First, however, I will leave the security of academic discourse to describe my own personal struggles with apparent conflicts of science and religion and the roles of problem identification and priorities in the search for understanding.

PROBLEMS AND THE QUEST FOR ANSWERS:
AN ETERNAL PERSPECTIVE

Solving any problem requires correct problem identification and a sagacious search for answers. Although this general prescription is probably acceptable to all, its application presents different challenges to each of us because of our individual talents, strengths, and weaknesses. Some weaknesses are simply the result of our mortality or the consequence of sinful choices, but it appears that others were "planted within our individual personality and genetic characteristics by a loving God for his divine purposes," as suggested by the scripture "I give unto men weakness that they may be humble" (Ether 12:27).[4]

If we remain faithful and humble as we strive to overcome weaknesses and dispel doubts, we are promised increased understanding and strength: "for if they humble themselves before me, and have faith in me, then will I make weak things become strong unto them" (Ether 12.27); and "for now we see through a glass, darkly; . . . now I know in part; but then shall I know even as also I am known" (1 Corinthians 13:12).

The following personal account is offered in hope that, first, it might help others avoid similar difficulties arising from incorrect problem identification and lack of humility and, second, that it may reassure those who struggle in like manner that they too can find "the peace of God, which passeth all understanding" (Philippians 4:7).

I can say, as did Nephi, that I was born of goodly parents, for they had long and strong traditions in the Church. Unlike Nephi, however, my testimony ranged from nonexistent to a mere desire to believe. In fact, I was often plagued with doubts about the very existence of God. Given the teachings and examples of my parents, those doubts were a source of guilt and distress, for I could see no reason for them other than some failure on my part. I used to marvel that my peers, who came from similar backgrounds, could testify of their knowledge of the gospel and the divinity of Jesus Christ while I could not. It was in this state that I began my college education in geoscience at Brigham Young University. Unsurprisingly, the geologic history of Earth and the paleontological evidences of evolution exacerbated my doubts and raised additional questions. Moreover, lacking a testimony of the gospel, I had a great need to find conformity of religious teachings with science, reasoning that true religion should be verifiable by science.

Improper Problem Identification and Lack of Humility

In retrospect it is clear that apparent conflicts of religion with science were merely disguises of my real problems. Unacknowledged at the time, and to some degree not recognized, were some major obstacles to receiving a witness born of the Holy Spirit. First among those obstacles, and perhaps most important, was an aversion to and distrust of the emotional aspect of testimony and spiritual experience. I was particularly troubled by the seemingly nonaccountability of God: when a prayer was answered directly, that answer was attributed to the power of prayer and a loving God; but if a prayer was not answered directly, that too was attributed to a loving and omniscient God who does best by each of us. That relationship between man and God presented me with a dilemma: how could I resolve my doubts and "prove" God in an unemotional, objective way if he were not accountable?

Inappropriate Quests for Answers

The arrogance and naïveté of my seeking to "prove" God is obvious, although it was not so at the time. "Behold, there are many that harden their hearts against the Holy Spirit, that it hath no place in them" (2 Nephi 33:2). Clearly, this is not the way to obtain a testimony. As Elder Boyd K. Packer observed, "There are those who have made a casual, even an insincere effort to test the scriptures and have come away having received nothing, which is precisely what they have earned and what they deserve."[5]

Spiritual Laws and Knowledge

As a testimony is in essence spiritual, it can be obtained only by abiding spiritual laws. Accordingly, I did not obtain a witness until I became properly humble and receptive to the Holy Spirit. Did this answer the mysteries or eliminate all apparent conflicts of science with religion? No, but it enabled proper perspective and the setting of appropriate priorities: *Once the love of Christ has been experienced at the personal level, all perspective is forever changed.*

Priority and Order

Man's first priority is to come unto Christ. "To be learned is good if they hearken unto the counsels of God" (2 Nephi 9:29). My own experience is that although science can enrich understanding and testimony, science does not of itself bring anyone to Christ. That experience is consistent with scripture and counsel from prophets, both ancient and modern: "Man, by searching, cannot find out God. Never, unaided, will he discover the truth about the beginning of human life. The Lord must reveal Himself, or remain unrevealed"[6]; "no man knoweth of his ways save it be revealed unto him" (Jacob 4:8); and "the things of God knoweth no man, but [by] the Spirit of God" (1 Corinthians 2:11).

The message is clear: acquisition of a witness of the divinity of Jesus Christ and of the truth of his gospel are man's first priorities, and this witness comes only from the Spirit of God. That is the order established by God. "In this area of knowledge [God and the doctrines of the gospel], scholarship and reason are insufficient."[7] Reversing this order does not lead to a spiritual witness, but it may lead to other problems. For example, President Gordon B. Hinckley is quoted as saying, "Following mortal, fallible man instead of God leads to remorse, . . . [and to] avoid such a result, we need to stay close to the Spirit and make the Gospel of Jesus Christ first in our lives."[8] Moreover, when close to the Spirit, man is receptive to inspiration in all righteous endeavors that advance God's work and plan for man, including science. "Seekers who have paid the price in perspiration have been magnified by inspiration. . . . Many of the great discoveries and achievements in science and the arts have resulted from a God-given revelation."[9]

Typically, the scientist employs theory to structure (interpret) limited factual information as a means to mental exploration of that which is imperfectly known. Accordingly, there may be more than one scientific interpretation or inference that is consistent with the available factual information. Gospel understanding may enable a more informed selection among alternative interpretations, as it does for mineral resources and environmental issues.

Resources, Science, and Religion: Seduction of the Intellect

In a courageous First Presidency message published in the *Ensign,* President James E. Faust addressed some complex issues that currently confront society and contrasted gospel answers and teachings with those inspired by Satan.[10] For example, he cited abortion as a Satan-inspired means to achieve sustainability. That is one example of how Satan can and does employ a notion or principle that of itself may be basically good, such as concern for the welfare of future generations of our unborn brothers and sisters, to seduce man into wrongheaded ideas and evil practices, such as abortion. Although particulars vary, his approach is familiar, for it began in the premortal existence. There is nothing wrong per se with the desire for all spirits to return and live with God, our Eternal Father, but Satan's plan for achieving this end served only Satan, not God or man. Similarly, knowledge about God's creations is desirable, but the pursuit of this knowledge in ways that disavow spiritual laws is not God's way, and it is not necessary for the advancement of science. "That which is demonstrated, we accept with joy; but vain philosophy, human theory and mere speculations of men, we do not accept nor do we adopt anything contrary to divine revelation or to good common sense."[11]

In accordance with the plan of salvation, our mortal state presents us with many difficulties and challenges. Satan employs many crafty ways to lead man away from God's revealed word, such as appealing to man's ego, exploiting man's limited knowledge, and heightening man's anxieties about a future that in terms of mortal man's references and limited vision is inherently uncertain. Following President Faust's lead, I next examine two additional issues of sustainability: exhaustible (or nonsustainable use of) mineral resources and the environment.

MINERAL RESOURCES: PERCEPTION OF CRISIS AND IMPENDING DOOM

Consider the following statements: "We are facing a global mineral resource crisis. Earth's finite supply of minerals is being used by a population that is growing faster than at any time in history. . . . To make matters worse, mineral consumption is growing even faster than the population."[12] These comments, taken from a college textbook on resources, economics, and the environment, at the very least provoke concern; for some, they may even create anxieties about their future or the future of their children. Are these concerns and anxieties justified? What confirmation or refutation of impending crisis is there in the scriptures and the inspired words of our prophets?

Scriptural References to Resources

The foregoing quotations about mineral resources contrast sharply with scriptural references: "The earth is full, and there is enough and to spare; yea, I prepared all things, and have given unto the children of men to be agents unto themselves" (Doctrine and Covenants 104:17). "I have made the earth rich" (Doctrine and Covenants 38:17). "O Lord, how manifold are thy works! in wisdom hast thou made them all: the earth is full of thy riches" (Psalm 104:24). "Behold, my brethren, this is the word which I declare unto you, that many of you have begun to search for gold, and for silver, and for all manner of precious ores, in the which this land, which is a land of promise unto you and to your seed, doth abound most plentifully" (Jacob 2:12).

Complex Issues

Is Earth richly endowed with mineral resources, as the scriptures and as our understanding of a loving God suggest? Or is man doomed to a future of suffering from the scarcity of necessary mineral and other resources, as some professional and lay persons firmly believe? Intellectually, the issues are complex and challenging, for they involve on the one hand the undeniable finiteness of Earth and on the other hand the increasing needs of ever-growing populations, societies of increasing complexity, and environmental pollution. These components can be easily used to create various doomsday scenarios, as they have been historically.

Scarcity Doctrine Not New

Near the end of the eighteenth century, Thomas Malthus foresaw a dismal future: man's capability of producing food, which was limited by a finite and fixed amount of agricultural land, would be exhausted and overrun by an exponentially growing population, resulting in starvation and death.[13] Stanley Jevons concluded that the rapid increase in coal consumption in England coupled with the finite nature of coal supply would soon cause progress to cease.[14] The 1970s witnessed a sophisticated statement of the Malthusian scarcity doctrine as a computer model that predicted the collapse of society sometime around the year 2050.[15] That predicted collapse is to be the result of declining mineral and energy resources and declining per capita food production combined with environmental pollution. By that prognostication, per capita food and per capita industrial production should now be approaching their maximum levels, and by now about one-half of available mineral and energy resources should have been depleted.

Malthusian-like views and prognostications share two common features: a fixed or linear component, which man cannot change, pitted against an exponentially increasing antagonist, which man also is incapable of changing. The most recent version of the Malthusian scarcity doctrine pits a limited capability of man to clean up the environment against an inexorably and exponentially increasing production of pollutants. Implicit in all Malthusian models is the incapability of man to learn and to take corrective actions to mitigate resource constraints or environmental problems. Such a depiction is not compatible with our knowledge of man and his relationship with God.

GOSPEL PERSPECTIVE ON RESOURCES AND MAN

God, the Creator of all, knows exactly the magnitude and quality of Earth's mineral resources, as well as Earth's future inhabitants and their needs. Yet, despite the finiteness of the world that he created, God tells man through the scriptures that there is plenty for all. As God is omniscient, any interpretation or prognostication by man that is contrary to God's word must be based on incorrect premises or incomplete information. Accordingly, it is wise to use God's word as a guide to possible intellectual resolutions of man's knowledge.

One resolution is that man's perception of the limits to mineral resources is generally correct, but the number of future generations that will need the use of those resources is far fewer than anticipated by man. Of course, this could be the case, but is restricting the number of future generations the only possible resolution?

Consider a second and more powerful resolution, one that does not require the restriction of future generations: The resources of the scriptures are not fixed, static physical assets like tons of coal, but dynamic functions of man's knowledge. For example, man does not need coal per se, but he does need energy, and collectively Earth matter (land, sea, and the atmosphere) and exogenous energy (energy from the sun) provide many different ways of obtaining energy. Historically, man's knowledge of energy resources has increased greatly. This second resolution allows that man's knowledge of God's creations will continue to increase, and as it does so will his perception of needs change, and the means to meet those needs will increase. In this view man's resources are dynamic functions of Earth matter, exogenous energy, and man's knowledge. Knowledge becomes the mother of all resources, and knowledge need not be limited by the finiteness of specific mineral assets like tons of coal. Moreover, knowledge is not dissipated by use, but grows by being shared.[16]

Does this second resolution describe our world? Such a world would, of course, be consistent with scriptural references to resources. And for such a world any prognostication by man that is constrained by his current perception of the finiteness of specific mineral assets and by the present knowledge of the use of those assets to meet needs as we now perceive them would be simplistic and would seriously understate the potential of man and Earth. Can science be used to test this resolution? What would be a useful empirical measure of resource scarcity and abundance that would reveal the presence or absence of the dynamics implicit to this second resolution?

MEASUREMENT OF RESOURCE SCARCITY

Those scientists who have sought to measure resource scarcity have concluded that the most meaningful measure is economic, not physical scarcity. The argument is simple but compelling: scarcity of a resource is measured by what man is willing to give up (sacrifice) for an additional unit of that resource. Thus, although physical scarcity may impact economic scarcity, it is not a sufficient measure of scarcity. For example, if a particular natural resource is very limited physically but man has no need of it, it is not economically scarce. Or, if there are technically good and abundant substitutes for a particular resource, that resource is not economically scarce, even though it may be very limited in a physical sense.

Empirical Tests of Economic Scarcity

Measures that have been used to investigate the economic scarcity of mineral resources include unit cost (cost of capital and labor per unit of mineral output) and unit labor cost,[17] price of the mineral commodity relative to labor wage,[18] price of minerals sector products relative to the price of nonextractive sector products,[19] and real (inflation-adjusted) mineral commodity price.[20]

Generally, the objective, scientific examination of mineral-resource scarcity leads to a startling finding: although the quantities of specific kinds of deposits of minerals and fuels are in a physical sense finite, and although we have depleted some of the richest of these deposits, *so far there is no evidence of economic scarcity.* Unit costs, real prices, and relative prices of mineral commodities have decreased and continue to do so, indicating increased economic abundance, not economic scarcity!

Such a result seems counterintuitive and incredulous to many in view of the finiteness of Earth and specific mineral assets. How is this result rationalized in terms of man's experience and current understanding? Mineral resource scarcity has been mitigated by (1) the ingenuity of man's God-given intelligence in expanding options in usable materials, (2) continuing discovery of mineral deposits of known types, (3) the identification of previously unknown kinds of mineral deposits, (4) the substitution of abundant for scarce mineral resources, (5) the substitution of nonmineral resources for scarce mineral resources, (6) scrap recovery and recycling, and (7) changes over time in mineral-using products and mineral-production technologies. Generally, the impact of technological change over time has been to decrease the amounts of mineral-derived materials used in a given manufactured product. "The finite limits of the globe, so real in their unqueried simplicity, lose definition under examination."[21] "Resources are highly dynamic functional concepts: they are not, they become."[22]

Simply stated, economic scarcity of mineral resources is not present, because man is not powerless, as he is depicted in Malthusian-like models, to alter his future; instead he reacts in many God-inspired, complex ways to mitigate scarcity and to expand his resources. "Resources are dynamic not only in response to increased knowledge, improved arts, expanding science, but also in response to changing individual wants and social objectives."[23]

CONFORMITY OF SCIENCE AND RELIGION

Interestingly, science confirms the promise of LDS scriptures regarding the sufficiency of mineral resources (see Doctrine and Covenants 104:17). The capability of man to avoid resource scarcity in a finite world led Julian Simon to refer to man as the "ultimate resource."[24] He almost had it right, but not quite: The ultimate resource is God. *Through inspiration from God, man's resources will continue to increase as needed to fulfill the purpose of his creation and that of Earth.*

THE ENVIRONMENT: A PERSPECTIVE

Few subjects elicit more diverse ideas and foster more intense discussion than do environmental problems and prescriptions for their solutions. Man does now and will in the future have to deal with pressing environmental problems, problems that were for a time either ignored or trivialized. Moreover, some of those problems are related to man's use of mineral resources: "Although we need more minerals to supply civilization, we are becoming increasingly aware that their production and use are polluting the planet. Just when we need to expand mineral production, there is concern that Earth is reaching its limit of mineral-related pollution."[25]

The issues are complex, as they involve not just science but also personal and societal values. As with the issue of mineral resource scarcity, desirable solutions to environmental problems need to be consistent with both science and spiritual laws. However, unlike mineral resource scarcity, Christianity is incorrectly seen by some to be a source of our environmental problems, not their solution. Moreover, environmental concerns are the new "cause célèbre" for Malthusian "doomsdayers." What, then, is the proper balance of environmental responsibility with man's temporal and spiritual welfare? The following comments are directed generally to these issues, but especially to correcting the false impression regarding the environmental teachings of Christianity in general and of the Church of Jesus Christ in particular.

THE MATLTHUSIAN POLLUTION DOCTRINE AND OTHER EXTREMES

In a Malthusian pollution model, gross emissions to the environment are proportional to economic activity; consequently, as society grows, meeting established environmental standards requires increasingly greater effort to remove increasingly greater amounts of pollution. Given Malthusian assumptions, pollution increases inexorably and costs rise, leading to the inevitable collapse of society.[26]

A Malthusian view of man and the environment is just as misleading as it is for other natural resources. Contrary to such views, man is not helpless and incapable of learning about environmental pollution and of taking corrective actions to mitigate environmental problems! Although it is an incorrect model of man and the environment, the Malthusian pollution doctrine seems to be at least politically powerful because of the evangelical-like passion for the environment and because of great anxieties about uncertain adverse consequences of environmental pollution. Naturally, these uncertainties and anxieties can be easily misused to play excessively upon man's fears with doomsday messages and serious distortions of man's future welfare.

Some prescribed solutions to man's environmental problems are so radical that they lead to speculation as to their source or to the motives of their advocates. Consider, for example, the comments of David M. Graber, research biologist with the National Park Service: "We become a plague upon ourselves and upon the Earth. . . . Until such time as Homo sapiens should decide to rejoin nature, some of us can only hope for the right virus to come along."[27] Or consider the recommendations of Rudolf Bahro, the theoretician and one of the founders of the German Green movement: "People should live in socialist communities of no more than 3,000, consuming only what they produce and . . . they should be restricted from trading with other communities. There should be no mechanized transportation, no computers, no modern technology."[28] Such radical prescriptions are just as serious in their implications to the welfare of man today and in the future as those that demean all environmental concerns on the grounds that they hinder industrial development and that pollution is not an important issue. Both are incorrect and exaggerations, and both impede the progress and welfare of man.

Implicit in extremists' views and to Malthusian pollution models is the proposition that the great explosion of knowledge since the Dark Ages suddenly has ceased with man's recognition that some of his activities are polluting Earth's environment. To hold such a view is to attribute all scientific and social progress to a badly misguided mortal intelligence. This is essentially a denial of a divine creation of Earth and man and a denial of divine influence. The greatest of all possible distortions, however, and one that most assuredly is inspired of Satan, is that man's environmental problems are due to Christian teachings.

Religion and Environmental Problems

One day, while reading from a widely used textbook on natural resources and environmental economics, I was startled by the following passage: "[Lynn White Jr.'s] thesis,[29] simply put, is that the environmental crises is due to the teachings of Judaism and Christianity which in Western culture have created a warped view of the proper relationship between humans and their environment. The basis for this is to be found in the first book of the Old Testament."[30] The biblical reference cited was Genesis 1:26: "And God said, Let us make man in our image, after our likeness: and let them have dominion over the fish of the sea, and over the fowl of the air, and over the cattle, and over all the earth, and over every creeping thing that creepeth upon the earth."

Incredibly, environmental problems are attributed to those very characteristics that most dignify man—his creation in the image of God and his God-given stewardship of Earth! Those who hold this view also advocate that man must adopt new values that reject the primacy of humans and elevate the stature of nature.[31] When carried to its extremes, that thesis has misled some followers to a new religion in which nature is God and man is an undesirable intruder. "Indeed, some turn ecology into a separate pantheistic religion of earth worship, often joined with New Age doctrine."[32] Consider the following, for example: "Human happiness and certainly human fecundity are not as important as a wild and healthy planet. I know social scientists who remind me that people are part of nature, but it isn't true."[33]

Companion to the creation of a new religion is the creation of a world order of socialism as a means to enforcing environmental protection. "It is often said that the only remaining socialists are in the environmental movement and continue to seek statist solutions based on government fiat."[34] Consider, for example, the words of Judi Bari of Earth First!: "I think if we don't overthrow capitalism, we don't have a chance of saving the world ecologically. I think it is possible to have an ecologically sound society under socialism. I don't think it's possible under capitalism."[35] Setting religion aside, the idea that the environment is better protected under socialism is bizarre in view of the rampant environmental pollution in the previous Soviet Union and other Eastern bloc countries under communist regimes. "In those areas of the world that most reflect the socialist economic system preferred by regulating-via-government environmentalists— as in Eastern Europe and the former USSR—an environmental mess has been made, a mess, however, that Western companies and Western technology, far from harming the environment, will actually help clean up."[36]

Deceptions and Seductions

Addressing resource problems and preserving the environment for future generations of our unborn brothers and sisters are of themselves good and noble goals, goals that are consistent with the restored gospel of Jesus Christ. However, the proposition that achieving these goals requires that man abandon Christianity is ridiculous, as also is the idea that preserving the environment requires man to abandon democracy for a world order of socialism. Those who espouse these ideas have been seduced to believe that the environment can be preserved only through a political system that provides for command-and-control enforcement. Such an approach would eliminate personal agency and responsibility and is not in keeping with the revealed word of the Lord: "I prepared all things, and have given unto the children of men to be agents unto themselves" (Doctrine and Covenants 104:17).

TEACHING OF THE CHURCH OF JESUS CHRIST ON THE ENVIRONMENT

The charge that Christian teachings constitute a license to pollute Earth reflects an uninformed view of Christianity in general and of the restored gospel of Jesus Christ in particular. Doctrines and teachings of The Church of Jesus Christ of Latter-day Saints do not advocate damaging Earth's environment or vindicate those who do so. Unlike some Christian religions, which are just now trying to become "green,"[37] the LDS Church has always taught responsible stewardship over Earth and its resources. When members of the Church have failed to properly care for the environment, it is either because of ignorance or because of personal failure to observe gospel teachings. The source of these failures is not doctrinal, as Doctrine and Covenants 104:13–17 makes clear:

> For it is expedient that I, the Lord, should make every man accountable, as a steward over earthly blessings, which I have made and prepared for my creatures.
>
> I, the Lord, stretched out the heavens, and built the earth, my very handiwork; and all things therein are mine.

And it is my purpose to provide for my saints, for all things are mine.

But it must needs be done in mine own way; and behold this is the way that I, the Lord, have decreed to provide for my saints, that the poor shall be exalted, in that the rich are made low.

For the earth is full, and there is enough and to spare; yea, I prepared all things, and have given unto the children of men to be agents unto themselves.

The message from the scriptures is clear: Earth is the Lord's; man is only a steward. And as a good steward, man is accountable and must be respectful of Earth and its inhabitants. There is no evidence that God intended man's authorized dominion over Earth to be taken as an entitlement to exploit Earth wantonly. Quite to the contrary, God counsels man through the scriptures to "hurt not the earth" (Revelation 7:3), to care for the poor, and to be a prudent and responsible agent: "It pleaseth God that he hath given all these things unto man; for unto this end were they made to be used, with judgment, not to excess, neither by extortion" (Doctrine and Covenants 59:20). Certainly the pursuit of personal gain with disregard for the environment and the rights and welfare of others is a violation of God's will. Our responsibility for the environment was affirmed by President Spencer W. Kimball, who considered deterioration of the environment as one of the prime evils of his time, the others being the quest for affluence and trust in force of arms.[38]

BALANCE AND AN ETERNAL PERSPECTIVE

The gospel of Jesus Christ clearly teaches that man is created in the image of God and that he does have dominion over all earthly things. Accordingly, environmental, mineral, and nonmineral resources are for the prudent use of man to meet his righteous needs. Extremist views that elevate nature above man are not in accordance with teachings of the restored gospel of Jesus Christ. However, man's special place in God's creations is due to his godly potential when he lives the gospel of Jesus Christ, and that gospel clearly teaches man to respect and care for Earth and its inhabitants, giving no license for abuse for personal gain. "The Bible speaks of man having dominion over the earth (Psalm 8:6), but the scriptures also warn us to be wise in how we exercise that dominion. It is no small thing to be made the caretaker of the Lord's house and overseer of His Creations."[39]

The restored gospel of Jesus Christ teaches that Earth is our home and that in its celestial state it will be our eternal home; consequently, although man has dominion over all earthly things, Earth must not be misused or polluted. As each of us is a member of a great patriarchal order, we need have concern for our yet unborn brothers and sisters as well as those who currently occupy Earth. A comprehensive and righteous concern dictates that (1) we use Earth's resources wisely to care for our currently living brothers and sisters everywhere, (2) we preserve Earth's environment for use by future generations, and (3) we empower future generations with increased knowledge of Earth's resources and improved technology for the use of those resources to enrich their mortal experience. "The gospel of Jesus Christ as taught by His church in these latter days can provide full answers to these [ecological] problems."[40]

We will continue to be confronted with challenging mineral resource and environmental problems. Yet "we need not . . . be troubled by world conditions, as long as we walk in that light which a gracious Father has so abundantly shed forth upon us in this final gospel dispensation."[41] Jesus the Christ, the Creator of this world, is the source of all knowledge, scientific as well as spiritual. He is our Savior and Redeemer; his gospel is the greatest of all influences in changing lives and bringing joy to mankind; and through inspiration from him will all problems and difficulties of this life be solved and overcome. "Be not afraid, only believe" (Mark 5:36). "Peace I leave with you, my peace I give unto you: not as the world giveth, give I unto you. Let not your heart be troubled, neither let it be afraid" (John 14:27).

SUMMARY

I often express my gratitude to Heavenly Father for the wonders of this second estate, for the beautiful and rich Earth, and for the challenging and exciting adventure of learning of him and his creations! I am grateful for the opportunity afforded me to be involved in research and teaching and to share with students and peers the excitement of new ideas. The calling to be bishop of the University Third Ward of the Tucson Arizona Stake, an institute ward of young singles, was a great blessing to me and my lovely wife, Sandra, who was the secretary of the Tucson Institute of Religion. Sandra's love and concern for others is remarkable and has provided me with a great example. Serving as bishop greatly enlarged my understanding of the power of Christ's love and gave me great admiration for today's youth in the Church. To share with them their love for Christ, to experience even a very small portion of Christ's love for them, and to witness the gospel of Jesus Christ at work in their lives was a great blessing! That experience enhances my appreciation of the words from that wonderful hymn "I Stand All Amazed": "I stand all amazed at the love Jesus offers me, confused at the grace that so fully he proffers me."[42]

NOTES

1. See my *Mineral Exploration Decisions: A Guide to Economic Analysis and Modeling* (New York: John Wiley & Sons, 1990).

2. See my article "Mineral-Resource Assessment—Perspectives on Past and Present and Speculation on Future Directions," *Nonrenewable Resources* 4, no. 3 (1995): 213–32.

3. See my *Mineral Resources Appraisal: Mineral Endowment, Resources, and Potential Supply—Concepts, Methods, and Case Studies* (New York: Oxford University Press, 1984).

4. *Melchizedek Priesthood Study Guide, 1977–78*, p. 95.

5. *Ensign*, May 1974, p. 95.

6. Joseph Fielding Smith, John R. Winder, and Anthon H. Lund, "The Origin of Man," *Improvement Era* 12 (1909): 80–81.

7. Dallin H. Oaks, April 1989 general conference address, quoted in *Church News,* 27 January 1996, p. 14.

8. Ibid.

9. Ibid.

10. James E. Faust, "Serving the Lord and Resisting the Devil," *Ensign,* September 1995, pp. 2–7.

11. "First Presidency Christmas Address," *Deseret News,* 17 December 1910, p. 3.

12. Stephen E. Kessler, *Mineral Resources, Economics, and the Environment* (New York: Macmillan, 1994), p. 1.

13. Thomas R. Malthus, "An Essay on the Principle of Population as It Affects the Future Improvement of Mankind" (1798), *Population. The First Essay* (London: Macmillan, 1926); and *Principles of Population,* 5th ed. (Homewood, Ill.: Irwin, n.d.).

14. See Stanley Jevons, *The Coal Question: An Inquiry Concerning the Progress of the Nation and the Probable Exhaustion of Our Coal Mines* (London: Macmillan, 1865).

15. See Donella H. Meadows et al., *Limits of Growth* (New York: Universe Books, 1972).

16. See William N. Peach and James A. Constantin, *Zimmermann's World Resources and Industries,* 3rd ed. (New York: Harper & Row, 1972).

17. See Harold J. Barnett and Chandler Morse, *Scarcity and Growth: The Economics of Natural Resource Availability* (Baltimore: Johns Hopkins University Press, 1963).

18. See Julian Simon, *The Ultimate Resource* (Princeton: Princeton University Press, 1981).

19. See ibid.

20. See Thierno Sow, "Multivariate Forecasting of Mineral Commodities Price: Implications for Natural Resource Scarcity" (Ph.D diss., University of Arizona, 1996).

21. Ibid., p. 45.

22. Peach and Constantin, *Zimmermann's World Resources and Industries,* p. 156.

23. Ibid., p. 12.

24. Ibid.

25. Kessler, *Mineral Resources,* p. 1.

26. See Harold Barnett, "Scarcity and Growth Revisited," in *Scarcity and Growth Reconsidered,* ed. Kerry Smith (Baltimore: Johns Hopkins University Press, 1979).

27. David M. Graber, Book Review, *Los Angeles Times,* 22 October 1989, p. 9; quoted by Walter Williams in *State Journal-Register,* 25 June 1992. Williams is quoted by Dixie Lee· Ray and Lou Guzzo in *Environmental Overkill: Whatever Happened to Common Sense?* (Washington, D.C.: Recency Printing, 1993), p. 204.

28. Rudolf Bahro, "Building on Unlimited Future," *Imprimis,* January 1992; also excerpted in Barry Asmus, "The 'Green Brick' of Socialism," *Abundant Wildlife* 5 (1992) and quoted by Ray and Guzzo, *Environmental Overkill,* p. 203.

29. See Lynn White Jr., "The Historical Roots of Ecological Crisis," *Science* 155 (March 1967): 1203–7.

30. Tom Tietenberg, *Environmental and Natural Resource Economics* (Glenview, Illinois: Foresman, 1984), p. 56.

31. See ibid.

32. James L Malone, "Mineral Resources and the International Environmental Agenda," *Mining Voice* 1, no. 5 (November/December 1995): 32.

33. David Graber, Book Review, *Los Angeles Times,* 22 Oct. 1989, p. 9.

34. James L. Malone, "Mineral Resources . . . ," p. 32.

35. Judy Bari, quoted by Walter Williams in *State Journal Register,* 25 June 1992. Williams is quoted by Ray and Guzzo in *Environmental Overkill: Whatever Happened to Common Sense?,* p. 203.

36. Ray and Guzzo, *Environmental Overkill: Whatever Happened to Common Sense?,* p. 25.

37. Ray and Guzzo in *Environmental Overkill: Whatever Happened to Common Sense?,* p. 202.

38. See Hugh W. Nibley, *Approaching Zion,* vol. 9 of The Collected Works of Hugh Nibley (Salt Lake City: Deseret Book Co. and F.A.R.M.S., 1989), p. 480.

39. Viewpoint, *Church News,* 17 February 1996.

40. Alexander B. Morrison, "Our Deteriorating Environment," *Ensign,* August 1971, p. 9.

41. Joseph Fielding Smith, quoted in *Come unto the Father in the Name of Jesus,* Melchizedek Priesthood personal study guide, 1971, p. 7.

42. *Hymns,* 1985, no. 193.

J. EDWIN SEEGMILLER *studied at Dixie Junior College and the University of Utah and received his M.D. from the University of Chicago. He did postdoctoral work at the National Institute of Health and at the Thorndike Memorial Laboratory in Boston and focused his career on medical research. He has held positions at the National Institutes of Health in Bethesda, Maryland; the University College Hospital in London; and the School of Medicine of the University of California, San Diego, in La Jolla, California. He was the founding director of the Institute for Research on Aging at the University of California, San Diego, and the associate director of the university's Sam and Rose Stein Institute for Research on Aging. He was a visiting scholar at the Basel Institute for Immunology and at the Sir William Dunn School of Pathology and the Department of Biochemistry at Oxford. He was also a Guggenheim Fellow at the Swiss Institute for Experimental Cancer Research.*

A recipient of the U.S. Public Health Distinguished Service Award in 1969, Dr. Seegmiller was elected a member of the National Academy of Sciences in 1973 and of the Institute of Medicine of the National Academy in 1978. The recipient of many honors and awards, he is the author of more than 300 articles and books.

He has served in many Church callings, including two bishoprics. He married Roberta Eads, and they had four children and seven grandchildren. Following the death of his first wife, he married Barbara Davies Ellerston. He is now professor emeritus at the University of California, San Diego, in La Jolla, California.

CHAPTER 11

EXPANSION OF KNOWLEDGE OF HUMAN GENETICS: A MORMON PERSPECTIVE

J. EDWIN SEEGMILLER

In this essay I will share highlights of new insights into hereditary diseases and human genetics that I have learned in the course of nearly half a century of a professional life of medical research. By design, my discussion will freely reflect my own Mormon cultural perspective.

This period of time has been a most enlightening epoch in which to live, for our understanding of the field of genetics and, in particular, human biochemical genetics has seen remarkable progress. Such advances bring to my mind the ultimate purpose of our life here on Earth, concisely stated in a couplet by LDS Church president Lorenzo Snow: "As man is, God once was; as God is, man may become." I feel we are well along on our way, and I can think of no greater destiny for each of us to aspire to.

Acquiring the greatest intelligence possible and the fullest knowledge of the natural laws governing our lives here on Earth becomes a major objective for Latter-day Saints. It should not matter if we now catch a glimpse of the creative, godlike powers we may start to control even here in this mortal existence. This goes well with the scripture "the glory of God is intelligence" (Doctrine and Covenants 93:36) and the admonition "ye shall know the truth, and the truth shall make you free" (John 8:32), which is the essence of science. Thus a life dedicated to the study of science comes easily to Mormons. Perhaps this philosophy is one reason for the fact that in 1943 the state of Utah had a per capita figure of 45 percent more men listed in *American Men of Science* than any other state in the Union.[1] This lead has persisted with more highly educated Mormons also being more religious than less highly educated Mormons. A summary by Mark W. Cannon[2] of nine studies over a seventy-year period found that Utah (in relation to its population) has led the nation in production of scientists and continues to do so despite substantial recent migration of non-Mormons into Utah. The fact that scientists and engineers have been among the Church's leaders from its inception and continue to do so is also worth noting. Over a near half century, the state of Utah has led the nation in the portion of its college graduates who go on to receive the Ph.D. degree. In the same period, Utah has consistently shown a higher proportion of its population honored by listing in *American Men [and Women] of Science* than any other state in the Union. It is therefore not surprising that a higher proportion of graduates of Utah universities received this recognition of contributions to science than even the graduates of MIT, Harvard, or Stanford, according to a 1944 study. The importance of learning and education has been long recognized as an integral part of the philosophy of the Church. The well-known challenge given by every missionary to each prospective convert to "prove for yourselves the truth of this doctrine" becomes, in effect, an application of the scientific method to religion.

PERSONAL BACKGROUND AND EARLY MAJOR DECISIONS

In retrospect a rather unusual set of events catalyzed the early steps in my transition from a rural agricultural environment to an interest in scientific pursuits. I was born in St. George, Utah, a member of the second generation of descendants of the settling pioneers who were hand-picked by Brigham Young to raise cotton in this region of more temperate climate in the southwest corner of Utah. I am aware of at least three university presidents who trace their origins to this same small farming community of around twenty-five hundred people whom I knew in my early years. My decision to prepare myself for a research career, initially in chemistry, was the result of a memorable contact of only a few hours with another descendant of the original settlers who was one of the most inspiring men I have known, Dr. Henry Eyring, then a professor at Princeton University. He had a brilliant mind, a warm personality, and a strong belief in the truths of our religion. I had just turned seventeen. I remember well his words "You can't make a mistake going into chemistry," followed by advice to pay attention to grades so I could qualify for a fellowship to cover the expenses of graduate school. This occurred before I had been exposed even to high school chemistry. Eyring's own parents were part of the first generation growing up in St. George and had been close friends of my own parents. The families of both of his parents had been included in a group selected by the Church to immigrate to Mexico to found a Mormon colony in the 1890s. Henry Eyring came with his wife and two sons to St. George to bring his parents back to visit their old friends there during his own summer vacation.

I took Dr. Eyring's advice, and during my senior year at the University of Utah I was accepted at several graduate schools, including Princeton, when World War II intervened. However, a war research project to which I was assigned brought me in contact with physicians at the National Institutes of Health (NIH) in Bethesda, Maryland. I found some were working on human diseases caused by chemical abnormalities of the body. I found that these disorders presented problems even more fascinating to solve regarding the chemical mechanisms producing human diseases than anything I had found in the chemistry laboratory. After my discharge from the army, I promptly enrolled in medical school at the University of Chicago. While interning in medicine at Johns Hopkins Hospital, I learned that a clinical research center was under construction on the grounds of NIH. In addition, a new basic biochemical research group was being assembled, including some of the research doctors I had met during my work there. Feeling the need for more intensive training in biochemistry to be most effective in the field of clinical research that had captured my interest, I applied and was accepted. It was an excellent choice since the leader of the group, Dr. Arthur Kornberg, won a Nobel Prize for his elucidation of the biochemical mechanisms for the replication of DNA after he moved to Stanford less than a decade later.

EARLY PHASES OF CLINICAL RESEARCH

In preparation for more clinically oriented research, I then worked for a year as a research associate at Harvard Medical School's Thorndike Memorial Laboratory identifying chemical abnormalities of the blood in patients with hepatic coma. During my medical training I had been intrigued by the fact that we were still lacking a full explanation of the basic abnormalities causing gouty arthritis. I was, therefore, most gratified when the newly appointed clinical director of the Institute of Arthritis and Metabolic Diseases of NIH, Dr. Joseph J. Bunim, suggested that I start working on gouty arthritis with Dr. Dewitt Stetten at the Public Health Research Institute of the City of New York. Stetten's pioneering earlier work while he was still on the faculty at Harvard involving use of heavy isotopes for studies of a chemical abnormality of gout had already attracted my attention.

DISTINCTIVE FEATURES AND HISTORY OF GOUT

Gouty arthritis has a fascinating history.[3] It is one of the most anciently recognized forms of arthritis first described by Hippocrates in the fourth century B.C. He noted that gouty arthritis is a disease primarily of mature young men after the age of "venality" and that it is much less frequently seen in women, and then only after menopause. Far earlier evidence of gout has been found in ancient Egyptian mummies, and it may very well have afflicted a portion of the human race from the beginning. The remarkable number of social and political leaders in past ages who have been afflicted with the gout ties the disease closely with this aspect of mankind's history as well. I have therefore undertaken to open new vistas of self-worth and potential accomplishment to numerous young patients who have come to me with their first attack of gout by informing them that they are suffering the initiation rites to the world's most illustrious and exclusive fraternity.

Through the more recent centuries, the chemical abnormality in gouty patients had provided a meeting ground for the interests of both early chemists and physicians. The classic description of the clinical features of gout was published in 1683 by a British physician, Thomas Sydenham, based on his thirty-four years of personal affliction with this disease. The Swedish chemist Scheele was the first to isolate uric acid from a urinary stone in 1776. In 1797 a British chemist, Wollaston, was the first to isolate uric acid from a gouty tophus that he is purported to have removed from his own ear. In 1848 another British physician, Alfred Baring Garrod, was the first to demonstrate the elevation above normal of uric acid in the serum of gouty patients by collecting uric acid crystals formed on strands of huckaback or other unwashed linen fibers added to acidified serum in a shallow glass dish exposed on a mantelpiece for thirty-six to sixty hours.

But neither the cause of this elevation nor the mechanism causing the recurring, debilitating acute attacks of gouty arthritis had yet been clearly defined. These episodes usually involve a single peripheral joint that rapidly becomes swollen, red, warm, and exquisitely painful and tender. Even if untreated, symptoms gradually disappear over a period of days or even weeks but with time recur at progressively shorter intervals with development of firm nodules called tophi over tendons, joints, and, not infrequently, the outer edges of the ears. Advanced cases show a progressive destruction of joint cartilage and subchondral bone and virtually constant pain and disability. Development of kidney stones composed of uric acid or calcium oxalate are not infrequent, and a progressive kidney damage accelerates progression of the disease and can lead to death from kidney failure.[4]

In 1890 Garrod, in his "Propositions on Gout," proposed that deposits of crystals of sodium urate found in tophi (nodules) in and about the affected joints of gouty patients was the cause of the exquisitely painful attacks of acute gouty arthritis. However, this view had been discounted when other investigators failed to find any ill effects from injecting similar urate crystals into rabbits. I could find no report of the effect of injecting urate crystals into a human volunteer, which I kept in mind as a project I must do when I returned to the clinical center of NIH.

BEGINNING OF RESEARCH ON GOUT

I found that my new research project with Dr. Dewitt Stetten Jr. at the Public Health Research Institute of the City of New York was a great joy. He had both an M.D. and a Ph.D. in biochemistry and was a most inspiring mentor with a contagious enthusiasm for research. He had a brilliant mind and was a most effective teacher and a man of great integrity and compassion.[5] My first assignment was to synthesize a chemical precursor of purines, 4-amino-5-imidazolecarboxamide (AIC) incorporating a heavy isotope of carbon (C-13). I found there was a chemist, Dr. D. Wayne Woolley at the Rockefeller Institute, who had synthesized this compound. I promptly made an appointment to visit him.

I had been told that he was completely blind. In talking with him, I found he had grown up a member of a Mormon community in western Canada and had received his Ph.D. in biochemistry from the University of Wisconsin even though he had problems with diabetes at that time. While in his postdoctoral fellowship at Rockefeller Institute, he had become completely blind as a complication of his diabetes. I was most impressed with his remarkable ability to continue his productive life as a biochemist despite his handicap. With our Mormon heritage in common, he had me visit his home and meet his wife, who was also scientifically trained and could therefore be of special value to him by reading the current scientific literature to him. We became good friends although he never seemed interested in talking about religion. Whenever I saw him at annual biomedical meetings, I always spoke to him and he always recognized me from my voice.

My organic synthesis was successful, and I became the first normal control for our study by eating a portion of my newly synthesized product with my breakfast one morning. I decided that this would be a good ethical principal to follow in my research career. I could not go far wrong if I ask a patient to undergo only procedures that I, myself, would be willing to undergo. As a result I have been one of the normal controls for virtually all of my human investigative studies. Our studies showed that AIC is a ready precursor of uric acid and that it substantially inhibits the new synthesis of uric acid from glycine-N15 given simultaneously.[6] This was our first evidence for the presence of a regulatory system for the control of the rate of synthesis of purines. We eventually showed that the elevated serum urate of gout patients resulted from an increased rate of urate synthesis in some patients, a decreased efficiency of elimination of uric acid by the kidney in most patients and occasional patients show evidence of both processes.[7] In some families we have even found the enzyme defect that has in most cases been an absence or diminished activity of an enzyme, but in one family an overactive rate-limiting enzyme was found as the genetic basis of their gout.

After a year and a half in New York, I returned to NIH in 1954 as clinical investigator in the Arthritis and Rheumatism Branch of the National Institute of Arthritis and Metabolic Diseases located in the newly completed clinical center. Since Dr. Stetten soon joined the same institute as research director, we continued our research on gouty arthritis. I recall preparing the needle-shaped crystals of monosodium urate of size comparable to those found in gouty tophi and injecting a sterilized suspension of these crystals into the skin of my forearm. The next morning I was most pleased to see an intense red and slightly swollen area at the injection site. When I showed this to Dr. Stetten, he was delighted to see it but soon asked me if I had received permission from the Human Investigations Committee for doing this procedure on myself. I told him I had not thought that was necessary and pointed out that I was in reality merely following the ethical standard that I had set up for myself. However, I did agree to obtain that important committee's approval before I administered the crystals to any of my volunteers.[8, 9]

CRYSTALS AS THE CAUSE OF ACUTE ATTACKS OF GOUTY ARTHRITIS

I recall having several volunteer gouty patients in the clinical center with typical attacks of acute gout in the single joint, which they had consented to have me inject with a small dose of sterile crystals. It happened to be at the time of the annual meeting in the Washington, D.C., area of the American Rheumatism Association. When some of the association's members visited our institute, I showed them my patients. Even when they were permitted to examine the patients' joints themselves, none of them even spoke to me. It was only then that I realized I had just shown them a phenomenon that completely violated the dogma they had been taught about gout. This common reaction to new ideas that are not yet accepted by the establishment can be a deterrent to progress if the investigator becomes discouraged too soon. It was obviously difficult for them to face this truth about the origin of these attacks even though they had seen the results themselves. I find that this skepticism, although difficult to take, is probably a healthy part of the scientific establishment. Demonstrating the truth usually requires the presentation of supporting evidence from several different sources.

Our group and other investigators did furnish supporting evidence of the ability of the urate crystals to induce an inflammatory response as part of the acute gouty attack by showing an additional aspect of the inflammatory reaction. During either the spontaneous or the urate crystal–induced acute attacks of gout, more than 90 percent of the crystals readily visible in the synovial fluid obtained from the affected joint were found engulfed in white blood cells (phagocytes).[10]

These were the same type of cells that are normally attracted to areas of bacterial invasion in the body and were obviously treating the crystals as the equivalent of invading bacteria by engulfing them with a burst of increased oxygen consumption and in effect placing them into the cellular counterpart of our kitchen garbage disposal known as a lysosome. These organelles in the cytoplasm of the cell are capable of generating an abundance of "free radicals," molecules with a single unshared electron generated from the burst of oxygen consumption via the direct oxidative pathway of glucose, thus delivering single electrons to oxygen molecules to generate the highly active oxygen radicals. The resulting strongly oxidizing environment serves to kill the bacteria taken up by the phagocytes and is an important factor in our defense against infection. The lysosomes can even generate the same active oxidizing ingredient that is found in our laundry bleach to kill bacteria and bleach out stains: sodium hypochlorite. We found that even urate crystals engulfed by these phagocytes could be destroyed,[11] which might very well contribute to the gradual recovery of the patients from each acute gouty attack even if they have not received treatment with anti-inflammatory drugs. In addition, the destruction of urate crystals by phagocytosis was demonstrated and was diminished by addition of colchicine,[12] a drug with a long medical history of being an effective and specific treatment of the acute attack of gouty arthritis.

A BENEFICIAL ROLE FOR URIC ACID IN THE HUMAN SPECIES

I have mentioned the remarkable number of political and social leaders of past ages who have had gouty arthritis. This may have prompted Dr. Stetten to do a study of army inductees at an army base that showed a low but nevertheless statistically significant positive correlation of their serum urate concentration with their score on the Army General Classification Test, which was regarded as a measure of intelligence.

Among all mammals, the human species and possibly closely related primates are the only ones in whom gouty arthritis develops. Early biochemical investigators showed that all mammals but man and the higher apes and some Western monkeys excrete allantoin instead of uric acid as their end-product of purine metabolism. The reason for this biochemical difference was traced to the absence of the enzyme uricase, which in all other mammals converts the sparingly soluble uric acid to the more soluble substance allantoin before excretion. If uric acid is merely a waste product, this leaves two unanswered questions. Why does the human kidney excrete uric acid so inefficiently? Kidney physiologists have shown that the normal human kidney is very inefficient at eliminating uric acid from the body. It actually excretes into the urine only around 5 percent of the uric acid that passes into the kidney from the bloodstream.

The second question is closely related: If uric acid is merely a waste product, why is the mean concentration of serum urate of normal human males of 6.4 mg per deciliter so very close to the limit of solubility of urate we have found in human serum of 7.0 mg per deciliter? All gouty patients have more than this upper limit so their serum is supersaturated with urate as was noted by A. B. Garrod in the middle of the last century. The fact that the mean value for serum urate of women is 5.4 mg per deciliter until after the menopause explains very well Hippocrates' observation of their being protected from the gout until after the menopause. It should also have pointed the way for successful treatment of gout in the preventive mode.

Actually, the answer to the two questions above was a completely new function for urate in serum and other body fluids shown by a former colleague of mine at NIH, Dr. Bruce Ames, now on the faculty of the University of California, Berkeley. In 1982 he proposed a new role for uric acid as a very effective natural scavenger of free radicals.[13] He has since shown that although ascorbic acid (vitamin C) is the first line of defense the body has against free radicals in the water-soluble compartments of the human body, in some systems uric acid is actually as effective as vitamin C in its free-radical scavenging ability. Furthermore, it does this without having a hazard shown by vitamin C. In laboratory studies of free radicals, a convenient source is found by the simple addition of trace metals, iron or copper, to a solution of vitamin C. Iron, of course, is an essential component of hemoglobin of red blood cells and of the cytochromes involved in transmitting electrons from the mitochondria inside cells where food is oxidized by the oxygen delivered by the hemoglobin to form water. It makes good reason for storage forms of iron in the body to be found encased in a protein sheath.

These considerations are of even further interest when we remember that humans are incapable of making vitamin C. That is why it is called a vitamin. We find that the same human progenitors who lost the enzyme uricase also lost the activity of the last enzyme that in other mammals is involved in their synthesis of vitamin C. Other investigators have proposed that this high level of uric acid in serum from the loss of the enzyme uricase and loss of the ability to synthesize ascorbic acid may account for the fact that the human species has the longest average life span of all mammals.[14] In the overall plan, gouty arthritis in a small segment of the population was thus the price the human species pays for having a longer and perhaps a more intelligent life than any other mammal.

CONTROL OF GOUTY ARTHRITIS IN A PREVENTIVE MODE

In the last four to five decades, research into the basis of the disease by numerous investigators and the development and application of new drugs have made gouty arthritis readily controlled in a preventive mode by primary care physicians throughout the world. Once the primary role of crystals of monosodium urate was demonstrated as the cause of the acute attacks of gouty arthritis, the rational solution was to remove the cause by lowering the serum urate from the supersaturated range generating the crystals to the normal unsaturated range that would allow the crystals to be dissolved by body fluids. The first really effective drug was probenecid (Benemid), which increases uric acid excretion by diminishing the reabsorption of urate in the distal tubule of the kidney and eventually mobilizing gouty tophi and preventing recurrence of attacks.[15] Another drug, allopurinol (Xyloprim), is an inhibitor of the enzyme xanthine oxidase (responsible for making uric acid) and was first synthesized by an LDS chemist, Roland K. Robins[16] for enhancing the clinical effectiveness of an anticancer drug, 6-mercaptopurine. It was later shown to be very effective for lowering the serum urate for the long-term treatment of gout by Wayne Rundles and associates[17] and later by James Klinenberg and colleagues in my group.[18] If either of these drugs that lower serum urate to the normal (unsaturated) level is initiated during an acute attack of gout, it usually makes the acute attack worse. Since we still found urate crystals engulfed by phagocytes during these attacks, we presume they are dispersed from a disaggregation of clumps of crystals so that it is the equivalent of injecting additional urate crystals into the joint. An herbal drug extracted from the autumn crocus, colchicine, is so specific in suppressing the acute attacks of gout that response to colchicine was used for many years as the diagnostic test for gout and is still of value in suppressing this tendency to develop gout if it is given daily during the first few months treatment with probenecid or allopurinol. More modern anti-inflammatory drugs are also effective in terminating acute attacks of gout.[19]

Origin of Free Radicals

Detailed studies by Dr. Irwin Fridovich at Duke University showed that xanthine oxidase, the enzyme generating uric acid, also generates free radicals and that these agents are formed by all enzyme systems that deliver single electrons to oxygen.[20] Free radicals are very reactive and are strong oxidizing agents that damage virtually all organic molecules in their vicinity. All life forms that consume oxygen for energy generation have developed free-radical scavenging enzymes and reducing agents such as ascorbic acid (vitamin C) in aqueous compartments and vitamin E in lipid and lipid membrane compartments to destroy free radicals and thereby minimize their damage.[21] In the human species uric acid is another important free-radical scavenger quite comparable in many systems to ascorbic acid. Investigators are now finding that many degenerative diseases of later life may well be caused in part by free radicals.

Insight from Study of Inherited Diseases

I soon came to realize that each inherited metabolic disease was in reality an experiment of nature caused by a single mutation, usually in a gene directing the synthesis of a single protein. If that protein happens to be an enzyme, the mutation results in the impairment in carrying out a specific chemical reaction, which results in the accumulation of the precursor.

The gene enzyme relationship was first proposed by British physician Archibald E. Garrod (the son of Alfred Baring Garrod) in 1908 in the Croonian Lecture,[22] a full thirty years before microbiologists at Cal Tech developed the same gene-enzyme concept from their studies of bacterial systems. Garrod's theory was first developed to explain the clinical features of a rare human hereditary metabolic disease called alcaptonuria. The excessive accumulation of an intermediate compound of metabolism announces its presence by turning into a dark pigment in the diapers and urine while standing exposed to oxidation by air. The chemical from which the pigment is formed was identified by an early organic chemist as homogentisic acid, a close structural relative of one of the amino acids called tyrosine. This suggested to Garrod that its accumulation in the body fluids and the urine of affected patients was from a lack of the chemical machinery (enzyme) for its normal further processing, which resulted in its accumulation in the bodies of affected patients. Although this chemical disorder is benign during early decades of life, it leads to a severe crippling arthritis in mature adult life. At autopsy these patients show the deposition of a dark pigment in and about the cartilage of the joints and tendons associated with severe degenerative changes in virtually all of the joints. Under the microscope this pigment has an ochre color, so the pathologists named the clinical disease "ochronotic arthritis." In his 1931 book *The Inborn Factors in Disease,* Garrod listed this disorder, gout, and only four or five other such disorders.[23]

Concurrent with the rapid development of our understanding of metabolic pathways in the field of biochemistry has come a substantial expansion in the recognition of human diseases with biochemical abnormalities. Nearly six thousand aberrations of genetic disorders are now listed in McKusick's most recent listing.[24] In 1957, just a few years after I had begun working as a clinical investigator in the Institute of Arthritis and Metabolic Diseases in the newly opened clinical center of the National Institutes of Health, I received a referral of a patient with alcaptonuria and well-advanced ochronotic arthritis. I was surprised to find no report in the literature of the actual documentation of Garrod's proposal of a missing enzyme as the actual cause of this disease. On his second admission the patient required surgery for stopping a severe gastrointestinal hemorrhage and had consented in advance of the surgery for the surgeon to remove a small piece of his liver for this determination. Quite by chance, Bert LaDu, a physician with a recent Ph.D. thesis from Berkeley on tyrosine metabolism, had just joined our institute with a laboratory near mine. We worked together in determining the activity of each of the enzymes of tyrosine metabolism in the liver sample and were able to show the virtually complete absence of the single enzyme homogentisic acid oxidase as had been postulated by Garrod nearly half a century earlier.[25]

In subsequent studies Dr. LaDu's group demonstrated the step-wise oxidation of homogentisic acid to benzoquinone acetic acid was required for homogentisic acid to bond with cartilage with formation of fairly stable intermediates that were carrying an unpaired electron and so were free radicals. In subsequent work in my laboratory, a medical student showed that a large dose of vitamin C would reduce the deposition of isotopically labeled homogentisic acid into rat-tail tendon and chest (xyphoid) cartilage in rats on a high tyrosine diet.[26] We have, therefore, shown subsequently an inhibition of growth of cultured cartilage cells induced by homogentisic acid at the concentrations we have found in serum of affected patients that is partially prevented by vitamin C.[27] Vitamin C given to infants with alcaptonuria was effective in significantly reducing the amount of benzoquinone acetic acid found in the urine,[28] which was taken as evidence of a beneficial effect and is now being recommended for treatment of affected children and adults.[29]

It has been fascinating to have had the opportunity of actually having a hand in proving the truth of Garrod's hypothesis for this disease, to participate in the identification of additional such diseases, and to gain a better interpretation of others that are well known. In the case of gout, for example, this progress in our understanding of human genetics has also introduced new prospects for the treatment of at least some of these genetic diseases by the new technologies of medical genetics. The possible introduction into the patient's cells of a normal gene to provide the missing enzyme produced by a mutant or damaged gene becomes a rational therapy for the treatment of a number of genetic diseases in the near future. At one point the religious leader Jerry Falwell had a group of his followers assemble in Washington, D.C., to persuade elected representatives on Capitol Hill to make a law outlawing the introduction of any gene into humans and thereby "spoil God's handiwork." When notified of this pending action, the director of NIH, Dr. James Wyngaarden, told me how he had to drop everything he was doing to rush down to Capitol Hill to prevent such a bill from being introduced.

This incident provided to me a current example of the contrast of the doctrines of conventional Christian religions with the LDS view of the potential of mankind. The LDS view that man is a God in embryo carries the expectation that we must each eventually learn how to put genes together and even to create new life forms as part of our preparation to be creators. The inhospitable environment of adjacent planets might well yield to remodeling with the help of specific life forms yet to be developed by modern technology.

INSIGHT FROM STUDY OF LESCH-NYHAN DISEASE

In 1964 I was in London for a year's sabbatical to learn more about human genetics from Dr. Charles Dent at University College Hospital and to learn the technology of tissue culture from another laboratory nearby. Dr. Dent was aware of my interest in abnormalities of uric acid metabolism and one morning asked me to go with him to see a patient at Hammersmith Hospital who had an elevated level of uric acid in his blood. Upon arrival we were escorted to a crib where a six-year-old boy with a severe form of cerebral palsy was lying down with his hands tied to the side of his crib. As I started to untie one hand, the child started crying and his mother said, "He is afraid you will not hold his hands, and if his fingers get into his mouth, he will bite them, and it hurts." I then saw scars on the ends of his fingers from previous biting. He was violating some of my assumptions about life: that we all have instincts that protect us from injuring ourselves, that we all can control our actions and are responsible for them, and that we all have free agency to make all choices. I then told Dr. Dent and the other doctors of a similar case of which I had been told a few weeks before I had left the NIH for London. It was a young boy of similar age and similar neurological problems at Johns Hopkins Hospital who had been first seen in the emergency room because of blood in the urine. Under the microscope his urine had shown many crystals, so his doctors collected all of the urine the child passed in a twenty-four-hour period and analyzed it and could not believe the presence of three to four times the normal amount of uric acid for a child of that age. They were concerned that the test being used for determining the uric acid was nonspecific and was reacting with some other chemical, so my laboratory at NIH was given a small sample of the urine to analyze using a highly specific enzymatic method that we had developed for our studies of patients with gout. The test confirmed that it was indeed uric acid. An older brother of the child at Johns Hopkins Hospital had suffered from the same neurological disease and had died from it, suggesting to the doctors that both cases may have been caused by a genetic defect.[30] To the doctors at Hammersmith Hospital I predicted they would find a similarly excessive amount of uric acid in this child's twenty-four-hour collection of urine, which proved to be true. I knew immediately that eventually I must study this disease in detail and find the enzyme defect responsible.

Enzyme Defect in Lesch-Nyhan Disease

Upon my return to NIH, I soon had my tissue-culture system working well, but it was nine months before I had a patient with this same disease under my care in the clinical center. We began cultures of his fibroblast cells from a small skin biopsy. It took another nine months for us to find the enzyme defect that was responsible—a gross lack of activity of an important enzyme of purine metabolism that I think of as a thrifty Scottish enzyme that reutilizes the purine bases hypoxanthine and guanine.[31] It is named hypoxanthine-guanine phosphoribosyltransferase, generally abbreviated to HPRT.

The disease was eventually named Lesch-Nyhan disease after the authors Michael Lesch, a medical student, and Dr. William Nyhan, pediatricians who published a detailed study of the clinical description of the original patient under their care at Johns Hopkins Hospital.[32] We soon found a less-severe deficiency of this same HPRT enzyme in a family of three gouty brothers who all produced an excessive amount of uric acid in their daily urine but had no neurological disease and had been participating in our clinical studies for several years.[33] Evidently even a small amount of residual enzyme activity from a slightly different mutation in the same gene was enough to prevent the neurological problems. In still other patients we found even less residual enzyme correlated with relatively mild neurological symptoms. Eventually this gene was shown to be located on the X chromosome, which meant that it affected only males and was transmitted only through the mother's side of the family.

By incubating the cultured skin fibroblasts with hypoxanthine labeled with radioactive tritium, we had a simple way of demonstrating the presence or absence of normal or mutant HPRT-deficient cells by exposing the cells to photographic film and developing it. The normal cells took up substantial radioactivity, and the mutant ones did not. We used this same procedure to demonstrate the presence of both normal and mutant cells in fibroblasts cultured from mothers of Lesch-Nyhan patients. This showed the correctness of genetic work done by a British investigator, Dr. Mary Lyon, in studies of coat color in cats some years before demonstrating the random inactivation of one of the two X chromosomes carried in female cats to account for the spotted fur markings of certain strains of female cats.

Dr. Ted Friedmann used the above radioautographic procedure in 1967 while working with me at NIH to see if the simple addition of DNA isolated from normal human cells to cultures of the HPRT deficient human cells would show any evidence of restoration of the HPRT activity. DNA isolated from the HPRT deficient cells showed no restored cells, while DNA isolated from normal cells showed correction in one in five thousand cells to one in one hundred thousand cells. However, the corrected cells failed to increase in number with additional replication in fresh media. In fact, they were lost. We took this to mean that the extracted normal DNA carried the HPRT gene into the cell but failed to insert it into the replicating DNA of the chromosomes of the mutant cells. Dr. Friedmann then left my laboratory to go to work at the Salk Institute in La Jolla to find out just how RNA viruses could be used to insert genes into host cell DNA. This was the first human condition found where an identifiable gene defect was correlated with a stereotyped compulsive behavior.

The first Lesch-Nyhan patient under my care at the NIH Clinical Center was a bright-eyed seven-year-old boy who was very alert and intelligent. In response to my question as to why he bit his fingers, lips, and tongue, he said with a glint in his eye, "My uric acid is too high." I think he was telling me that it was not his fault and that he had no desire to do it. The answer I obtained from another patient, a fourteen-year-old black boy, was informative. He said he felt an urge to bite whenever he was worried and upset. I immediately faced the fact that when concentrating on a problem I often find I am biting at my own lips, but rather gently and not hard enough to cause bleeding. I also thought of several friends of mine who have the compulsion to bite at their fingernails when under pressure. Could children with Lesch-Nyhan disease have a fairly common compulsion but with the volume turned up? Other investigators have reported substantial decreases in the brain concentration of serotonin and L dopamine involved in transmission of nerve signals found in a Lesch-Nyhan patient at autopsy. Affected children seem quite willing to wear Velcro-fabric splints around their elbows that are sufficiently tight to prevent their hands reaching their mouth but also sufficiently loose so they can reach their mouth with a spoon to feed themselves. They then still have freedom of choice as long as their fingers do not reach their mouth. Thus the moment of free decision is shifted to an earlier action.

Treatment of some aspects of Lesch-Nyhan disease has been found, but the major problems remain. The large amount of uric acid produced leads to deposition of uric acid stones in the kidneys and urinary tract with resulting development of progressive kidney damage. This can be largely avoided by using allopurinol and by increasing the fluid intake to give a larger volume of urine with which to carry the load of uric acid out of the body. Allopurinol also prevents childhood gout seen in some of these patients.

In 1969 I left NIH and joined the new medical school that had just opened at the University of California, San Diego, in La Jolla. William Nyhan was the chairman of the Department of Pediatrics and I was director of the Division of Arthritis in the Department of Medicine. Upon completing his fellowship at the Salk Institute, Dr.

Ted Friedmann joined the Department of Pediatrics and eventually cloned the normal HPRT gene and inserted it into a defective retro virus that could not replicate and cause disease. I soon had funding with William Nyhan for a project grant from NIH to support our program on human biochemical genetics that allowed us to continue our research activities on Lesch-Nyhan disease and other enzyme defects of human purine metabolism for a total of fifteen years. We collaborated with Ted Friedmann in testing the effectiveness of his retro viral vector for carrying the normal HPRT gene into a permanent line of lymphoblasts cultured from peripheral blood of a Lesch-Nyhan patient. We found from 3 to 23 percent of normal HPRT activity restored in different cloned colonies of lymphoblasts.[34] We felt we had demonstrated that this gene transplant could be done, but the variability of response in the different clones might very well be a result of the great variability in the location of this newly transplanted gene in the chromosomes of the genetically corrected cells. This variability would then have a substantial effect from the genes adjacent to the transplant site. It would be much better if the gene could be inserted in a uniform site surrounded by its own normal regulator systems. We think that we may need to deal with the development of a system that will carry the gene into cells of the brain. The prospects now in view for genetic modalities for treatment of human ailments is rapidly expanding and presents a most fascinating range of diseases to be treated and additional modalities for introducing these genes.

Further studies of the detailed biochemical mechanism responsible for the marked overproduction of purines in HPRT-deficient patients revealed an elevated concentration of the nonpurine substrate for the missing enzyme called phosphoribosylpyrophosphate (PRPP), which is also a substrate for the rate-limiting enzyme for the first step of purine synthesis.[35] This in turn led to the identification in 1972 of an increased activity of this first enzyme, PRPP synthetase, as another hereditary cause of an excessive rate of purine synthesis and gouty arthritis by Dr. Sperling's group in Israel.[36] The detection of additional families was made by Dr. Becker in our group soon after.[37]

The PRPP synthetase gene was mapped to the X chromosome quite close to the HPRT gene.[38]

CONCLUSION

I have a strong conviction that we have a Father in Heaven who created our universe and developed the life forms we see about us using natural laws that we are still discovering. I have never had a direct conversation with or vision of the Lord. He is probably too busy. I do feel that I have been given during my life unusual opportunities to help bring knowledge of these creative endeavors to our brothers and sisters now occupying Earth. A special pleasure has been the opportunities to obtain glimpses of mutations the Lord must have created in the generation of some of the characteristics of modern man to give this species a longer life than any other mammal so we will have time to learn and absorb the new information that is developing. In my studies I feel very strongly that I have been repeatedly presented with most unusual opportunities to make incremental increases in human knowledge, and I thank my Creator for this privilege to work with him.

If we make the search for truth an objective for our personal everyday life as well as our religious life and views as advocated by Henry Eyring,[39] I feel confident we can each add a greater meaning to life's experiences and an enrichment of our appreciation of our own potential for interaction with our Creator. In my own lifetime we have all seen modern science verify the validity of a revelation known as the Word of Wisdom, given to the Prophet Joseph Smith in 1833 "in consequence of evils and designs which do and will exist in the hearts of conspiring men in the last days" (Doctrine and Covenants 89:4). In effect it can be viewed as the counterpart of the manufacturer's brochure enclosed with this new machine you have just purchased, giving advice on how to obtain the best performance and how to avoid damaging it.

A recent study of the health of Mormons of southern California by Dr. James E. Enstrom, a non-Mormon epidemiologist on the faculty of University of California, Los Angeles, has shown the lowest death rate yet found for cancer and for cardiovascular disease. From an eight-year follow-up study (1980–1987) of 5,231 Mormon high priests and 4,613 wives twenty-five to ninety-nine years of age, the Mormon men showed one-half the expected number of deaths from cancer and from cardiovascular diseases. The wives showed 72 percent of the expected death rate from all cancers and 64 percent of the expected death rate from cardiovascular diseases. The take-home message given by Dr. Enstrom in an interview with a writer for the *Wall Street Journal* was his finding that active Mormon males have a life expectancy of eleven years longer than the average for the American males, and Mormon females have a life span six years longer than the average for American females.[40] If I had seen his publication a bit earlier when I was facing mandatory retirement from the university at age seventy, I might very well have challenged this ruling. I could have argued that because of my cultural heritage I should not face mandatory retirement until at least eighty-one years of age!

NOTES

1. See Edward L. Thorndike, "The Production, Retention, and Attraction of American Men of Science," *Science* 92 (August 1940): 137–41; Edward L. Thorndike, "The Origin of Superior Men," *Scientific Monthly* (May 1943): 424–33; and Kenneth R. Hardy, "Social Origins of American Scientists," *Science* 185 (August 1974): 497–506.

2. See David John Buerger, "Highly Educated Mormons Are More Religious, Study Shows," *Sunstone* 10 (March 1985): 51; Brent Harker, "Academic Minds, Religious Hearts," *BYU Today*, April 1985, p. 16; and, most recently, Mark W. Cannon in Virginia McClairo, "Mormons and Science" (14 May 1998), a still-unpublished, concise summary.

3. See my paper "Conquest of Gouty Arthritis," in *Landmark Advances in Rheumatology,* ed. Daniel J. McCarty (Atlanta: American Rheumatism Association, 1985), pp. 89–101.

4. See my study "Genetic Diseases: II. Gout and Lesch-Nyhan Disease," in *NIH: An Account of Research in Its Laboratories and Clinics,* ed. DeWitt Stetten Jr. and William T. Carigan (New York: Academic Press, 1984), pp. 314–23.

5. See my work *Biographical Memoirs of DeWitt Stetten, Jr.* (Washington, D.C.: National Academy Press, 1996).

6. See J. Edwin Seegmiller, L. Laster and D. Stetten Jr., "Incorporation of 4-amino-5-imidazolecarboxamide-4-C13 into Uric Acid in the Normal Human," *Journal of Biological Chemistry* 216 (1995): 653–62.

7. See the letter to the editor by DeWitt Stetten Jr. et al., "The Pathogenesis of Gout," *Metabolism* 6 (1957): 88–91.

8. See J. Edwin Seegmiller, Rodney R. Howell, and Stephen E. Malawista, "The Inflammatory Reaction to Sodium Urate: Its Possible relationship to the Genesis of Acute Gouty Arthritis," *Journal of the American Medical Association* 180 (1962): 469–75.

9. See Stephen E. Malawista and J. Edwin Seegmiller, "The Effect of Pretreatment with Colchicine on the Inflammatory Response to Microcrystalline Urate," *Annals of Internal Medicine* 62 (1965): 648–57; Rodney R. Howell and J. Edwin Seegmiller, "Inflammatory

Response to Injected Sodium Urate," Eighth Interim Scientific Session of the American Rheumatism Association, December 1961 (abstract); J. S. Faires and Daniel J. McCarty Jr., "Acute Arthritis in Man and Dog Produced by Intra Synovial Injection of Sodium Urate Crystals," *Clinical Research* 9 (1961): 329.

10. See Daniel J. McCarty Jr., "Phagocytosis of Urate Crystals in Gouty Synovial Fluid," *American Journal of Medical Science* 243 (1962): 288–95.

11. See Rodney R. Howell and J. Edwin Seegmiller, "Uricolysis in Human Leucocytes," *Nature* 196 (1962): 482–83.

12. See Stephen E. Goldfinger, Rodney R. Howell and J. Edwin Seegmiller, "Suppression of Metabolic Accompaniments of Phagocytosis by Colchicine," *Arthritis and Rheumatism* 8 (1965): 1112–22.

13. See Bruce N. Ames et al., "Uric Acid: An Antioxidant Defense in Humans against Oxidant- and Radical-Caused Aging and Cancer: A Hypothesis," *Proceedings of the National Academy of Sciences, United States of America* 78 (1981): 6858–62.

14. See Richard Cutler, "Urate and Ascorbate: Their Possible Roles as Antioxidants in Determining Longevity of Mammalian Species," *Archives of Gerontology and Geriatrics* 3, no.4 (1984): 321–48.

15. See Tsy F. Yu and Alexander B. Gutman, "Mobilization of Gouty Tophi by Protracted Use of Uricosuric Agents," *American Journal of Medicine* 11 (1951): 765; A. B. Gutman and T. F. Yu, "Benemid (p-di-n-Propylsulfamyl-Benzoic Acid) as Uricosuric Agent in Chronic Gouty Arthritis," *Transactions of the Association of American Physicians* 64 (1951): 279–88; and J. H. Talbott et al., "The Clinical and Metabolic Effects of Benemid in Patients with Gout," *Transactions of the Association of American Physicians* 64 (1951): 372.

16. See Roland K. Robins, "Potential Purine Antagonists. 1: Synthesis of Some 4,6-Substituted Pyrazolo-3,4-pyrimidines," *Journal of the American Chemical Society* 78 (1956): 784–90.

17. R. Wayne Rundels et al., "Effect of a Xanthine Oxidase Inhibitor on Thiopurine Metabolism, Hyperuricemia, and Gout," *Transactions of the Association of American Physicians* 76 (1963): 126–40.

18. See James R. Klinenberg, Stephen E. Goldfinger and J. Edwin Seegmiller, "The Effectiveness of the Xanthine Oxidase Inhibitor, Allopurinol, in the Treatment of Gout," *Annals of Internal Medicine* 62 (1965): 639–47.

19. See J. Edwin Seegmiller, "Goals in Gout," *Postgraduate Medicine* 45 (1969): 99–103.

20. Irwin Fridovitch, "Quantitative Aspects of the Production of Superoxide Anion Radical by Milk Xanthine Oxidase," *Journal of Biological Chemistry* 245, no.16 (1970): 4053–57.

21. See J. Edwin Seegmiller, "Future Directions in Aging Research," in *Molecular Biology of Aging,* ed. Avril D. Woodhead, Anthony D. Blackett, and Alexander Hollander (New York: Raven Press, 1985), 29:461–63.

22. See Archibald E. Garrod, "The Croonian Lectures on Inborn Errors of Metabolism. Lecture II: Alkaptonuria," *Lancet* 2 (1908): 73–79.

23. See Archibald E. Garrod, *The Inborn Factors in Disease: An Essay* (London: Oxford University Press, 1931).

24. Victor McKusick, personal communication.

25. See Bert N. LaDu et al., "The Nature of the Defect in Tyrosine Metabolism in Alcaptonuria," *Journal of Biological Chemistry* 230 (1958): 251–60.

26. See Thomas J. Lustberg, Joseph D. Schulman, and J. Edwin Seegmiller, "Decreased Binding of C-Homogentisic Acid Induced by Ascorbic Acid in Connective Tissue of Rats with Experimental Alcaptonuria," *Nature* 228 (1970): 770–71.

27. See Adam P. Angeles et al., "Chondrocyte Growth Inhibition Induced by Homogentisic Acid and Its Partial Prevention with Ascorbic Acid," *Journal of Rheumatology* 16 (1989): 512–17.

28. See Jon A. Wolff et al., "Effects of Ascorbic Acid in Alkaptonuria: Alterations in Benzoquinone Acetic Acid and an Ontogenic Effect in Infancy," *Pediatric Research* 26 (1989): 140–44.

29. See J. Edwin Seegmiller, "Ochronosis and Alkaptonuria," in *Internal Medicine*, ed. Jay H. Stein (Boston: Little, Brown and Co., 1994), pp. 2508–11.

30. See Michael Lesch and William L. Nyhan, "A Familial Disorder of Uric Acid Metabolism and Central Nervous System Function," *American Journal of Medicine* 36 (1964): 561–70.

31. See J. Edwin Seegmiller, Frederick M. Rosenbloom, and William N. Kelley, "Enzyme Defect Associated with a Sex-Linked Human Neurological Disorder and Excessive Purine Synthesis," *Science* 155 (1967): 1682–84.

32. See Lesch and Nyhan, "A Familial Disorder of Uric Acid Metabolism and Central Nervous System Function," pp. 561–70.

33. See William N. Kelley et al., "A Specific Enzyme Defect in Gout Associated with Overproduction of Uric Acid," *Proceedings of the National Academy of Sciences, United States of America* 57 (1967): 1735–39.

34. See Randall C. Willis et al., "Partial Phenotype Correction of Human Lesch-Nyhan (Hypoxanthine-Guanine Phosphoribosyltransferase-Deficient) Lymphoblasts with a Transmissible Retroviral Vector," *Journal of Biological Chemistry* 259 (1984): 7842–49.

35. See Frederick M. Rosenbloom et al., "Biochemical Bases of Accelerated Purine Biosynthesis de Novo in Human Fibroblasts Lacking Hypoxanthine-Guanine Phosphoribosyltransferase," *Journal of Biological Chemistry* 243 (1968): 1166–73.

36. See Oded Sperling et al., "Altered Kinetic Property of Erythrocyte Phosphoribosylpyrophosphate Synthetase in Excessive Purine Production," *Revue Europeenne d'etudes Cliniques et Biolofiques* 17 (1972): 703–6.

37. See Michael A. Becker et al., "Purine Overproduction in Man Associated with Increased Phosphoribosylpyrophosphate Synthetase Activity," *Science* 179 (1973): 1123–26; see also Michael A. Becker and J. Edwin Seegmiller, "Recent Advances in the Identification of Enzyme Abnormalities Underlying Excessive Purine Synthesis in Man," *Arthritis and Rheumatism* 18 (1975): 687–94.

38. See Michael A. Becker et al., "Regional Localization of the Gene for Human Phosphoribosylpyrophosphate Synthetase on the X-Chromosome," *Science* 203 (1979): 1016–19.

39. See Henry Eyring, *The Faith of a Scientist* (Salt Lake City: Bookcraft, 1967).

40. See James Enstrom, "Health Practices and Cancer Mortality among Active California Mormons," *Journal of the National Cancer Institute* 81 (1989): 1807–14.

INDEX

Clark, J. Reuben, on personal
   revelation, 9–10
clay, absorbent nature of, 24
"closed timelike curves" (CTCs), 165
closure temperature, 32
colchicine, 211
comets, inactive, 145
consciousness, 171–72
Copenhagen interpretation, 169–70
Copernicus: astronomy principles
   discovered by, 56; solar system
   described by, 144
cosmology, definition of, 57
Creation, 134; scriptures on, 15–16;
   measurement of time during, 16;
   nonspontaneous nature of, 18;
   purpose of, 41–42; echoes of, 57;
   alternate events possible in, 132;
   order of, 158
Creations, endless, 38
Crick, Francis, 171–72
criticism, higher, 72
Cuvier, Georges, fossil theories of,
   94–95

d-amino acids, 53–54
Darwin, Charles, 69, 72, 134
day: definition of, 42; concept of,
   163, 164; duration of, 174
de Chardin, Teilhard, 134, 172
death, LDS understanding of, 64
decay, 30
Deep Sea Drilling Project, 143–44
defects, genetic, 218
design, of universe, 161
determinism, 169
dictatorship, 63–64
discoveries, scientific, 127
diseases, inherited, 214
disorder, 17
DNA, 73, 206, 219
Dobzhansky, Theo, 134
dogmatism, 10–11
Durant, Will, on science and religion,
   72

Dyson, Freeman, 29, 157–58, 173;
   on readiness of universe for
   human life, 80

Earth: age of, 1, 4, 14–18, 35, 37, 93,
   117, 128, 174–75; divine creation
   of, 40, 122; evolution of, 96;
   ancientness of, 96, 106; rotation
   of crustal plates of, 129, 131;
   changing climate of, 129–30;
   prepared for human habitation,
   133; latter-day revelations
   concerning, 141; geography of,
   174; ample resources of, 189;
   gospel teachings regarding,
   197–98; gratitude for, 199–200
earthquakes, specific causes of, 133
eclipses, accurate prediction of,
   54–55
economic scarcity, 192
ecosystem, Arctic, 130
Einstein, Albert, 101, 163–64;
   probability and chance studied by,
   170
elements: refined, 20; heavy, 113,
   117–18; formation of, 117
energy, 52
energy crisis, 191
Enstrom, James E., 222–23
entropy, 17, 136, 172–73
environment, 184; problems of,
   193–97
enzyme, missing, 215
error, human, 10
eternity, 41
ether, 20
Ethington, Raymond L.: background
   of, 92; healing of grandson of,
   98–100
events: probability of, 22; random,
   131–33
Everett, Hugh, 162
evidence, scientific, 8
evolution, 1, 35, 128, 175; unlikely
   sequences of, 22; controversies

helium, 104, 116
Herschel, William, Uranus discovered by, 144
Hinckley, Gordon B., on inspiration, 187
hindsight, 70–71
Hintze, Lehi F., 36–37
holism, 171–72
Holy Ghost: as tool for finding truth, 9–10; light and, 20–22
honesty, 138
Hoyle, Fred, on evidence of divine Creator, 161
HPRT, 218–22
Hubble, Edwin, 57
human body, 137
human life, 137
humility 39–40, 185
humus, 25–26
Hutton, James, 93
Huxley, on human evolution, 134
hydrogen, 104
hypotheses, scientific, 81, 112; untestable, 137

"If You Could Hie to Kolob," 100–101
immortality, cellular, 23–24
Inborn Factors in Disease, The, 215
In Search of Truth, 86
inspiration, 9–10, 152, 187; in use of resources, 193
Institute, 78
intelligence, 43, 168, 203–4
interpretation, 8–9
intuition, 151
iron, 116–17
isotopes, radioactive, 30–32
isotopic dating, 30–32

Jesus Christ, 186–87; light and, 19–22; atonement of, 27; role of, in Creation, 40; gospel of, 63, 72; as Creator, 199
Jevons, Stanley, coal supply theories of, 190

Johnson, Frank, 53
Johnson, Hollis R.: background of, 102; early experiences of, 105
Joseph Smith as Scientist, 20
judgment, 154
justice, God's, 62

Kierkegaard, Soren, on hindsight, 70
kingdoms: revelation on, 147; universe filled with, 163
Kirkham, Don, 79
Klinenberg, James, gout studies of, 213
knowledge, 11, 43, 121, 150–51, 191; faith a precursor to, 2; perfect, 12–13; sacred and scientific, 150–53; future, 155–56
Kolob, 163, 174–75
Kornberg, Arthur, 206
Kowallis, Bart J.: background of, 28; early experiences of, 33–37

Lacks, Henrietta, 23
LaDu, Bert, 215–16
l-amino acids, 53–54
land, mapping of, 147
lands, bounds of, 142–44
latitude-longitude system, 142
Latter-day Saints, health of, 222–23
law of the harvest, 166
laws: physical and spiritual, 13–14; eternal, 60–61
leaders, Church, 152
Lesch, Michael, 218
Lesch-Nyhan Disease, 218–22
Leverrier, Neptune discovered by, 145
life: evolution of, 1; origin of, 52; intelligent, 58; lessons of, 71–72; premortal, 141
light: truth and, 12–13; and matter, 21–22; nonvisible, 22; speed of, 56
Light of Christ, 19–22
light years, 58; definition of, 56
Linde, Andrei, 41

"little God," concept of, 42–43
love, God's, 62
Low, Philip F.: background of, 6; early experiences of, 11; testimony of, 26–27
Low, Philip S., 22
Lyon, Mary, 219

magma, 133
Malthus, Thomas, 189–90
man: creation of, 14–18; spirit of, 21–22; as child of God, 63, 103, 222; existence of, 168; origin of, 175; as steward of Earth, 195–96; life span of, 212–13
mankind, nature of, 39–40
"many worlds," theory of, 162
maps, accuracy of, 142
Mars, fossils from, 119
Mason, Grant W., on four sources of knowledge, 151–52
matter: conservation of, 18–19; spirit, 167; nature of, 167–68; study of, 169–71
McConkie, Bruce R.: on length of days during Creation, 42
McMullin, Ernan, on the Big Bang, 160
media, inaccuracy in, 109
method, scientific, 82
microorganisms, role of, 25–26
Milky Way galaxy, 38, 56, 145–46; size of, 113; origin of, 118; enrichment of, 119; boundaries of, 146–47
mineral resources, abundance of, 193
minerals, 184
miracles, beyond medical explanation, 98–100
missionary service, 107
molecules, 50–52, 104; of ammonia, 51
moon, magnetic field of, 144
Moroni, promise of, 69

Moses, scientific implications of vision of, 38–42, 96–97
mountains, underwater, 143
muscles, composition of, 53
mutation, 135–36

National Academy of Sciences, 5; on creationism, 158
nature, pessimistic views of, 158; chance in, 169
Neptune, discovery of, 144
Newton, Isaac, 8, 54; on the solar system, 157
Noah, 173
Norman, Keith E., 160
nucleus, atomic, 49; process of studying, 49–50
nutrients, water-soluble, 25
Nyhan, William, 218

ocean, evolution of, 128–30
oceans, depth of, 143
ochronotic arthritis, 215
Of Stars and Men, 57
one billion, definition of, 37
orbit, prediction of, 54–55
organisms, life and death of, 23–24
organs, vestigial, 175

Packer, Boyd K., on efforts to test scriptures, 186
paleontology, 95, 96
parity, theory of, 50
participatory universe, theory of, 162
Paul, 10–11
Penrose, Charles W., on light, 20
perception, spiritual, 22
perspectives, various, 100
phagocytes, 210, 213
Phelps, W. W., 100
philosophers, renowned, 84
physics, study of, 77–79
plan, gospel, 64
Planck, Max, on scientific truths, 9
planets: life-supporting, 57–58;

ancient knowledge of, 144; motion of, 156

plates, crustal, 129

plates, movement of, 144

Pluto, discovery of, 144

pollution, 193–99

postulates, 61

Pratt, Parley P., on refined substances, 20

prayer, 27; power of, 98–100

premortal life, 16–17, 63; council during, 141

pride, 154

priesthood ordinances, 99–100

principles, mutually exclusive, 83–84

priorities, correct, 187; false, 196

probabilities, 184

probenecid, 213

progress, definition of, 132

progression, eternal, 64, 66, 85, 150

Provine, William B., on evolution, 134–35

Proxima Centauri, 57

pulsars, 116

quantum mechanics, 51, 79; definition of, 169

quarks, 50, 100, 167

Quebec Mission, 35

radar, 142

radiation, electromagnetic, 21

randomness, 17, 128, 131–33, 136

Raup, David M., on fossil record, 136

reactions: photochemical, 21; chemical, 52

reality, photographs vs., 97–98

reason, 151

red giant, 114–15

reductionism, 171–72

religion, gaining testimony of, 11–12

religious beliefs, uncertainty in, 9

repetition, 71

research: scholarly, 109–10; inappropriate, 154–55; geological, 184

resonance, 161

resource scarcity, 191–93

resources: mineral, 188–93; righteous use of, 198–99

respect, 199

resurrection, 89–90, 103

revelation: personal, 9–10, 151, 187; of "things of the earth," 29; divine, 188

revelations: to be received line upon line, 142; future, 153; 176–77

reverence, 43

Richards, L. A., 80

Richards, Robert J., 135

Roberts, B. H., 3; on truth, 150

Robins, Roland K., gout studies of, 213

Rundles, Wayne, gout studies of, 213

Ruse, Michael, on evolutionary progress, 135

Sagan, Carl, on religion and science, 42

Satan, 63, 188

satellites, 54–55, 142–43

Schrodinger, Erwin, probability and chance studied by, 170

science and God, 79

science and religion: conflict between, 1, 65, 70, 109, 127–28, 176; compatibility of, 7, 14,155–58

Science and Religion: Toward a More Useful Dialogue, 173

science, 9, 138, 156; LDS views on, 3; methods of, 11–14; limitations of, 73; disagreements in, 153

scientific data, interpretation of, 8–9

scientific findings, 8

scientists, LDS, 4–5, 69–70, 173–75, 204

Scopes, John T., 73

scriptures, 10; purpose of, 15; nonscientific nature of, 38, 97–98

seafloor spreading, 143

seas, bounds of, 142–44

seed, word compared to, 12

Seegmiller, Edwin, J.: background of, 202; early experiences of, 204–6; testimony of, 222

senses: spiritual, 14; physical, 14, 151–52

Shapley, Harlow, 57

Smith, Joseph, 18, 27, 66; on erroneous scripture translations, 10; difficult issues addressed by, 84; on revelation, 141, 153; on salvation and ignorance, 152

Smith, Maynard, on evolutionary progress, 135

Smith, William, fossil theories of, 95

Snell, Heber C., 78

Snow, Lorenzo, on eternal progression, 203

soil: concept of divine creation supported by, 24–26; complex nature of, 26

soil physics, 78–79

solar mass, 114

solar system, 1, 157; elements available in, 119; age of, 145; ancient beliefs about, 146

sonar devices, invention of, 143

space: gaseous clouds in, 113; human understanding of, 163

space travel, 57–58, 165

special relativity, theory of, 163

specific heat capacity, 25

spectrum, 21

Spencer, Herbert, 134

spirit, refined nature of, 167

Sputnik, 55

St. Augustine, on belief and understanding, 85

star: white dwarf, 115; neutron, 116

starbirth, 113

stardeath, 115

stars, 55–60, 114; beliefs about, 55–56; composition of, 111; life of, 111–12; death of, 118; red giant, 118; early, 119

"Steady State" universe, 159–60

Stetten, Dewitt, Jr., gout studies of, 208

Stokes, William Lee, background of, 140

strong anthropic principle, 161

structures, geological, 131

study, appropriate topics of, 150

subduction zones, 143

sun, 111, 146; as giant furnace, 59–60; creation of, 60; energy sources within, 113–14; age of, 117; motion of, 173–74

supernovae, 118

Sydenham, Thomas, gout studies of, 207

system, closed, 17–18

Talmage, James E., on ancientness of earth, 36; on nonscientific nature of scriptures, 38

Tanner, C. B., 87

teaching, 150

technology, value of, 197

teleology, 161

telepathy, 168

telescope, discoveries facilitated by, 56

testimony, 86; growth of, 11, 37, 76; emotional aspects of, 186

theories, scientific, 14, 112

theory: thermodynamic, 17–18; scientific, 112

Theory of the Earth, 94

Thorne, Kip, 165

time: questions regarding, 1; human vs. divine perspective of, 42, 163–64; dimension of, 58; arrow of, 136, 173

time travel, 165

Tipler, Frank, 172

Tombaugh, Clyde, discovery of Pluto by, 144

truth, 43; search for, 9–11, 64–65, 86–87, 101, 149–77, 204, 222; single source of, 66; borrowed, 70; physical and spiritual, 71, 98–100, 107, 121
truth and error, 9
Truth, the Way, The Life, The, 3–4
truths, religious, 71, 107; scientific, 86

understanding, belief impossible without, 85
universe, 1, 38, 41, 163; magnificence of, 43, 120, 157; exactness of, 51; size of, 56, 79–80; activity and motion in, 58–59; evolution of, 73; chemical composition of, 104; boundaries of, 147; pessimism regarding, 157–58; creation of, 158–59; designed for human life, 161; participatory, 162; God's, 166; recollapse of, 172–73
universes, many, 160
uranium-238, 30–32
Uranus, discovery of, 144
urate crystal, 209–10
uric acid, 207–8; elimination of, 211

vitamin C, studies on, 212

Warner, C. Terry, on truth, 149
Wasatch Fault, 32
Wasatch Mountains, age of, 31–32
water, plant-nourishing role of, 24–25

water bodies, mapping of, 147
weak anthropic principle, 161
weaknesses, human, 185
Weinberg, Steven, 81, 158
Wheeler, John Archibald, 79, 162; "wormhole" theory of, 165
white blood cells, 210
Widtsoe, John A., 85–86; on light and Holy Spirit, 20; on ancient nature of Earth, 36
Wigner, Eugene, on pointlessness of universe, 158
Williams, George, on evolution, 135
Wilson, Edward O., 29
wisdom, 43
word of mouth, 9
Word of Wisdom, as "manufacturer's brochure," 222
words of God, experimenting on, 12–13
works of God, endless, 38
world, predictable properties of, 55; governed by divine powers, 65–66; handiwork of God evident in, 162
worlds: other, 19, 57–58, 119, 163; many, 41, 159; physical and spiritual, 49–62
Wright, Thomas, on vastness of universe, 157

Young, Brigham, 42, 150; on need for personal revelation, 10; on the Creation, 45, n. 33; on religion and science, 150